Future of Business and Finance

The Future of Business and Finance book series features professional works aimed at defining, describing and charting the future trends in these fields. The focus is mainly on strategic directions, technological advances, and challenges and solutions which will affect the way we do business tomorrow. We also encourage books which focus on the future of sustainability and governance. Mainly written by practitioners, consultants and academic thinkers, the books are intended to spark and inform further discussions and developments.

More information about this series at http://www.springer.com/series/16360

Peter Wollmann · Frank Kühn ·
Michael Kempf
Editors

Three Pillars
of Organization
and Leadership
in Disruptive Times

Navigating Your Company
Successfully Through
the 21st Century Business World

 Springer

Editors
Peter Wollmann
Bonn, Germany

Frank Kühn
Dortmund, Germany

Michael Kempf
Bad Honnef, Germany

ISSN 2662-2467   ISSN 2662-2475   (electronic)
Future of Business and Finance
ISBN 978-3-030-23226-9   ISBN 978-3-030-23227-6   (eBook)
https://doi.org/10.1007/978-3-030-23227-6

This Springer imprint is published by the registered company Springer Nature Switzerland AG.
The registered company address is: Gewerbestrasse 11, 6330 Cham, Switzerland

Contents

About the Authors

Tim Burmeister is a learning transformation manager for GP Strategies, with a focus on EMEA, working with large, global corporate clients. One of his main goals is to help clients identify an approach to learning that is fit for the future, which involves integrating current best practices. Having worked in learning and development (L&D) for 18 years (2 of those with GP Strategies), he sees the learning profession and learning industry on the verge of a profound change driven in part by emerging digital technologies.

Alberto Casagrande is actively involved in the angel investment ecosystem both in California, where he has been member of a 150-member angel community since 2016, and in Italy. For the last 15 years, he has managed The Core Inc., a boutique firm devoted to strategic, ICT, and economic consulting. During this period, Alberto has advised both the World Bank and several central banks across the world on financial infrastructure reforms and SME finance. He has acted as senior advisor for several banking sector restructuring projects across the world, and has advised several global players in the insurance sector on strategic issues, also supporting various economic ministries on growth strategies and debt management. Project locations have included North and Latin America, Europe, the Middle East, and North Africa. Alberto was previously project manager at McKinsey in Italy and economist at Italy's Central Bank.

Bernadette Cass is an organizational change consultant and executive coach. Much of her work today is accompanying and supporting leaders in their thinking as they grow and develop their organizations. Bernadette's commitment to creating sustainable change developed when she held IT directorships for a number of blue chip organizations and was responsible for the development and delivery of complex global technology programs. Bernadette is accredited by the International Coach Federation, a practitioner of Organizational Transactional Analysis, and a member of the European Association for Transactional Analysis. She leads professional education groups in York, UK. Bernadette is a regular speaker and presenter at International Coaching Week and International Supervision Week. She has published numerous publications and case studies.

James Chamberlain is the acting Director of the Language Centre at the Bonn-Rhein-Sieg University of Applied Sciences in Germany. He has studied, taught, and worked in the USA, the UK, Israel, France, and Germany. He has been teaching intercultural skills since 1994 in both academic and corporate contexts and has also supported international team building in cross-border corporate project contexts. His specialist areas can be summarized as training intercultural communication competence for all levels of management, train-the-trainer seminars for intercultural communication trainers, and facilitating international project team performance. James is a coauthor in the field of international communication with numerous publications.

Bob Dignen works as a director of York Associates, an organization that supports clients with leadership training, C-suite and executive coaching, international team building, and consultancy on learning design to achieve better international results. He supports his clients in meaningful ways in complex contexts spanning environmental, organizational, cultural, and personal multilayered challenges. He recognizes that digital transformation threatens to bring yet more disruption to his clients' ability to perform. Bob is the author of several books.

Volker Hische has been working as a consultant, trainer, and manager/managing director for more than 25 years in a global American technology company. Nowadays, he works as a leadership coach for his clients. He has already published and written books on leadership and project management. Volker has a strong background in HR management. He is an Associate Professor for the Human Capital Management MBA at Lake Constance Business School and a Certified International Project Manager and Certified International Project Management Trainer, IPMA.

Nicole Hönig de Locarnini is a senior advisory member within one of the "big 4" companies. To date, she has devoted her professional life to developing deep technical insurance/reinsurance expertise at a major global insurance company (she originally trained as an actuary) and later leveraged this, matched with a diverse skills set in strategic transformation architecture and execution, operations, innovation, digital enablement, and people and organizational design within the management consulting industry. Her work spans companies and business units within the financial services, life sciences, and producing industries. To satisfy her continuous passion for learning and growth, she recently completed the Consulting and Coaching for Change Specialized Executive Master/MBA Program at Oxford Saïd Business School and HEC Paris.

Isabell Huschka likes the fascination of good questions that help to find new ideas and ways into the future. As a consultant, the uniqueness of her clients and the joint journey into something new drives her work. After her apprenticeship and studies (business administration), she worked in different HR-management functions in the Foods and Automotive Industries, before providing clients with an outside perspective as a consultant. Isabell managed the Academy for Modern Leadership at a well-known consulting firm and created numerous complex leadership development processes. The focus of her work in change projects and organizational development is leadership. Her passion is identifying, developing, and cultivating a more collective leadership force inside organizations.

Michael Kempf has been an experienced Management Consultant for over 20 years. The driving force of his professional activities is his strong ambition to design processes and organizations in a sustainable manner. He relishes identifying key challenges, diagnosing complex relationships, and assisting in shaping the future. Gaining experience and learning something new are indispensable part of his life, which is why he likes to seize new chances. He began his career as a carpenter before studying social work, education, and business administration. His career has spanned various jobs in social work, 10 years as a manager (HR and logistics) in industrial and retail companies, and, since 1998, in advising people, leadership teams, as well as working teams and organizations that are all very different. Michael has coauthored numerous publications in the field of leadership and organizational development.

Frank Kühn has been facilitating projects on transformation, organization, and leadership for over 25 years. His work connects experience, future thinking, and getting into rapid action with people. Some of his recent projects have been building a Business Unit 4.0, helping a bank to transition toward agile working, and developing rapid product development processes. Frank graduated in engineering and received his doctorate in work science. After gaining leadership experience in research and industry, he became a partner at HLP in Frankfurt and ICG Integrated Consulting Group in Berlin and Graz. Today, he is a self-employed consultant and business partner of ICG and is associated with further development and project partners. He has published a wide range of publications and teaches courses at universities.

Christal Lalla is a certified sommelier, working in Italy, Germany, France, and the USA since 2012. She has established a fast-developing, innovative business around wine, wine services, and wine education under the name VinAuthority as well as providing out-of-the-box leadership training. She has a holistic approach which understands wine as something that appeals to all the senses including music, the winemaker's philosophy and approach, the visual and haptic sensations of the vineyards and the cellars with their barrels, and the taste of the wine combined with different varieties of food. Before 2012, Christal worked in the entertainment industry in Las Vegas and Nashville.

Sharon Lalla has worked in industry and higher education for over 30 years. In industry, she learned the importance of leadership, deadlines, project management, effective communication, and team building. In higher education, she adopted a collegial style of leadership balanced with relationship building and shared governance. After being awarded a doctorate in Education Technologies at Pepperdine University, Sharon took a leadership role in the administration of education technologies at New Mexico State University. As a College Assistant Professor, she taught a variety of classes at the undergraduate and graduate level. Currently, Sharon is a New Leadership Academy fellow and Vice President of Instruction at Luna Community College at Las Vegas, New Mexico.

Alfred Mevissen has been working as a European project manager at Novartis Pharma for the last 8 years (retired on January 1, 2019). Prior to this, he worked as Head of Sales in two other companies after a classic career in sales and marketing. He holds a university degree as a teacher and is a certified coach. In his last role, he was responsible for identifying and implementing "strategic capabilities." He has managed several change management processes and was part of the core group in an important merger. Following his passion for sculpting, he has published the books *Perfekt kann jeder—Steine als Wegweiser zu neuen Perspektiven* and *Ich bin die Freiheit—I am the Freedom*. He is the initiator of the international art projects www.pillars-of-freedom.com and www.art-moves-europe.eu.

Mersida Ndrevataj is an architect and urban planner based in Venice. Her professional objective is to help better shape the built environment through a multidisciplinary research-based and human-centered design process. To this end, she is currently working and learning, immersing herself in the field of environmental psychology. For the last 3 years, she has been working as a Cultural Mediator and Project Manager for the Venice Biennale. This experience brought her international exposure and provided her with considerable knowledge in cross-cultural and communication abilities.

Reto Püringer has worked for more than 20 years in the banking and insurance industry. He has held various senior positions in global companies. His practical experience ranges from strategy development, business model design, product/proposition development/management, enterprise-wide portfolio management, program/project management, operations/IT management, large-scale change program delivery to financial/actuarial management over different geographies and time zones, hierarchies and units, cultures and systems. Reto has managed multinational and multicultural change and transformation efforts across the globe and managed teams of various sizes both on-site and remotely. Reto holds a degree in economical informatics and marketing and completed an Executive MBA program at the University of Zurich.

Fernando Sanabria is a Computer Engineer and Program Director with broad experience in managing complex global projects. He specializes in starting up developing and implementing international programs with a good track record in developing high performing teams and becoming a trusted advisor to his business partners. He has held senior management positions in the global consultancy and insurance industries, working with IBM and Zurich Insurance Company, with a special focus on delivery, especially in scenarios with high organizational complexity. Fernando has spent more than 15 years working closely with business partners, acquiring in-depth understanding of real business needs, and taking business capabilities to the next level by developing enabling technology solutions and services.

Hannspeter Schmidt Following his studies of communications, ethnology, and religious science at the University of Cologne and Marburg, Hannspeter studied psychology at the University of Bonn where he graduated in 1980 with a PhD in psychology. From 1986 to 1995, he lectured at the University of Applied Sciences in Cologne and the University of Bonn focusing on the sciences of binding, interaction, group dynamic theories, and psychotherapy in groups. Since qualifying as a psychoanalyst and psychotherapist in 1990, he has worked as assistant professor, trainer, and supervisor for psychotherapists and psychoanalysts. He was head of the psychological counsel in Cologne from 1992 to 2017 and has meanwhile worked as an independent management consultant in the field of human resources management focusing on coaching and team development.

Marie Schmidt studied Health Economics at the University of Rotterdam and SDA Bocconi School of Management where she graduated in 2012. She specialized in Market Access of pharmaceuticals and medical devices throughout her professional career. As Associate Director Market Access EMEA, she has led pricing and reimbursement processes of innovative medicines and medical devices for a global research-based pharmaceutical and device company since 2016. Her projects are driven by strong cross-functional collaboration across organizational entities and healthcare authorities, always engaging multiple disciplines in decision-making processes. With her international working culture, she effectively manages diverse teams and projects in changing environments.

 **Peter Wollmann** has been program director for global transformations within Zurich Insurance Company (ZIC) and acting as a senior mentor, sparring partner, and catalyst for leaders in new roles and responsibilities and for organizations. His experience is based on a broad career spanning over 38 years in diverse project/program roles with a global scale or line management roles such as leading project portfolio management, strategic business development, and strategic planning and controlling units in ZIC, Deutsche Bank Insurance Group, and Deutscher Herold. Peter has a degree in mathematics and physics from the University of Bonn. He is the author and publisher of a range of books and articles on strategy, leadership, and project and project portfolio management. Finally, he founded and runs a wine business start-up: VinAuthority.

Part I

About this Book and the Three Pillar Model

Why and How the Three-Pillar Model Has Become a Reality

Peter Wollmann, Frank Kühn, and Michael Kempf

Abstract

We have experienced that traditional organizations don't offer reliable structures any longer. New reliability has to be different. An international team of authors, practitioners, and consultants has worked on this issue and defined three basic building blocks: sustainable purpose, travelling organization, and connected resources. These building blocks are based upon many years of experience in transformation projects and facing the current development and future changes. We have summarized them in the "three-pillar model of organization and leadership." The model is exemplified by a practical case and provides the framework for the articles and clusters in this book.

The editors of the book introduce themselves:

Peter Wollmann is now acting as a senior mentor, sparring partner, trusted advisor, and catalyst for leaders in new roles and responsibilities and for organizations. Before he has held over nearly 40 years diverse senior positions in the finance industry and worked in the last few years as program director for

(continued)

P. Wollmann (✉)
Consulting Partner, Bonn, Germany
e-mail: pw@peterwollmann.com

F. Kühn (✉)
Consulting Partner, Dortmund, Germany
e-mail: fk@kuehn-cp.com

M. Kempf (✉)
Consulting Partner, Bad Honnef, Germany
e-mail: michael@kempf-cp.com

© Springer Nature Switzerland AG 2020
P. Wollmann et al. (eds.), *Three Pillars of Organization and Leadership in Disruptive Times*, Future of Business and Finance,
https://doi.org/10.1007/978-3-030-23227-6_1

global transformations within Zurich Insurance Company (ZIC). He is the author and publisher of a range of books and articles on strategy, leadership, and project and project portfolio management.

Frank Kühn has been facilitating projects on transformation, organization, and leadership for over 25 years. Frank graduated in engineering and received his doctorate in work science. After gaining leadership experience in research and industry, he became a partner at HLP in Frankfurt and ICG Integrated Consulting Group in Berlin and Graz. Today, he is a self-employed consultant and business partner of ICG and is associated with further development and project partners. He has published a wide range of publications and teaches courses at universities.

Michael Kempf has been an experienced Management Consultant for over 20 years. His career has spanned various jobs in social work, 10 years as a manager (HR and logistics) in industrial and retail companies, and, since 1998, in advising people, leadership teams as well as working teams and organizations. Michael has coauthored numerous publications in the field of leadership and organizational development

Disruptive Times and Need for Action

Peter Wollmann, Frank Kühn, and Michael Kempf

Abstract

In this chapter, the authors explore and discuss key design building blocks for organization and leadership, derived concrete principles, and test their efficacy to get the indispensable ones which make the difference. They derive, analyzing a huge number of cases across industries, enterprises, and institutions as well as existing literature, exactly three of such building blocks with an overwhelming fundamental importance and leadership significance, far more than a purely technical perspective, and call them "pillars": the sustainable purpose of an organization (bringing new orientation and certainty to the people that are wanted to engage for the joint endeavor), the mind-set of an organization in a permanent state of flux and how to cope with this—called a "travelling organization"—and the capability of connecting the valuable resources such as aims and concepts, strategies and processes, experiences and competencies, balancing and inter-linking peoples' interests and ideas in a flexible manner towards joint success.

P. Wollmann (✉)
Consulting Partner, Bonn, Germany
e-mail: pw@peterwollmann.com

F. Kühn (✉)
Consulting Partner, Dortmund, Germany
e-mail: fk@kuehn-cp.com

M. Kempf (✉)
Consulting Partner, Bad Honnef, Germany
e-mail: michael@kempf-cp.com

© Springer Nature Switzerland AG 2020
P. Wollmann et al. (eds.), *Three Pillars of Organization and Leadership in Disruptive Times*, Future of Business and Finance,
https://doi.org/10.1007/978-3-030-23227-6_2

We are living in special times with opportunities and threats brought about by an epochal transformation with new political and social developments, significant scientific progress, disruptive technologies, new ways of communication and virtual cooperation, and new concepts for energy, mobility, and environmental protection. Enterprises and private individuals cannot avoid being highly impacted, and there is a feeling that, tomorrow, nothing will ever be the same again, but nobody knows what the "new" will look like in detail. It is more than likely that the old traditional state and different shades of new states will exist in parallel for some time—similar to the situation at the end of the nineteenth/beginning of the twentieth century—and, likewise, disruptions; personal, systemic, and political catastrophes; or break-throughs might be around in a different guise.

The significant uncertainty, the lack of orientation, and increasing number of additional players and factors to cope with need a strong leadership response, especially in the case of enterprises, social organizations, and public institutions. This response has to be technically simple but intellectually sophisticated in diverse facets—and the response, interpreted and well specified, has to have the potential to give sustainable orientation and to lead to successful action. It goes without saying that it is a tremendous challenge but one which must be attempted.

We already touched upon some of the challenges in our book *Leading International Projects* (Dignen and Wollmann 2016) and continued the discussion on our experiences with change projects and transformative concepts. Our exchange seemed so fundamental to us that we have focused on it in our next step.

We decided to explore the epochal transformation described above inclusive of the various gaps between diverse organization design concepts from classical to agile, and we were confident to have good preconditions in spite of the dimensions of this task. The cooperation of people from different geographies, nationalities, careers, industries, and professions over nearly 2 years had created a desire to continue working together.

It was—certainly—helpful that the exchange on "what's next" took place in Tuscany, where the joint endeavor had started years ago, and was nurtured by an environment far from each contributor's business routine, easily connecting intellectual, sensual, and emotional perspectives and supporting every kind of lateral thinking. Those environmental—non-ritualized—preconditions have become very rare in daily business life and are thus highly appreciated if something new has to be developed.

Ultimately, it is our strong belief that if you have a challenging topic of major interest and coverage of a burning issue and if you blend amazing and different people with ambition and curiosity, experience, and creativity in such an environment, you always will have an amazing and sustainable outcome. One advantage is that various perspectives from different industries, enterprises, and institutions, different personal experiences, and different personalities produce a lot more than merely a pure compendium of articles and arguments: meta-insights and solid support to help the reader to find their own leadership way in a competent manner. Figure 1 gives a rough impression of how our topic developed.

Our Connected Journey

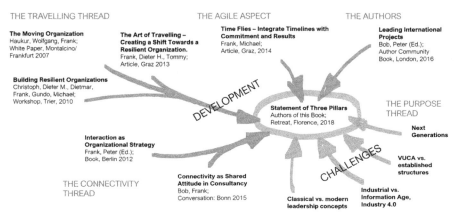

THE TRAVELLING THREAD

The Moving Organization
Haukur, Wolfgang, Frank;
White Paper, Montalcino/
Frankfurt 2007

Building Resilient Organizations
Christoph, Dieter M., Dietmar,
Frank, Gundo, Michael;
Workshop, Trier, 2010

**The Art of Travelling –
Creating a Shift Towards a
Resilient Organization.**
Frank, Dieter H., Tommy;
Article, Graz 2013

**Interaction as
Organizational Strategy**
Frank, Peter (Ed.);
Book, Berlin 2012

THE CONNECTIVITY
THREAD

**Connectivity as Shared
Attitude in Consultancy**
Bob, Frank;
Conversation: Bonn 2015

THE AGILE ASPECT

**Time Flies – Integrate Timelines with
Commitment and Results**
Frank, Michael;
Article, Graz, 2014

DEVELOPMENT

Statement of Three Pillars
Authors of this Book;
Retreat, Florence, 2018

CHALLENGES

**Classical vs. modern
leadership concepts**

THE AUTHORS

**Leading International
Projects**
Bob, Peter (Ed.);
Author Community
Book, London, 2016

THE PURPOSE
THREAD

**Next
Generations**

**VUCA vs.
established
structures**

**Industrial vs.
Information Age,
Industry 4.0**

Fig. 1 Focus of the book developing from various roots (authors' own figure)

The severe and demanding issue for the book has already been touched upon from a broad bundle of perspectives above, covering political, sociological, technological, cultural, organizational, and especially leadership aspects. Let's go now a bit more into detail.

For the world of enterprises, it is some sort of "common—at least often shared—knowledge" that the "old business world" is going to die as a consequence of an epochal transformation based on new technologies, especially concerning data management, communication styles and platforms, global cooperation with a cut in value chains, politics, trade, changes to tax and customs regulations, etc. "Old world" means in the perspective of organizations—only to take some buzz words—top-down decisions, Taylorism, command and control, hierarchical and departmental silos, micromanagement, short-term thinking, focus on career and position, etc.

All of this will vanish, or at least change significantly, in the new digital and data-oriented world as a consequence of one of the biggest paradigm shifts for business in the last two centuries. And it is obvious that things are already changing for enterprises. The impact of huge enterprises from places like Silicon Valley such as Apple, Google, Amazon, Uber, and also of upcoming start-ups and the respective demands and decisions of customers have obviously changed daily life.

That can all be regarded as challenges from outside that bump up against organizational conditions and ideas of further development. It can be described by some key observations which are perfectly expressed in the song "Everything at Once" by Lenka which was used to launch a new Windows version some years ago and which covers the current situation in organization design for companies quite well. Lenka sings about the ambition to be everything at once, and we observe that:

- Companies want to be like a fleet of start-ups but at the same time be a big strong organization controlled by a sustainable financial and organizational background.
- Units want to start from scratch with zero "contaminated" history but with the service of an established organization and with collected professional experience and expertise.
- Enterprises want to have an explorative "learning from our mistakes" culture but run a traditional performance management system with fixed objectives to keep results consistently stable.
- Organizations want to be agile and flexible but at the same time predictable (e.g., in terms of budgets, profits, etc.) over a long period.
- Enterprises want to offer customers individual treatment but use quite inflexible algorithms for customer interaction, denying that mathematical models have to be optimized to fit to reality and not the other way around.

To summarize, companies would love to have a combined new and old world, only based on the advantages (which increases the range of different interests and opinions of the key stakeholders of an enterprise tremendously).

So, to repeat the reference to Lenka's song: the interesting observation and hypothesis is that an organization today wants to be everything at the same time. We will challenge this exciting hypothesis in all our cases. Assuming the hypothesis is right, this means that issues such as ambiguity and ambidexterity are not coincidental. For leaders, this means to continuously travelling with their teams through multi-polar fields of tensions and having to make decisions, step by step, milestone by milestone. This must not be arbitrary but needs fast management and decision-making processes and rules that are intertwined with the company's purpose.

As one might expect, such a situation is a good starting point for a collection of business and management literature and presentations to support leaders and experts. In such books, a lot of reasonable theory and concepts have been drafted—and also instructions in the form: "The 10 tools you have to use for success."

From our perspective, there are four main deficits recognizable:

- Firstly, current practice is far away from the proposed theories and concepts (Fig. 2), especially in the context of organizational design and culture.
- Secondly, the existing concepts and their practices—e.g., between classical organization design and agile organization design—show significant gaps which are not covered so far all, neither theoretically nor in practice.
- Thirdly, and connected to the first two reasons, there are not so many concretely applicable ideas for the transition of the organization to the future state. Instead, we have to understand that, as each situation is more or less unique, significant work has to be done to apply concepts in an ideally tailored way and to discuss how such tailoring might work.
- Fourthly—and a bit connected with the second point—we frequently experience that the different parts of large organizations are in very different maturity and cultural states, whereas one part is a modern mature network organization, another part is in the pioneer or start-up phase and the third in the phase of systemizing achieving a functional orgchart the first time. So, concepts fitting for

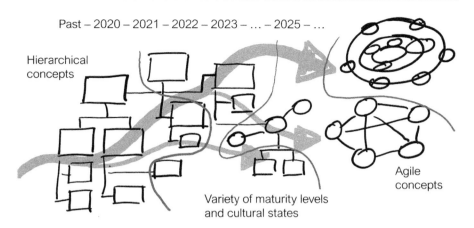

Past – 2020 – 2021 – 2022 – 2023 – … – 2025 – …

Hierarchical
concepts

Agile
concepts

Variety of maturity levels
and cultural states

Fig. 2 What is our shared understanding of past, present, and future; of organization, development, and maturity; of gaps, contradictions in our pictures of organization, and transformation? (authors' own figure)

the one part do not fit necessarily for the other parts. In general, a gap between the classical theory of organization design (mostly driven top-down) and the theory of agile organizations (nearly exclusively driven bottom-up) has to be urgently closed.

This all underlines that the current book is about one of the most important, challenging, and urgent leadership challenges for organizations facing developments that are more complex and ambiguous than they have been for decades: a situation where nobody can exactly know what the—even near—future will bring although many people with a great deal of confidence pretend to do so (and even publish recipes and solutions to remedy the situation).

In contrast to this, none of our author and editor team believed that they have any absolute truth, but rather a strong belief that most of the challenges are solvable with a well-selected group of reasonable people who are able to discuss—honestly and calmly—all the aspects and commit to going on a journey of exploration where directions and destinations might change in order to get the best result.

In this context, we explored and discussed key design building blocks ("pillars"), derived concrete principles, and tested their efficacy to get the indispensable ones which make the difference. It was quite striking that—when analyzing the huge number of cases across industries, enterprises, and institutions as well as existing literature—not many fundamental design building blocks for leadership remained consistently relevant: we found exactly three with an overwhelming fundamental importance and leadership significance, far more than a purely technical perspective, and called them "pillars."

- The sustainable purpose of an organization (bringing new orientation and certainty to the people that we want to engage for our joint endeavor)
- The mind-set of an organization in a permanent state of flux and how to cope with this—we will call it a "travelling organization"
- The capability of connecting our valuable resources such as aims and concepts, strategies and processes, experiences and competencies, balancing and interlinking peoples' interests and ideas in a flexible manner towards joint success

We will describe and define these pillars in detail below.

As we all—also the authors—are looking for meaningful orientation, especially under volatile conditions, the concepts developed have already been quickly tested in practice, and their application in the authors' practice has already turned out to be very helpful during the finishing of the book. Our business life became more effective, and we succeeded in coping with complex situations faster.

So, we are confident that the book will be also helpful for our readers. It is especially thought as an inspiration for:

- Leaders who are prepared to radically rethink and redesign their enterprises and its journey in the light of the epochal transformation in which it finds itself, in order to create a true shift in performance and value by giving a sustainable purpose, forming organizations and teams that are ready for an explorative journey, and introducing connectivity as a pillar for organization and leadership.
- Program and project heads and teams who are expected to consistently make the necessary transformations in this environment, bringing the three aforementioned pillars to life and revitalizing them on an ongoing basis. They have to be encouraged to act as travelers and connectors, following their committed purpose, facing organizational conditions that are characterized by barriers, bottlenecks, and belief in classical structures such as top-down settings.
- Consultants and trainers who support individuals, teams, and organizations to build up the required mental and methodical capabilities.
- Advanced students and academics who want to develop their understanding of modern creative organizational strategies.

Reference

Dignen, B., & Wollmann, P. (Eds.) (2016). Leading international projects: Diverse strategies for project success. London: KoganPage.

Three Pillars of Organization and Leadership

Peter Wollmann, Frank Kühn, and Michael Kempf

Abstract

In this chapter, the identified and explored unchanging building blocks or—how the authors name them—pillars for "good organization, leadership, management, and governance" are described in detail.

We strongly assume that in volatile, uncertain, complex, and ambiguous (VUCA) businesses, enterprises need to be organized and managed in a dynamic way, committed to a clear direction and belief, developing and connecting the valuable resources they need to create impact and value. And facing this VUCA world, they must neither wait nor take long-term decisions but have to take next steps, again and again: experimenting, prototyping, and piloting their ideas and approaches so as to find the right development path.

As mentioned above, following our key idea was to identify and explore something like the unchanging building blocks or—how we name them—pillars for "good organization, leadership, management, and governance" in the described new business world, and for the transition to the future, we found exactly three pillars. To be competent in building on them will become a key success factor in the future.

P. Wollmann (✉)
Consulting Partner, Bonn, Germany
e-mail: pw@peterwollmann.com

F. Kühn (✉)
Consulting Partner, Dortmund, Germany
e-mail: fk@kuehn-cp.com

M. Kempf (✉)
Consulting Partner, Bad Honnef, Germany
e-mail: michael@kempf-cp.com

© Springer Nature Switzerland AG 2020   11
P. Wollmann et al. (eds.), *Three Pillars of Organization and Leadership in Disruptive Times*, Future of Business and Finance,
https://doi.org/10.1007/978-3-030-23227-6_3

Sustainable Purpose

The people in the organization need to know why they are doing what they are doing and why they are making the decisions. The purpose has to remain very stable, be supported by leaders and employees, be inspirational, and be lived out in practice, starting with the top management.

Or in other words: the purpose is giving clear and convincing orientation on the right level that aligns and inspires the people to a joint endeavor, which makes them confident and proud to be part of it and contribute to it. This is vastly different to visions that are reduced to mere figures and financial goals, as is the case in many companies, and which only serve to alienate people from their valuable work. In contrast to strategy and goals, the sustainable purpose remains unchanged for a longer period, as it is formulated on a meta-level but is concrete enough to inspire the people and make them engage for success of the company or institution.

Travelling Organization

The organization's understanding has to be that it is continuously on a journey towards the best possible results and joint success in partly unforeseeable influences. On the map, it will potentially have to zigzag, always exploring the best path between poles, alternatives, and options. Sometimes, the people in the organization don't know them, and then they have to make smaller steps and explore the land— based upon their sustainable purpose and enabled by their connected resources.

Even if they don't know what they will have to face around the next bend and what the best result will then be, they believe in their motivation and joint capabilities to manage it. This makes a fundamental difference to the illusion of business consistency, strategic stability, and structural continuity in disruptive times, as is sometimes promised to the managers and employees after completion of a change project. Travelling organizations need holistic agility in their mind-set and DNA, covering an agile mentality, self-reflection, readiness to embrace change, and willingness to deliver. People in a travelling organization are curious, open, and impartial, have the capacity for self-reflection, are experimental, and cope well with uncertainty, special challenges, and unforeseen obstacles.

Connecting Resources

The organization has to be aware that impact, value, and efficiency need connectivity between individuals, between people and organization, between ways of working and customer needs, and between strategy and skills. This means managing connectivity, preventing unconnected strategies and processes from developing, and continuously re-arranging connectivity on the company's journey. This is in marked contrast to the compartmentalization of the company's resources in terms of structural silos, hidden agendas, boxed competencies, individual incentives, and behaviors. And there is one additional huge advantage: only with an intelligent and flexible connectivity is it possible to balance the (increasingly) different interests within the company and between its multiple key stakeholders. This is a systemic asset that is not to be underestimated.

Model Testing via a Case Study

Peter Wollmann, Frank Kühn, and Michael Kempf

Abstract

In this chapter, the developed model of the trio of pillars for organization and leadership in disruptive times is seriously tested in a concrete case study of a company producing high-tech electrical components for manufacturing plants. The test is successful and proves the dimension and concrete impact of the model in detail.

After having identified this trio of pillars for organization and leadership in disruptive times, we discussed how to test their usability, how to exemplify them, and how to convey their relevance to the organization design community. From there, we developed the idea to prototype an article on a real case. The case description refers to the pillars and is based upon the micro-article approach, i.e., developing an outline of the situation, followed by analyses of the issues and possible solutions, and finally some take-aways. In the following, you can read an overview with some excerpts; you will find the longer version of the article later in the book.

P. Wollmann (✉)
Consulting Partner, Bonn, Germany
e-mail: pw@peterwollmann.com

F. Kühn (✉)
Consulting Partner, Dortmund, Germany
e-mail: fk@kuehn-cp.com

M. Kempf (✉)
Consulting Partner, Bad Honnef, Germany
e-mail: michael@kempf-cp.com

© Springer Nature Switzerland AG 2020
P. Wollmann et al. (eds.), *Three Pillars of Organization and Leadership in Disruptive Times*, Future of Business and Finance,
https://doi.org/10.1007/978-3-030-23227-6_4

15

Context

The case is about the travel of an electrical company that started its transformation from a solid product supplier to an agile solution provider, learning how to continuously adapt the organization to dynamic markets and customers' business journeys. In terms of competencies, it meant connecting the humans' expertise and creativity across the global organization and collaborating in changing teams. In terms of leadership, it meant taking the people on this expedition through uncertain territory, with rapid reflecting, learning, and re-alignment loops—and understanding that this would be an ongoing and continuous process in the future.

Situation

For decades, the company had produced high-tech electrical components for manufacturing plants. The development teams had used all their knowledge, ambition, and pride in realizing brilliant products. But in the last 2 or 3 years, they had had to accept that their customers were looking for reasonable and specific solutions for their complex systems rather than highly sophisticated catalogue (off-the-shelf) products. Thus, the Executive Team decided to replace their classic, sequential Product Development Process (PDP) with a progressive and co-creative Solution Creation Process (SCP), including a framework of concrete agile process management principles. This approach had two goals: rapid installation of a radical customer-oriented process and—using the process as a vehicle—starting the transformation of the organization as a whole (Fig. 1).

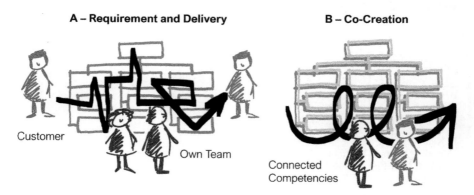

Fig. 1 From (**a**) a rather complicated process for understanding customer demands, working on them, and delivering the outcome to (**b**) a co-created solution more suited to the customer's journey (figure: Frank Kühn)

Issues and Solutions

The challenges and the solutions were manifold. The following paragraphs give an overview of both: What barriers and hurdles arose, and how were they tackled in order to advance both the transformation project as a whole and the new Solution Creation Process (as core process and entry project to the transformation).

There wasn't much shared experience in the organization concerning the larger dimension of transformation. Therefore, the question was how to staff a Core Team and a Champion Team who should coordinate and support the project, and how to get them on board? Research was started across the global organization and candidates were identified. A real breakthrough was a joint workshop with the Executive Team, the future Core Team, and the Champion candidates. They met on an equal footing and co-created the roles and tasks each of them were to take on. This initial workshop created a huge commitment to the project and its purpose. Resources were connected across the hierarchical structures, and the "travel group" had formed.

The next question arising was about the employees: How to involve them? Change projects and organizational transitions have to face various unforeseeable developments, uncertainties, barriers, and resistance. And, in this case, they suffered from the negative bad experiences that employees had had and personal survival strategies they had developed. The ambition was to make the employees a real Change Community. Vertical communication was applied to discuss the transformation, with participants from all organizational levels in a common market place: Executive Team, local headquarters, middle management, works council, and operational teams. Most questions and action items focused on the three pillars: how to communicate, internalize, and realize the purpose, how to create the joint journey together with the people, and how to respect and connect the resources they were willing to bring.

As a main hurdle, the participants in the workshops addressed bad collaboration across structural, functional, and local borders. Often, the differences between functions (e.g., classic conflict between Sales and R&D) seemed even bigger than those between regional cultures. Thus, the Executive Team stated again and again that there was no alternative but to build a new quality of collaboration as a prerequisite to realize the purpose. Cross-functional workshops were used to connect the resources in depth and shift mutual understanding, with true deep dives into the variety of individual perceptions, professional expectations, and behavioral patterns. Joint working on the future Solution Creation Process turned out to be a good anchor to connect personal and social findings with business requirements.

An additional barrier was the hierarchical management practice that had been exercised over many years. Leadership was understood as a position, not as a task, and the guiding management principle was command and control. But they felt that this practice didn't work any longer in view of increasing uncertainty and complexity, decentralized units looking for more autonomy, and a younger generation with different expectations of leadership. Some of the managers were very open-minded, understanding very well the need to shed classical management practices, distribute their territory, and take on a new role, e.g., in encouraging and supporting self-organized teams and serving customer-oriented processes. Others were reluctant. In the end, each manager had to make his or her individual decision whether to join the expedition or to leave it, whether to stand for the purpose and vision or not, and whether to be open to trustful connectivity or not.

Decision-making turned out to be one main hurdle that slowed down the Product Development Process as well as the management processes in general. Participants in decision meetings used the opportunity to distinguish themselves instead of solving problems effectively. Hidden conflicts arose everywhere. In addition, meetings and workshops were badly prepared, facilitated, and followed up. New conflict management and decision-making practices seemed necessary. The managers learned how to make smaller and quicker decisions, how to better prepare decisions, and how to apply, e.g., sociocratic practices such as consent. Conflict management workshops were run, using the future Solution Creation Process as an example for uncovering contradictory views and interests, and how to solve them. The results confirmed the identified pillars: shared purpose as guidance for effective decisions and conflict management, connectivity for integrating different experiences and interests, and speed as key to managing the travelling organization successfully.

The need to shift the collaborative mind-set met the lack of experience concerning how to involve other functions and customers in co-creative processes. One action was to design and run cooperation workshops around the Solution Creation Process that included participants from Marketing, Sales, R&D, and Production as well as participants from the customer side. The workshops were designed as vivid platforms for connecting experiences, needs, and ideas for future solutions and shared processes. They set the next milestones for the organization's travel.

Besides all these activities, some doubt was perceived among the employees; some of them didn't really believe in their managers' capability and motivation to change and to be true role models of the future organization, and especially the Solution Creation Process. Responding to this perception, specific measures were agreed: managers were offered coaching before taking on their new roles, critical meetings were facilitated by the champions, specific workshops were set up to convey tools for managing a travelling organization and connectivity, and peer consulting sessions supported the exchange of experience and ideas. In addition, the initial vertical communication was followed up by the so-called communication circles where managers and employees experienced another kind of connectivity: a new place, a new format, a new quality of communication, and a new cross-structural openness, each connected to each other.

Often, people are theoretically told that a sustainable purpose is a must in travelling organizations, giving the direction and keeping everything together, and that connecting internal and external resources is necessary to deliver progressive solutions and to avoid waste of scarce capacities. They will believe it or not. Instead, employees were involved and practiced the transformation and its advantages from the beginning. They experienced a new quality of collaborative process design. They connected their interests and knowledge, co-created solutions, solved conflicts, made rapid decisions, received customer feedback, and integrated it effectively, driven by a committed purpose and experience of connectivity.

Some Further Takeaways for the Travelling Mind-set

The most fundamental learning points were the following.

- Arrange the organizational journey together with the people. Ask them: What has happened to date, what is the current situation, what expectations and ideas do you have about the future? What are our strengths, and what should we do more of? Is there anything in our culture that could prevent us from succeeding?
- Transformation needs trust, and trust needs clarity. Communicate a clear purpose and reason, involve your employees in planning the joint endeavor, connect the people across the organization, again and again. Be aware: Resistance is caused by skepticism, fear, or bad treatment of people.
- Set up a balance of what the people will lose and what they will win when embarking on the journey. Consider the outcome: Do you need to strengthen the purpose? Do people need more connectivity between strategy and daily work, between purpose and urgency of change?
- Coach your managers and team leaders when taking on their new roles. Discuss typical interactions that are part of their new roles: Convey the purpose even with challenging audiences; take skeptical people on the journey; connect all available resources again and again.
- Create events that clearly demonstrate your understanding of how to connect your most valuable resources: Offer vivid platforms to make your employees interact with each other and with your providers and customers. Install such social hubs as key elements of your travelling organization.
- Check all organizational resources in terms of how they are connected with the intended transformation and its prototype, in this case the Solution Creation Process. What does it means for other processes, functions, projects, technologies, and skills? Learn together how to connect all those threads.
- Open the organization; otherwise it can't travel. Strategies, teams, functions and roles, processes, and practices may change. Resources migrate across organizational borders and contribute benefit wherever they can. Agree rules how to handle this agility and adaptability. The purpose will guide you; connectivity holds it all together.

Conclusion and Outcome Evaluation of the Testing: A "Practical Theory" on the Three Pillars

After the hypothesis, test by prototyping. In the example described above, it makes sense to develop a practical theory based on the three pillars for organization and leadership—which strongly correspond to the latest concepts of evolutionary organization, experimental change and innovation processes, self-organizing teams, and lateral leadership and circles that develop and work across structures—in order to face a VUCA world that can no longer be managed centrally.

First Pillar: Sustainable Purpose

It sounds so easy and yet is so difficult, especially for insiders, to formulate the final purpose of an enterprise, an organization. This is not about what the target for the next 3 years from a financial or strategic perspective might look like, it is about how the organization justifies its existence or why the world needs this organization. So, one has to think fundamentally and simply and outside-in. This contains, in many cases, an explicit customer perspective (not a self-interest-based view). If the purpose is easily understandable and obviously acceptable, it provides a strong direction for the organization and its leaders and employees.

Second Pillar: Travelling Organization

As mentioned above, organizations are a bit "spoiled" by an overkill of exact and detailed planning demands—as they strive for certainty and risk avoidance. The thinking created by this culture is inevitably not very entrepreneurial and causes the rigidity, immutability, and inflexibility of large organizations (the large tanker effect). The disruptive and accelerated development of the markets in general and, concretely, the environment of enterprises demands a start-up mentality of entrepreneurs: to embark on a journey to cover a relevant part of the sustainable purpose of the organization, to act on the journey on the basis of entrepreneurial capabilities, of fast analysis of environmental changes and their impact; of fast, stable, and definite decisions; and of very flexible understanding of plans and plan modifications. Perhaps, one of the most famous examples for this mind-set beyond the successful start-ups (intensively analyzed in Alberto Casagrande's article) is the Shackleton expedition, which was identified as a masterpiece of leadership in a travelling organization.

Third Pillar: Connecting Resources

There was an interesting announcement recently in the leading German newspaper *Süddeutsche Zeitung*. A new scientific interdisciplinary institute was founded by the German government to support ministries and their institutions. In the so-called

Fig. 2 Three pillars that are closely interlinked: purpose explaining the raison d'être and creating engagement, the shared understanding of a travelling organization to be ready for future challenges, and connected resources to manage them with joint efforts (authors' own figure)

BIMSB (Berlin Institute for Medical Systems Biology), scientists from Medicine, Biology, IT, etc. will cooperate. There will be no departments, no classic organizational chart, but merely the desire that everybody should interact and cooperate with everybody else. It is a milestone in Civil Service working style and methods.

Another dimension of connectivity has already been stressed several times above. It is the role of connectivity capabilities to realize stable and resilient commitments on interlinking strategies and processes, competencies, and working styles in a very complex enterprise (Fig. 2), in a landscape of epochal transformation where it is normal that the key enterprise stakeholders have a wide range of different interests, opinions, and ambitions. Solutions are only possible if all key players get involved flexibly, engage in prudent negotiations, personal communications, etc.—it is, in fact, a mammoth task akin to that of a diplomatic service in the multi-polar world. The enterprise-specific institutions and processes to support and facilitate this are also of high value for the enterprise's travel as they help in every unexpected situation.

So, radically speaking, the outcome of the case study is invest your valuable energy, deep motivation, and scarce capacities in working—in a self-organizing team environment—on an inspiring purpose, contributing to the corporate journey, building connections. Question everything else.

Practice Clusters of This Book

Peter Wollmann, Frank Kühn, and Michael Kempf

Abstract

Four practise clusters to structure the case studies in the articles are introduced.

The "practical theory" on the three pillars has been successfully applied, or at least thought through, in nearly 20 cases run and experienced in different industries and contexts worldwide by our community of authors. The articles are clustered into four main areas (Fig. 1):

- Leadership & Systems
- Projects & Interventions
- Humans & Enterprises
- Talents & Capabilities

These areas relate to, and overlap with, one another but should provide a first orientation.

The Leadership & Systems area is a fundamental one with contributions more on a meta-level and looking at how to cope with cardinal rules, demands, challenges, and issues.

P. Wollmann (✉)
Consulting Partner, Bonn, Germany
e-mail: pw@peterwollmann.com

F. Kühn (✉)
Consulting Partner, Dortmund, Germany
e-mail: fk@kuehn-cp.com

M. Kempf (✉)
Consulting Partner, Bad Honnef, Germany
e-mail: michael@kempf-cp.com

© Springer Nature Switzerland AG 2020
P. Wollmann et al. (eds.), *Three Pillars of Organization and Leadership in Disruptive Times*, Future of Business and Finance,
https://doi.org/10.1007/978-3-030-23227-6_5

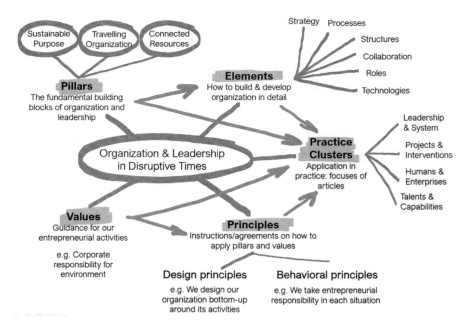

Fig. 1 The key terminology, contexts, and outcome of the book (authors' own figure)

The Projects & Interventions area is about designing and realizing real transformation with ideas how this might work and which preconditions are necessary.

The Humans & Enterprises area mainly focusses on how the necessary content-related and personal connectivity might be reached systemically and what this looks like in some enterprise contexts.

The Talent & Capabilities area has a strong Learning & Development (L&D) focus on a general level and in enterprise contexts.

Part II

Practice Cluster: Leadership and Systems

Frank Kühn, Michael Kempf, and James Chamberlain explore the three pillars for organization and leadership in detail before Isabell Huschka interlinks the pillars with leadership aspects in general, and Reto Püringer discusses them in the context of multinational enterprises. Fernando Sanabria focuses on aspects of connectivity and so-called trusted advisory, whereas Peter Wollmann goes into experiences of true travelling and how to transfer them to organizations. Finally, Peter and Mersida reflect how architecture might support the three pillars for organization and leadership.

The Concept of Purpose, Travelling, and Connectivity: Three Pillars of Organization and Leadership

Frank Kühn, Michael Kempf, and James Chamberlain

Abstract

The three pillars of organization and leadership are discussed as being fundamental because they enable organizations to continuously synchronize with business needs and opportunities and enable their employees to interact flexibly and successfully. The building blocks or pillars are interconnected with agile practices such as iterative procedures and minimum viable solutions. They also challenge our learning abilities beyond enriching our inner maps, i.e., adapting them and even managing their adaption.

The editors of the book introduce:

Frank Kühn who has been facilitating projects on transformation, organization, and leadership for over 25 years. Frank graduated in engineering and received his doctorate in work science. After gaining leadership experience in research and industry, he became a partner at HLP in Frankfurt and ICG Integrated Consulting Group in Berlin and Graz. Today he is a self-employed consultant and business partner of ICG and is associated with further

(continued)

F. Kühn (✉)
Consulting Partner, Dortmund, Germany
e-mail: fk@kuehn-cp.com

M. Kempf (✉)
Consulting Partner, Bad Honnef, Germany
e-mail: michael@kempf-cp.com

J. Chamberlain (✉)
University of Applied Sciences Bonn-Rhein-Sieg, Sankt Augustin, Germany
e-mail: James.Chamberlain@h-brs.de

© Springer Nature Switzerland AG 2020
P. Wollmann et al. (eds.), *Three Pillars of Organization and Leadership in Disruptive Times*, Future of Business and Finance,
https://doi.org/10.1007/978-3-030-23227-6_6

development and project partners. He has published a wide range of publications and teaches courses at universities.

Michael Kempf who has been an experienced management consultant for over 20 years. His career has spanned various jobs in social work, 10 years as a manager (HR and logistics) in industrial and retail companies and, since 1998, in advising people, leadership teams as well as working teams and organizations. Michael has co-authored numerous publications in the field of leadership and organizational development.

James Chamberlain who is the acting director of the Language Centre at the Bonn-Rhein-Sieg University of Applied Sciences in Germany. He has studied, taught, and worked in the USA, UK, Israel, France, and Germany and is a co-author in the field of international communication with numerous publications.

Introduction

The business world is transforming quicker than ever before, organizational charts and processes are being reinvented, and new business models are adopted. At the same time, we are told that people—at all times—have looked for stability in terms of orientation, structures, and finding their place therein (cf. Schön 1971). On the other hand, we learn that motivation is based on exploring, experimenting, and learning (Cable 2018). How should we interlink such aspects of life and work?

The authors of this book have defined three pillars for organization and leadership when tackling those manifold challenges, based on their own wide professional experience:

- *Sustainable Purpose*: Inspiring the people for their joint endeavor—enabling them to align their work and to proudly answer the question: What is our contribution to the world?
- *Travelling Organization*: Being aware of changing markets and needs, adapting our structures, believing in our team, motivations, and capability to manage even when disruptions arise.
- *Connecting Resources*: Connecting our strategy with our organizational set-up, our customers' needs with our processes, our motivation and skills with business opportunities.

These pillars are themselves connected with each other: The resources have to be connected with the purpose in order to be effective and the organizational dynamics need orientation through purpose and connectivity of all relevant resources; otherwise the organization will disintegrate. In the end, the purpose itself is the most relevant resource; it must be connected with everything so as to keep the joint endeavor on its volatile track.

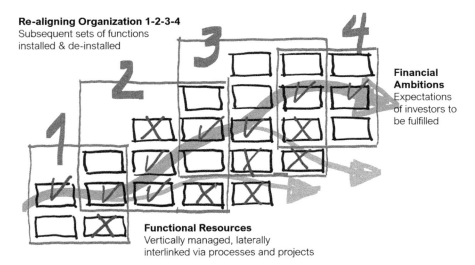

Re-aligning Organization 1-2-3-4
Subsequent sets of functions
installed & de-installed

Financial Ambitions
Expectations of investors to be fulfilled

Functional Resources
Vertically managed, laterally interlinked via processes and projects

Fig. 1 Classical organization trying to respond to business needs via repeated restructuring (authors' own figure)

In classical organizations, the relevant operational principles are often different: financial ambitions dominating the vision, restructuring projects halfway through, and separated functions only caring about meeting their cost-saving targets. People who initially deployed their talent and enthusiasm become alienated from their work, silo thinking emerges, and, as a countermeasure, processes and projects are installed to overcome these functional borders. And barely has the new multi-level structure been implemented, it has to be re-aligned to the changing business world, installing new functions and disassembling others, as displayed in Fig. 1.

Our approach makes a difference (Fig. 2); it goes with the organizational flow, continuously synchronizing with business needs and opportunities, providing the employees with the highest possible autonomy to enable quick and flexible action. There is a sustainable and shared purpose (what is our company's reason for being?) as a basis for meaningful work, offering the people an attractive perspective, allowing them to use their motivation, expertise, and creativity. The people connect all their resources because the purpose is worth it.

The connectivities themselves are the most valuable resources organizations have. Whenever adaptations and disruptions emerge or are foreseeable, concerted actions are taken to face and manage the challenge. The awareness is everywhere, and even weak signals are shared immediately: new technology opens new chances for solutions and processes, new business partners offer new opportunities for shared infrastructure, and next-generation colleagues with new skills develop progressive solutions for future customers. And everything is held together by the purpose.

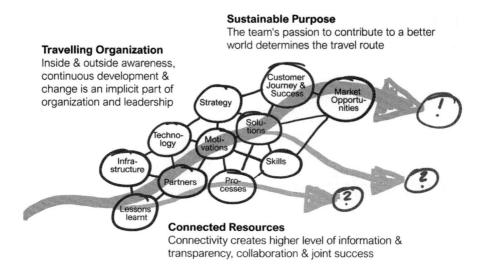

Fig. 2 A flexible organization constantly synchronizes its set-up with its purpose, market opportunities, and customers' journey, constantly connecting the relevant resources (authors' own figure)

Sustainable Purpose

The relevance of purpose is linked with the upcoming awareness of the VUCA world and the increasing realization that rigid structures and lengthy decision-making procedures are no longer appropriate to synchronize corporate activities with the complexity and dynamics of the market. Therefore, purpose is closely linked with meaningful leadership, taking people on a volatile corporate journey. The *Why* and *How* are crucial since the *What* may change. "It's not what you do, it's how you do your job and why—the strengths and passions you bring to the table no matter where you're seated" (Craig and Snook 2014). It is about "a company's core 'reason for being.' ... It provides consistency, unifies employees" and "anchor[s] them in firm values when making operational decisions." It is "creating passion and engagement among employees, resonating at a deeper and more individual emotional level, which builds and strengthens a personal commitment to the company's work. Contributing to something larger is something employees feel proud of and it creates energy. Several companies also mentioned how purpose helps to attract and retain talent, as people who are aligned with the purpose are drawn to the company" (Mazutis and Ionescu-Somers 2015).

Since moving targets, organizational change, and business transformation are omnipresent, purpose is one of the most relevant terms in search of stability, security, and guidance. When Google formulates their purpose, "To organize the world's information and make it universally accessible and useful," this inspires people and makes them proud to be part of the travelling team, contributing their part to the world.

This differs fundamentally from corporate visions reduced to figures and financial goals as found in many companies and alienating people from their valuable work, streamlining them, and making them slaves of production figures or output/input ratios: target met, work completed, and Taylorism perfected. Travelling organizations must be much more flexible, continuously synchronizing with the changing business environment. Therefore, we have to understand what reason we are working for—the *Why* —to be able and ready to adapt our targets, decisions, and structures whenever necessary.

Purpose is the strong core of companies that are able to open up to the outer system in order to interact with the challenges of the markets. This is a fundamental change of paradigm since we are used to thinking in clear borders and limiting structures, separating whatever we can separate: *Divide et impera*, as Julius Caesar recommended. In terms of opening up to the outer system, the companies will offer solutions that are designed from their customers' point of view; and that is why they are proud of them. In terms of limiting structures, they offer a catalogue of products, hoping they will suit their customers' requirements.

If structures are not stable any more, there must be something greater that creates cohesion, energy, creativity, and the courage to enter unknown territory. Thus, purpose is not only a formulation of the reason for the company's being, but it also implies behavior that makes us believe in the purpose. This context also leads to the discussion of identification and trust. Should people identify with their company? Should they trust their leaders? Exploring our own experiences and feelings, we see that we identify with purposes (more than with organizational constructions) and trust people, their competencies, and behavior (not their functions).

Therefore, the discussion of purpose includes aspects such as connecting our values and beliefs, the true meaning of our work with our motivation for connecting and setting free the potential in ourselves. To realize the power of purpose, we need to have a deeper look at human nature with its needs and potentials (beyond corporate structure and culture) when discussing the shape of future-proof organizations.

How to apply the idea of sustainable purpose:

1. Discuss with your team what your company contributes to the world. What makes you happy and proud to be part of it? How would you explain it to your family and your friends?
2. Discuss what your team can contribute to the purpose of the company. What is your team's reason for being? Why are they valuable for your company? What is the impact of your team?

(continued)

3. Formulate a purpose statement for your team that creates shared commitment and engagement for the extra mile for supporting your company on its way. Use your own words, "capture your essence"; and the purpose statement "must call you to action" (Craig and Snook 2014).

Travelling Organization

"The ability to 'travel' is crucial in order to develop organizations that are fit for the future. Travelers must be able to manage surprises, to cope with complexity and volatility. These are also the very skills needed to create a resilient organization" (Kühn et al. 2013). The ability to travel is crucial for developing and continuously adapting organizations to what is happening in the business world. Travelling teams have to face uncertainty and volatility and have to manage unexpected turns and surprises. They have to co-explore the territory and co-create the future, step by step: They have to agree on the right pace which itself can change, too, i.e., speeding up and slowing down. They have to agree on objectives iteratively because they don't know how the goals will develop in the future; perhaps there are some options. They learn from history but are not slaves to it. They have to realize that the blueprints of strategies, structures, and systems are momentary snapshots of a company that is always on the road.

We no longer have the time to complete an organization while business is passing by. The change curve—unfreeze, change, and refreeze—doesn't work any longer: The changes overlap each other. Change is always now. Change is part of the organization and the managers' permanent task. Before companies can realize their blueprints, reality will have moved on. The uncertainty and complexity of possible situations cannot been anticipated or even planned.

This is why organizations perform better if they enable and encourage their people to manage themselves. This covers awareness of what is happening inside and outside the company, taking and questioning decisions, solving conflicts themselves, sharing knowledge, and engaging in mutual coaching. The pre-condition is a clear purpose (giving the direction) and the connectivity of all resources (making this possible).

Thus, commitment to concrete working principles is crucial, e.g.:

- We discuss our working situation and working plan in a daily meeting.
- We address trouble and conflicts immediately.
- We ask for help and offer help.
- We each take responsibility for our tasks end-to-end.
- We take care of our connectivity and collaboration.
- We continuously reflect on our processes and outcomes: Do they support the purpose?

The dynamism of the market calls for a new quality of organization design. Agile practices for daily work have been proposed, such as collaborative conflict solving and peer consulting. And there are a number of tools such as rapid prototyping, design thinking, or microprojects that help us to speed up change and innovation, focusing on the customers' true needs.

See, for example, the development of business processes that are designed from the customers' point of view: What are the key touchpoints to the customer that have to work (instead of perfectionism along the whole value chain)? What are the crucial interactions between customers and employees? What are typical success situations? And then: How can we improve the processes in our organization and the qualifications of our teams in a way that will deliver true success? In this way, we will be able to speed up the development of our organization and pace the adaptation with market needs and opportunities.

> How to apply the idea of travelling organization:
>
> 1. Identify the markets (sales market, raw materials market, workforce market, technology market, etc.) and other influences with which your organization is connected and how they are affected by volatility, uncertainty, and change.
> 2. Set up communication platforms for sharing your insights and viewpoints and discussing the organizational situation. Benefit from humans' experience and creativity: Which influences are there that prevent the organization from synchronizing with current and future markets?
> 3. Explore the top influences. Apply the 5-why technique to understand them in depth. Follow the smoke to find the fire: Why aren't people open to peer consulting? Why do they mistrust their peers? Why does confidential information tend to be leak through the organization? Why is this kind of information culture relevant for the organization? Why do we lack professional information practices?
> 4. Then ask how to tackle barriers and create new opportunities. What interventions and organizational adaptations can be helpful? Think laterally to find unorthodox solutions.
> 5. Plan your travel in terms of next steps and people to take with you, some of them as expedition team or vanguard.
> 6. Walk the talk: Go on your joint journey—and communicate.

Connected Resources

The first known use of the word connectivity dates back to 1893. It has always been a technical term, used in such fields as topology and graph theory, ecology, urban planning, and image processing. Most recently, it has become associated with computer technology, in particular the ability of mobile devices to connect to, or communicate with, other devices, computers, or systems. This has led to an increasingly metaphorical use of the term to describe social connections between the users of such technologies and media.

Our approach is more comprehensive, extending the metaphor beyond its technical origins: In general, people are not effective if they are not connected in relationships, teams, or organizations. Business success, process optimization, and shared enthusiasm are always created out of connectivity. The interaction between an employee and a customer is the key experience of a customer (cf. the "touchpoints" mentioned above). Do the customers experience good support, do they feel that their problem is truly understood, are they offered a solution (and not a standard product?), do they develop trust?

But even this view is not enough. If the interaction is not connected to the purpose of the company, it is in danger of failing in business terms. If the conversation with the customer is interconnected with the employee's motivation to help the customer, but not connected to the company's purpose to offer highly standardized products, it will disorientate the customer and create additional costs in the form of a service not provided in the product portfolio and—consequently—not covered in the corporate process landscape.

And even this view is not enough. If the purpose of the company is not connected with the processes, the processes are in danger of wasting energy and money, and the purpose is in danger of not being fulfilled nor giving credible orientation to the employees. And because entropy is a natural law, everything tends to fall apart if we don't maintain connectivity. Often, we experience a lack of connectivity when strategies are presented from the top down: they are not connected to valuable resources such as the experiences and ideas of the staff, to knowledge incorporated in business processes, to current projects, and to the managers' perception of the business world and customers' needs. For instance, we experienced a fully committed CEO who unveiled her strategy during a management meeting but got little understanding from the participants. The discussion was certainly valuable, but she realized that they needed to restart the process and to co-create the strategy for quality and acceptance reasons. Finally, she adopted this kind of collaboration as a principle of her further leadership work, ensuring participant engagement through their connectivity with the process.

Both effectiveness and efficiency are based upon connectivity in a system and between systems. This means connectivity between individuals, between people and purpose, between purpose, products, and processes, etc. Without connectivity, the parts of the system are ineffective. No part can be realized by itself. Purpose is not effective if not connected with passion. This also means that connectivity doesn't work without mutual trust and true engagement—connectivity is much more than networking.

How connectivity can be used as key to success:

- Strategy needs to be communicated and connected with employees' skills and motivations—otherwise, it will remain the secret of the Management Board.

- Process improvement needs connectivity with available technology and infra-structure—otherwise, it will remain theory.
- Processes have to be closely interconnected to the purpose of the company—otherwise, the purpose will not be served, and a lot of energy and creativity will be wasted.
- Technology in terms of media and tools needs connectivity to the employees' and partners' skills—otherwise, their advantages won't be used.
- Solutions must be connected to customer journeys—otherwise, we will have invested in products that are not bought or customer relationships that won't survive.

How to apply the idea of connected resources:

1. Collect and display your resources together with your team (Fig. 2).
2. Describe and assess the connections between the resources.
3. Analyze the reasons and consequences of poor connections: little contact, unwillingness, differences in quality, maturity or interests, etc.
4. Derive an action plan to tackle the most urgent issues.

Many companies discuss their development by applying models such as the well-known 7S model (Waterman et al. 1980). You can use such models to check the connectivity between the factors defined within them. The distinction we make is that we see the relevance of active and vital connectivity as being more important than any aspects and their smart alignment. This means: The idea of connectivity drives any development, not the idea of elaborating a strategy or process for itself. From a consultant's view, this implies a disruption from offering standard expertise (focusing on one or two organizational aspects) towards penetrating into the company's inner logics and resources.

Consider the following case: The Quality Manager started to describe the business processes in order to be well prepared for an audit. When the auditor investigated not only the process descriptions but also how people applied them, there was little connectivity between process requirements and daily practice. Finally, the daily practices proved to be better connected to corporate principles that people believed in (such as customer satisfaction, knowledge sharing). The belief in the principles was based upon their strong connection to the company's purpose to provide their customers with top service. The principles also gave more space to manage daily volatile requirements in agile and adaptive ways of working—for fulfilling the company's purpose. Following from this, some meetings were set up to reconnect the processes to the teams' good practices and to learn from their valuable experiences.

Time and Pace

Having discussed the relevance of purpose, travelling, and connectivity as fundamental pillars, we now have to look at time. Time is one of the most difficult aspects; it isn't a fact on the table. It is about past, present, and (an unknown) future. Because of this, complex tasks are nowadays approached using iterative approaches, e.g., the developers of software apps build minimum viable products (MVPs), get customer feedback, and then plan the next development steps. Or managers make "time-limited" decisions to approach a solution that suits uncertain future challenges, instead of final decisions, not considering that business conditions will change during the course of the decided action line (cf. Dörner 2015).

Often, people look for a clear plan of activities end-to-end. This may be an appropriate procedure for "simple" tasks where we know what to do. Facing "complicated" issues that don't fit into well-prepared and standardized procedures, it is more appropriate to involve experts in order to explore the subject and agree on the procedure. "Complex" means that the issue is not plannable at all: We need, first, steps to explore the issue and understand the challenge, and then we continue step-by-step, in loops of trying, understanding, and continuing (Snowdon and Boone 2007).

Real-time data supports this development, also creating new attitudes and behavior. Let us consider Henry Beck's London Underground map, which was revolutionary at the time (Leboff and Demuth 1999), and how navigation has developed to date. There is an analogy to three learning levels as defined by Bateson and presented by Tosey (2006) and Oestereich and Schröder (2017): (1) learning by incorporating new information into our inner map; (2) learning and developing new inner maps; and (3) learning and reflecting on our way of developing and handling our inner maps.

In terms of travelling and connectivity, the exchange and mutual understanding of our inner maps are crucial. You won't be successful in explaining the common route to be taken if your people relate to different maps (Fig. 3).

Thus, let us come back to the London Underground map and apply the three levels to our way of navigation:

1. Using a familiar map: The presentation of the underground routes is embedded in a traditional city map. Travellers can immediately recognize relevant stations and trains.
2. Using a different, more abstract kind of map providing us with reduced information: All stations in the town and the underground lines connecting them, arranged as a geometric network. The travellers have to identify the relevant stations and connections, mirroring them to their (inner) city map—if they still have one.
3. Using real-time data: Follow the app on your smartphone, and you will reach the destination in the quickest time possible. Go to platform A and board train B. No need to know the town nor the timetable. But you can go to the app pages with more information if you are interested. And you can reflect on your way of

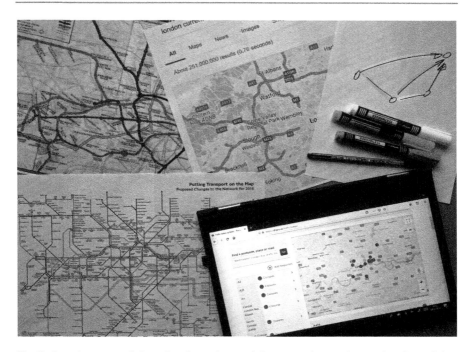

Fig. 3 Learning to travel: knowing the stations and the connections and managing the real-time situation (authors' own figure)

dealing with information, especially whether city maps and context knowledge still have any meaning for you.

That means we must always adapt and learn. This challenge addresses all elements of our organization. Sustainable purpose, travelling organization, and connected resources now mean that we have to synchronize the development and follow a shared rhythm, in order not to lose co-travellers, co-creators, nor the linkage between process reality and process blueprint, between strategy and market opportunities, and between our solutions and our customers' journeys.

How to transform your organization:

1. Set up a meeting with your team or a workshop with key people from different units.
2. Intro: Clarify the purpose of your company and keep it in mind during the following discussion.

(continued)

3. Create a shared understanding that your company has to enter unknown territory to reveal new opportunities and future-proof solutions.
4. Draft the resources and their connections. Identify substantial elements and connections. Separate elements that are not contributing to the purpose or are not connected. Mark elements and connections that don't work well.
5. Describe how the map is moving, what the speed and rhythm of movement is, and where it differs significantly between elements and connections. Identify the key issues, e.g., how to pace the connectivity between sales teams and supporting functions.
6. Analyze and discuss how the organization has dealt with such challenges to date, e.g., repeated conflict management.
7. Create ideas as to how to manage connectivity and travel in a more effective way, e.g., weekly meetings with key sales and support teams.
8. Discuss what is preventing your organization from realizing your meeting schedule, e.g., little time and weak self-management, and define activities how to tackle this, e.g., test weekly meetings and review in 4 weeks.

Conclusion

As a conclusion, we propose a dual model for any organizational transformation. First: focus on a strong and sustainable purpose; otherwise, you won't tap into the passion of your team. Communicate the picture of a travelling organization with a strong team of travellers who have the courage to embark on the joint endeavor; otherwise, change readiness won't be consistent. Connect the resources; otherwise, your strategies, processes, and competencies are not worth developing further. Second: manage the transformation in quick loops; otherwise, you will lose joint orientation and energy. This second part is increasingly being realized in modern change and project management approaches such as Scrum, Prototyping, Rapid results, or Micro projects; these approaches are based upon powerful communication processes and platforms. This second aspect is—relatively—easy as long as change and transformation projects happen from time to time. The first part seems much more difficult, because it attacks well-established power structures fundamentally, as Julius Caesar (and later Frederick Taylor) stated: divide and rule. That is why you need to involve your top management in experimenting with new approaches, being role models, and taking an active part in teams working on the challenge.

References

Cable, D. (2018, March 12). Why people lose motivation—And what managers can do to help. *Harvard Business Review*. Retrieved from https://hbr.org/2018/03/why-people-lose-motivation-and-what-managers-can-do-to-help?xing_share=news

Craig, N., & Snook, S. A. (2014, May). From purpose to impact. *Harvard Business Review*. Retrieved from https://hbr.org/2014/05/from-purpose-to-impact

Dörner, D. (2015). *Die Logik des Misslingens. Strategisches Denken in komplexen Situationen* (13. Auflage). Hamburg: Rowohlt

Kühn, F., Haselbach, D., & Gustafsson, T. (2013, February). *The art of travelling—Creating a shift towards a resilient organization*. ICG Change.

Leboff, D., & Demuth, T. (1999). *No need to ask! early maps of London's underground railways*. Berkshire: Capital Transport Publishing.

Mazutis, D., & Ionescu-Somers, A. (2015, February). *How authentic is your corporate purpose?* IMD Global Center of Sustainability Leadership.

Oestereich, B., & Schröder, C. (2017). *Das kollegial geführte Unternehmen*. München: Vahlen.

Schön, D. A. (1971). *Beyond the stable state*. New York: Random House.

Snowdon, D. J., & Boone, M. E. (2007, November). A leader's framework for decision making. *Harvard Business Review*.

Tosey, P. (2006, May). Bateson's levels of learning: A framework for transformative learning? Paper presented at: Human Resource Development Conference, Tilburg. Retrieved from http://www.ufhrd.co.uk/wordpress/wp-content/uploads/2008/06/12-2_tosey.pdf

Waterman, R., Jr., Peters, T., & Phillips, J. R. (1980). Structure is not organization. *Business Horizons, 23*(3), 14–26.

Further Reading

Bockelbrink, B., Priest, J., & David, L. (2017). *Sociocracy 3.0*. Retrieved from https://sociocracy30.org/the-details/history/

Cortese, J. (2015). *The future of work*. San Francisco: Designmind/Frogdesign.

Dörner, D. (1997). *The logic of failure: Recognizing and avoiding error in complex situations* (4th ed.). Cambridge, MA: Perseus.

Hofert, A. (2016). *Agiler Führen*. Wiesbaden: Springer.

Kahnemann, D. (2012). *Thinking, fast and slow*. London: Penguin.

Kegan, R., & Lahey, L. L. (2009). *Immunity to change*. Boston: Harvard Business Review Press.

Laloux, F. (2014). *Reinventing organizations*. Brussels: Nelson Parker.

Matzler, K., Bailom, F., von den Eichen, S. F., & Anschober, M. (2016). *Digital disruption*. München: Vahlen.

Pfläging, N. (2014). *Organize for complexity* (3rd ed.). Wiesbaden: Betacodex Publishing.

Purps-Pardigol, S. (2015). *Führen mit Hirn*. Frankfurt: Campus.

Rüther, C. (2018, August 12). Agile Selbstorganisation—Wie aus Mit-Arbeitern Mit-Unternehmer werden. *Skript*. Retrieved from http://www.christianruether.com/wp-content/uploads/2018/08/agile-selbstorganization-gesamt1.3.pdf

Leadership Creating Organizational, Interactional, and Individual Impact

Isabell Huschka

Abstract

Future-proof organizations need a sharpened understanding of leadership—as a power that takes influence and creates impact, as organizational, interactional, and individual performance. This article gives an insight into concepts and ideas that foster a more collaborative leadership approach. Ultimately, it is a question of re-examining and applying leadership concepts that serve the company on its way towards success based upon the three pillars of purpose, travelling, and connectivity.

The editors of the book introduce **Isabell Huschka** who is acting now as a senior consultant with the passion of identifying, developing, and cultivating a more collective leadership force inside organizations. Before she worked in different HR management functions in the Foods and Automotive Industries and having managed the Academy for Modern Leadership at a well-known consulting firm. The focus of her work in change projects and organization development is leadership.

Introduction

From the author's experience in organization development, there is still a significant difference in leadership practice and progressive leadership understanding: The concept of the individual heroic leader and of concentrating decisions on "the person

I. Huschka (✉)
HUSCHKA Organisationsentwicklung & Führung, Lauterbach, Germany
e-mail: isabell.huschka@huschka-consulting.de

© Springer Nature Switzerland AG 2020
P. Wollmann et al. (eds.), *Three Pillars of Organization and Leadership in Disruptive Times*, Future of Business and Finance,
https://doi.org/10.1007/978-3-030-23227-6_7

41

at the top," i.e., legitimated authority and purely focusing on the development of individuals with regard to the development of the leading forces, is no longer adequate for today's requirements.

Even though there are organizations that do operate according to the classical school of thought, although organizations and individuals do have difficulties letting go long-held ideas and concepts and though corporate cultures tend to change only with deliberate action, future-proof organizations need a "new" way of thinking and living leadership.

To justify the thesis above, there are many arguments in the relevant literature: Salicru (2017) refers to a leadership crisis and argues in consideration of ineffective, unethical, and untrustworthy managers. Winkler (2012) points to the growing need of employees to work independently, to influence or take part in decisions, and thus to refuse traditional hierarchical leadership structures. Heifetz (1994 and 2009) mentions the "adaptive challenges" in which it is no longer possible for an individual to cope with the solution to, or even the definition of, the problem alone. Weick and Sutcliffe (2016) emphasize that high reliability organizations cultivate diversity and shift decision-making processes "downwards and to the forefront" in the sense of having respect for expertise in order to raise awareness in more complex environments and not to lose pace. "Complexity in the network," as described by Baecker (2016), can no longer be led according to classical models of thinking and is no answer to current challenges—neither in society nor in organizations.

Against the background of the approach as described in this book by Chamberlain/Kempf/Kühn, and in view of the increasing complexity for and in organizations, the question arises as to how leadership in organizations can be understood, shared, lived, interconnected, and cultivated.

This contribution is certainly not a plea for the complete abolition of line management (Wassenaar and Pearce 2012) and non-transparency of leading roles, rules, and frameworks—quite the contrary. It aims to reveal concepts of how leadership should be designed when organizations become more and more agile. Furthermore, it is necessary to include the prerequisites for joint travelling: the ability to connect influences, forces, and design areas of the organization and to aim at a shared purpose and an inspirational common mission.

The article outlines how leadership and the development of leadership have to be rethought in a new or different way. To do so, it connects scientifically proven theories with the author's long-standing practical experience in facilitating organization development.

The first section is to examine how leadership is to be basically understood before relevant aspects of beneficial leadership approaches are highlighted. The third section then addresses the practical implementation and development of modern leadership.

Basic Understanding of Leadership

The theses in this article are based on the understanding that leadership (and management combined) has to be seen as an ability and performance of the organization which needs suitable leadership structures, decision-making processes, and an efficient leadership system—thus an effective interaction of all leading forces. In this context, leadership initiates internal resonance to and changes in the environment and shapes it by means of its answers (interaction), systematically makes decisions within its areas of responsibility, or applies intelligent decision processes. Leading contains target-oriented creating of social situations within an organized entity (osb international 2016).

With regard to the stakeholders involved, the view of Yammarino et al. (2012) is helpful and instructive: he understands leadership as a collectivistic phenomenon in which several individual persons interact by means of formal and informal structures and take on different leading roles during a certain period of time. These leading roles do not only exist in small groups or units but may also occur throughout the organization (or in all other sorts of networks). In addition, the roles have different informal relations, networks, and connections, including personal contacts in the organization and beyond. Within this construct, formal and informal relations, structures, and roles may change fundamentally over time (thus, they are neither static nor linear) and depend on the needs of the organization and the market.

This way, leadership is characterized by processes, dynamics, and fluidity (Fig. 1) and—according to the nature of the respective organization—is shared, connected, or bundled as well as being geared to an oriented common understanding.

When leadership is thus no longer seen as the purely individual achievement of a single person who is "set" on account of hierarchical superiority, authority, or exercise of power, it is necessary to identify who or what can be a "leading force."

Fig. 1 Leadership in the past—clear constellations for clear procedures. Leadership in the future—characterized by processes, dynamics, fluidity, and connectivity (figure: Frank Kühn)

Leading forces may be established communicative patterns, mind-sets, the purpose, the market, individuals, and groups or teams. Not only employees of an organization can exert leading power but also external partners and, most of all, customers. Who or what is leading at each moment depends on the situation or context and is specifically shapeable to a certain degree—according to the impact of the organizational culture and to the choice of a particular organization design. A fundamental necessity is that a deliberate decision has been made in the organization and that there is transparency as to who or what has a leading function or exerts a certain role, in which situation and for what they are taking responsibility.

According to this interpretation, there is no "one-size-fits-all" approach nor a best practice model which can be reproduced and deployed in any organization. One of the greatest achievements that leadership in organizations can demonstrate is the choice of a suitable leadership model and the way it is then developed.

Thus, the questions arise:

- Who is leading?
- How do we distribute responsibilities?
- Which control and decision processes should be employed?

These questions have to be answered depending on the following questions (Nagel 2014):

- What is the business problem that has to be solved?
- How do we generate products and/or services?
- How complex is the environment in which we are operating?
- How is the organization set up?
- How are individual organizational units/cells, etc. interconnected?
- How do we design our working conditions?
- How do we manage coordination between persons and organizational units?

In the end, interconnection between the individual elements significantly determines a company's success and is the fundamental responsibility of leadership itself. Moreover, it is necessary to permanently raise and answer these questions in order to ensure the viability of the organization.

The following sections examine some individual aspects of leadership more closely.

Directions of Leadership: Hierarchical, Horizontal, Interconnected Leadership, and Open Boundary Areas

More and more companies deliberately choose to reduce or completely do without strong hierarchies and strict line management. Where classical forms of organization are functional or not yet ready for change, it appears practicable to implement horizontal leadership alongside hierarchical structures as well as allowing collective leadership situations. For organizations which are changing or have deliberately chosen a hybrid version of leadership, it is particularly relevant to regard the boundary areas of leadership as being open and to think in terms of transitions rather than absolute positions. In the mind-set of collective leadership, there is no place for thinking in categories of "mine" or "yours."

To apply collective leadership does not mean that responsibilities do not have to be taken and that certain roles of leadership are obsolete or will sort themselves out—thus, this does not necessarily lead to negligence, anarchy, or rejection of responsibility. It is important to create responsibilities for design (Kaltenecker 2017) and mind-set in the organization as well as for the decision concerning the development of leadership—but these responsibilities need not be permanently fixed, irrevocable, or even concentrated in one person.

Key questions regarding this aspect of leadership are:

- Is leadership conceivable in the organization even without formal hierarchical structures and legitimized powers?
- How open is the organization and how open-minded are the people acting in boundary areas of leadership?
- Is there reflection and exchange of ideas on the question of who is currently the best to lead and which action and approach is the most appropriate?
- Does leadership act horizontally and in common and does it bundle forces?
- Do the leading forces of the organization (and beyond) interconnect in a reasonable way?
- Do we ask ourselves what we need to do to make leadership fully effective?

In organizations in which these questions can be answered in the affirmative, leadership is understood and experienced as a process that is shared and distributed and can be influenced jointly. In this context, Yammarino et al. (2012) state that in organizations with collectivistic leadership approaches, traditional powers and hierarchical structures are often ignored, de-emphasized, avoided, or redefined.

Ultimately, the shared goal seems to be a decisive factor: who or what answers which question and leads the context most effectively at any given moment.

Approaches of Collective Leadership: Shared, Distributed, and Joint Leadership

To give an overview of how leadership can be shared, distributed, and designed, the following paragraph describes a number of leadership approaches that seem relevant from the author's experience and which have been scientifically evaluated.

Shared leadership (Carson et al. 2007 in Contractor et al. 2012) is an approach that views leadership as a shared responsibility among team members, where a team is viewed quite broadly, both formally and informally. A key assumption is that leadership is a set of role functions that can be accomplished by a variety of individuals in various ways. Shared leadership suggests that leadership might be distributed around the team equally, unilaterally, or in any number of ways; and decisions and actions made by the team are not the result of a single leader acting on behalf of the team.

In the context of team leadership (Day et al. 2004), leadership is considered as a joint process of identifying necessary functions to ensure team effectiveness. It is not predetermined whether a function is performed by one or multiple people (so leadership is not necessarily shared (Bolden 2011)). Team leadership describes a process in which influencing is enabling versatility, agility, and adaptivity. Mainly the concept stands out by seeing leadership not as just an input but as the outcome of joint effort to achieve a common goal.

The concept of complexity leadership assumes that all leading processes are based on complex nonlinear interactions which, in turn, have interactions with complex adaptive systems (Uhl-Bien and Russ 2007). The connection between bureaucratic and administrative functions of the organization and emergent informal systems forms a dynamic relation—a typical feature of leadership as well as of change in organizations.

In addition, there are forms of leadership that have been described in theory and partially already implemented in practice, such as:

- Empowerment—(in hierarchical structures) responsibility and power are delegated from "above" to where decisions are made in day-to-day business and can produce immediate effects.
- Leadership substitutes—processes or procedures can substitute hierarchical functions.
- Follett's law of the situation—the person in a group who has the greatest knowledge in a given situation takes the decision.
- Hollander's leadership emergence—leadership emerges or is determined by the group or by a team itself.
- Self-leadership according to Manz and Sims—groups and teams lead themselves without formal leadership.

In practice, we see modern forms of leadership as described, for example, by Laloux (2017). They often rely on self-management and self-responsibility, i.e., efficient and fluid systems involving distributed authority and collective intelligence. Depending on the respective concept, interactions, roles, and responsibilities as well as decision-making procedures are more or less formally defined and lived. The decision-making power is given to those in the organization who are in the best position to judge the situation, having regard to the common goal, and whose actions receive direct feedback.

In organizational reality, shared leadership can also be seen in organizations or organizational units run according to the Scrum methodology or similar. Here, self-organization of the teams is supported by two clearly defined leading roles—one content-related function focused on the product and one coaching function which is to develop the people and secure the process.

Nowadays, more and more theoretical approaches developed in recent years are emerging in organizations as mixed leadership forms, i.e., in combination with classical leadership structures, or as hybrids that are developed continuously.

When "Non-members" of the Organization Lead

The discussion and reflection on leadership in view of the assumptions outlined so far are not limited merely to the direct members of the organization. In fact, it appears to be useful, and more than legitimate, to involve partners and other stakeholders from the organizational environment when the question arises as to which powers are sensibly the best to lead. It seems logical to include the market as a leading power, especially in the so-called peach or collegial circle organizations (Oestereich and Schröder 2017) in which the direction of leading runs from the environment of the organization to its inner circle (i.e., where in the end, after the creation of direct added value, indirect added value is created). The resulting forms of working together are extremely diverse.

The constant realignment towards customers and thus their role as a leading power becomes clearer and more sensitive than ever in cases where agility is described and actually realized. For some organizations and their members, it is apparently much more difficult to let other market participants take the lead, without fearing the loss of power and control. In this context, in addition to deliberate decisions and transparency, the mind-set and open boundary areas are essential and determine which forms of working together are possible and, thus, what effect can be initiated.

Purpose and Mind-set as Leading Forces

In the editorial of this book, Chamberlain/Kempf/Kühn point to the fact that purpose, as a strong core of the organization, is key particularly when change and travelling shape processes in the organization. Purpose in the context of leadership is more than the aim of the organization but includes the combination of aim and mission statement, the shared deep belief in a vocation (not only of the individuals, but also of the organization), and respects of the core values of those involved. A shared mind-set—i.e., assumptions, ways of thinking, and attitudes expressed in the behavior of the members of the organization—has an equally strong impact.

In this context, Hickman and Sorenson (2016) mention invisible leadership and formulate that the purpose is the invisible power that drives people to commitment, innovation, and success and that this effect can have huge influences.

Leading via a shared mind-set and purpose and deliberately applying this kind of leadership are obviously quite different from management solely based on KPIs (Key Performance Indicators) and thus require the leading persons to use different behaviors. Shared purpose and mind-set initiate inspiration, energy, and a common bond that connects the members of the organization (irrespective of their current role) so that particularly good performance can evolve.

In this context, leaders have to trust this power and have to foster purpose and mind-set and have to communicate and to agree on both. Similar to the issue of motivation, it is rather a question of which dysfunctional behaviors have to be avoided so that purpose and mind-set can be effective and of what has to be cultivated and released in order to enable the power to take its full effect. Shared purpose and mind-set are the basis as well as the result of leadership.

Cooperation of the Leading Forces

This section contains the transition from theoretical reflections to the practical needs within organizations with regard to the design of leadership.

Connectivity of all leading forces is essential for the overall performance of the organization. This refers to the level of leadership that focuses on the cooperation and interaction of all relevant elements and, first and foremost, of all relevant persons and has a comprehensive influence and impact.

In numerous approaches, leadership is described and understood as an input or a design principle for the organizational processes. In this context, it would seen appropriate to introduce another extended perspective before discussing the concrete requirements for designing leadership in practice.

Drath et al. (2008) concentrate on the outcome and consider direction, alignment, and commitment as a result of collective leadership. For these authors, direction means a widespread agreement in a collective on overall goals, aims, and mission; alignment means the organization and coordination of knowledge and work in a collective; and commitment means the willingness of members of a collective to subsume their own interests and benefit within the collective interest and benefit. Adopting such a mind-set would mean that talk of leadership would no longer necessarily involve talk of leaders and followers and their shared goals but would necessarily involve talk of direction, alignment, and commitment. Likewise, to practice leadership would no longer necessarily involve leaders, followers, and their shared goals but would necessarily involve the production of direction, alignment, and commitment.

Against the background of the theories discussed above, the following key questions for organizations arise concerning the implementation and efficiency of their leadership performance:

- How is the connectivity of the leaders designed?
- How are the formal and informal relationships realized?
- How is the construct interconnected with the shared purpose?
- What is being talked about together?

How Can Connectivity of Leadership Be Made Reality in Practice?

With the assumption that leadership is a dynamic and fluid process, the question arises as to the ability to constantly involve and interconnect different people as leading forces—this is a key ability for leadership. Besides the structural design of communication and the creation of appropriate scopes for subjects and occasions, the way people deal with each other plays an equally important role. Here, in turn, the shared mind-set forms the basis and is emergent at the same time. Designing formal and informal relationships and being open-minded with one another are core competencies, as are respect and interaction.

Another prerequisite for such a cooperation is confidence in another person's expertise and their responsibility. At the same time, it is not a matter of course to be able to share responsibility and to combine it at crucial junctures.

The significance of communicative design is not new at all. Transparency, exchange of information, and bringing together diverse perspectives as well as resolving controversies through negotiation and managing conflicts are the other key skills needed to foster beneficial connectivity.

At the beginning of this article, it was emphasized that organizations have to become more agile to be able to meet modern demands. The precondition of agility is the ability of the members of the organization and of the organization per se to reflect and learn. Leadership has a crucial influence on how the elements mentioned above are lived and applied.

According to Brinkmann and Lang (2018), clearly formalized rules, frameworks, and processes are needed in collectively led organizations to identify and exploit the potentials of self-organization. This means that structural and shaping aspects (such as organization design and its elements) are certainly not to be replaced by the key skills mentioned above, but rather that they complement and promote each other. Defining decision-making processes and delegating decision-making powers (to those junctures in the organization where the expertise needed is to be found) are leadership roles on a par with the conscious handling of power and the way of setting and meeting targets.

The Global Leadership Forecast 2018 (Development Dimensions International et al. 2018) lists special features in organizations acting according to a collective leadership approach, including the fact that they provide a high level of psychological safety that enables employees to work in an open and trusting environment. They also show a more active culture of learning and development as well as experiential practices to find out how leadership can be developed.

Rethinking and Implementing Leadership Development

In learning organizations where reflection and error analysis are functional, leadership development is emergent but is supplemented by the deliberate use of expanded leadership development interventions. The traditional development of individuals in terms of their leadership performance in the classical sense is still relevant; however, it is no longer sufficient for the needs of collective leadership (Petrie 2014).

The development and promotion of the individual person and his or her competencies—particularly with regard to communication and cooperation skills as well as the understanding of collective leadership—has to be complemented by forms of development which are rather characterized by classical features of organization development. Human Resources and Organization Development are inseparable functions of the organization and, as such, should be seen as being interlaced and be used accordingly.

Developing competencies that enable joint leadership performance stresses the interconnection of those involved in social contexts as well as the furthering of shared mind-set, of its components and practices and the exchange of views regarding the underlying elements of shared work. In addition, it emphasizes the process of achieving an understanding of systemic perspectives and of the development of capabilities to pursue culture development. The development of a leadership culture in the sense of shared leadership needs to pass through a discovery process of naming, investigating, evaluating, and reflecting together on the various sub-cultures in the organization (Cullen et al. 2012).

Then the development of leadership more and more often assumes the forms of team development or interconnecting interventions and increasingly loses event-based forms of development of the individual. Leadership development must provide space to enable collective communication on cooperation, on the benefit of diverse perspectives and skills as well as on conflict culture. Learning is successful when it is achieved via understanding and transparent exchange on the functioning of the group/team/organization.

In this context, there are new demands not only on leaders as such—those originally responsible for learning and development—but also on those responsible for leadership development as a departmental function, who now have to reorient and position themselves anew so that organizations can benefit from all leading forces. In organizations where leadership is already understood as a shared and dynamic function, for example, the responsibility for and competence of development are shifted back to the teams at the periphery of the organization where the employees on-site know best which additional resources they need to be successful together (Laloux 2017).

With these trends, an approach for learning and development is recognized which has been realized and promoted more and more consciously since the mid-1990s: the recognition that successful learning is achieved mostly through facing challenges and solving problems in practice as well as through cooperation with others (as opposed to formalized traditional learning away from working practice).

Conclusion and Some Further Takeaways

All considerations presented in this text are directly correlated with the three pillars: purpose, travelling, and connectivity. They are the starting point, object as well as the result of the leadership approaches discussed. Most of all changing and developing leadership towards future sustainability needs open-mindedness, reflection, and the common willingness to learn.

Today, leadership is understood and practiced in a more diverse way than ever before. This opens up opportunities but also calls for a deeper understanding of the different facets: What is relevant for us? Which mind-set do we want to encourage? Which leadership approach makes us fit for the future? How can we develop in this direction? What do we want to achieve in the future? Which pressure will be encountered on today's markets, one of which is the job market with its future talents?

Impulses for Practical Implementation in the Organization

- Use this article for a discussion with your colleagues. Talk about interesting aspects and document the results in a table with three columns: Which aspects do you think can be implemented in your organization directly, which of them are desirable, and which are irrelevant? What becomes apparent?
- Together with your colleagues, think about what leadership in your organization meant in the past, what it means today, and what importance it should have in the future. Focus the discussion on the three pillars—purpose, travelling, and connectivity. Where do you see differences between the current situation and the target?
- Summarize under the headings of the three pillars how a change can be initiated and what is to be done, which priorities you want to set, and which concrete steps are to be taken next. Also determine how you want to evaluate progress.
- Adopt the three pillars in your field of responsibility: What is the goal of the change you are considering and want to promote (purpose); where do you want to create agility and on which journey do you want to embark (travelling); which people with their special interests and skills, experience, and ideas do you need to invite on board; and with which design areas of the organization do you have to connect (connectivity)?

References

Baecker, D. (2016). *Digitalisierung als Kontrollüberschuss von Sinn*. Frankfurt am Main: Zukunftsinstitut.

Bolden, R. (2011). Distributed leadership in organizations. A review of theory and research. *International Journal of Management Reviews, 13*(3), 251–269.

Brinkmann, J., & Lang, M. (2018). *Selbstorganisation braucht klare Regeln*. Frankfurt am Main: Frankfurter Allgemeine Zeitung (F.A.Z.).

Carson, J. B., Tesluk, P. E., & Marrone, J. A. (2007). Shared leadership in teams. *Academy of Management Journal, 50*(5), 1217–1234.

Contractor, N. S., DeChurch, L. A., Carson, J., Carter, D. R., & Keegan, B. (2012). The topology of collective leadership. *The Leadership Quarterly, 23*, 994–1011.

Cullen, K. L., Palus, C. J., Chrobot-Mason, D., & Appaneal, C. (2012). Getting to "we": Collective leadership development. *Industrial and Organizational Psychology, 5*(4), 428–432.

Day, D. V., Gronn, P., & Salas, E. (2004). Leadership capacity in teams. *The Leadership Quarterly, 15*(6), 857–880.

Development Dimensions International, The Conference Board, & EYGM Limited. (2018). *Global leadership forecast 2018*.

Drath, W. H., McCauley, C. D., Palus, C. J., Van Velsor, E., O'Connor, P. M. G., & McGuire, J. B. (2008). Direction, alignment, commitment: Toward a more integrative ontology of leadership. *The Leadership Quarterly, 19*, 635–653.

Heifetz, R. A. (1994). *Leadership without easy answers*. Cambridge, MA: Harvard University Press.

Heifetz, R. A., Grashow, A., & Linsky, M. (2009). *The theory behind the practice—Adaptive leadership framework*. Watertown, MA: Harvard Business School Publishing Corporation.

Hickman, G. R., & Sorenson, G. J. (2016). *Unmasking leadership, leading organizations—Perspectives for a new era* (pp. 168–176). Thousand Oaks, CA: Sage.

Kaltenecker, S. (2017). *Selbstorganisierte Unternehmen—Management und Coaching in der agilen Welt*. Heidelberg: dpunkt.

Laloux, F. (2017). *Reinventing organizations*. München: Franz Vahlen.

Nagel, R. (2014). *Organisationsdesign: Modelle und Methoden für Berater und Entscheider (Systemisches Management)*. Stuttgart: Schäffer Poeschel.

Oestereich, B., & Schröder, C. (2017). *Das kollegial geführte Unternehmen*. München: Franz Vahlen.

osb international. (2016). *Leadership navigator. Führung von Komplexität—Komplexität von Führung*. Berlin: osb international. Retrieved July 29, 2018, from www.osb-i.com/fileadmin/user_upload/osb_leadership_navigator.pdf

Petrie, N. (2014). *Future trends in leadership development (white paper)*. Brussels: Center for Creative Leadership.

Salicru, S. (2017). *Leadership results*. Milton, QLD: Wiley.

Uhl-Bien, M., & Russ, M. (2007). *Complexitiy leadership: Part 1*. Charlotte, NC: Information Age.

Wassenaar, C. L., & Pearce, C. (2012). *The nature of shared leadership, the nature of leadership* (2nd ed., pp. 363–389). Thousand Oaks, CA: Sage.

Weick, K. E., & Sutcliffe, K. M. (2016). *Das Unerwartete managen* (3. Auflage). Stuttgart: Schäffer-Poeschel.

Winkler, B. (2012). Shared Leadership Ansätze nutzen. *Zeitschrift für Organisationsentwicklung, 3* (2012), 4–6.

Yammarino, F., Salas, E., Serban, A., Shirreffs, K., & Shuffler, M. L. (2012). Collectivistic leadership approaches. Putting the "We" in leadership science and practice. *Industrial an Organizational Psychology, 5*, 382–402.

Purpose, Journey Thinking, and Connectivity People to People in Global Companies

Fernando Sanabria

Abstract

The article shows that a first key factor and prerequisite for people connectivity is the "sustainable purpose." The teams require a context setting to find the "why" concerning what they are doing and need to feel that, to create meaning, there is a journey ahead, full of uncertainties and changes, that will need to be faced together as a travelling organization. The sustainable purpose is thus a source of energy and ensures that project teams have the required resilience for very demanding journeys with reflexive and self-empowered teams. The article highlights which skills are crucial for this and those right individuals who are indispensable who can generate and foster the required connections between team members and stakeholders and develop the required shared trust.

The editors of the book introduce **Fernando Sanabria** who is a Computer Engineer and Program Director with broad experience in managing complex global projects. He has held senior management positions in the global consultancy and insurance industries, working with IBM and Zurich Insurance Company, with a special focus on delivery, especially in scenarios with high organizational complexity.

F. Sanabria (✉)
Barcelona, Spain

© Springer Nature Switzerland AG 2020
P. Wollmann et al. (eds.), *Three Pillars of Organization and Leadership in Disruptive Times*, Future of Business and Finance,
https://doi.org/10.1007/978-3-030-23227-6_8

53

Foreword

In current volatile, uncertain, complex, and ambiguous (VUCA) businesses, it is well-known that data and information need to flow faster and broader through the different company departments and teams. Systems need to be increasingly connected, and the level of process automation needs to rise considerably in the coming years, which is a matter of life or death for many big companies. Companies are pushed continuously to be "faster" and more "agile." In addition, every change in the company, bringing in a new level of systems connectivity, information flow, and responsiveness can be made possible, thanks to the execution of projects that involve and require the active participation of different departments and teams.

As a general reference, International Data Corporation stated some years back that almost 25% of IT projects experience outright failure, 50% of projects require material rework, and 20–25% of them do not provide the return on investment (ROI) expected. We are convinced that one of the key reasons for those failures is the inability to manage people connectivity professionally.

Thus, we should find different pragmatic ways to develop the three fundamental pillars proposed in this book, in order to gain much more agility, responsiveness, and fluency in the complex organizations we deal with these days. Reality shows that, in the future, companies will drive every change as projects, at a much faster pace than before. But a key prerequisite is that the sponsors and the leaders of those teams and organizations are able to set the right context. This is their main responsibility: setting the context and the identity for the team. Why is it so important for teams to have a joint and sustainable purpose and for each individual to find out how she/he is delivering meaningful work? This is very important in this mass information environment as it makes everyone feel their work has meaning and that they are part of a true travelling organization.

In projects, there is a start and a destination that has to be reached (target state), which is sometimes not finally fixed before part of the project journey has been travelled. Resources have to be administered efficiently to reach this target. There are plenty of well-known and unknown risks to be managed. Uncertainty is the rule in many cases, and there are different stakeholders with different expectations to be managed. Experience tells us that the correct management of expectations is a fundamental part of every project. The management of expectations requires that aforementioned joint belief in the sustainable purpose of the project and the acceptance of a flexible journey. The project becomes a travelling organization in itself rather than a sequenced set of activities, where everything to be reached at the end is clear and transparent at the start.

Connecting resources, with people at the center, is required as a success factor in current global organizations. After all, in the end, all these facts and challenges are managed by people. People who have different nationalities, cultures, beliefs, and experiences (good and bad that have left a mark in them), and who work in different departments of the company and, last but not least, have slightly or totally different mind-sets and personal agendas. A systemic advantage of connecting across the whole organization is that it provides a brilliant vehicle to make different interests transparent, to discuss and agree with them to create a convergent view.

The main question that arises, which is by no means simple, is: How can we manage the "connectivity" between people running projects that aim to have better connected systems and information flow, in an era of digitalization?

Introduction to the Problem

As can be inferred from the foreword, achieving better connectivity between systems is not the key challenge. The real challenge is to achieve the right connectivity across people in practice that, when executing the projects, will enable the changes required to make companies' systems better connected.

In this chapter, we will focus on how to deal with people connectivity in complex projects, as a way of managing change in future organizations (travelling organizations). We will also consider the ubiquitous ambition/objective of these projects, which is business sustainability.

We have discovered a fundamental problem that needs to be solved before we can have better systems connectivity. The problem is about how to approach "people connectivity" in a correct and sustainable way, to deliver better projects. Again, we are convinced that the future of any company is driven by projects and their successful execution (in all senses).

Taking some previous experience with projects, you will probably remember cases where something as simple as a good chat, between two people sharing an "informal" coffee in the office, did actually alter the direction of the project and, in so doing, considerably changed the destiny of a company department or even the company itself. All projects start with people and of course ultimately come back to people.

Various different aspects may play a key role in people connectivity (to be covered in this chapter). However, it is important to understand that there are no secret formulae for success or infallible approaches that will ensure people connectivity in every project.

This chapter aims to elaborate some specific approaches (conceptual, but at the same time, pragmatic), for dealing with the problem described above. It deals with the issue of how to enhance connectivity between people in projects, which will enable better connectivity between systems in the "Digital Era."

Key Concepts and Proposed Approaches to Address Different Aspects of People Connectivity in Projects

Here we will elaborate various different, albeit related, concepts and factors to contextualize the possible approaches to the problem covered in this chapter. All of them have much broader implications in the context of projects, but we want to develop them here with a specific focus on the problem of people connectivity. By reading and reflecting on all of them from a high-level view, we can start to observe the need to consider people connectivity in projects as a key success factor.

In order to make the development of these concepts, as simple and concise as possible, we have structured them in six main aspects. While they may be initially perceived as very diverse, we expect the reader will be able to find the idea that links all of them:

1. The natural gift of some people to create rapport with others (the connectivity skill)
2. The trusted advisor curve
3. People first react and think on the basis of emotions rather than doing so rationally
4. Storytelling: impacting on people's need to identify
5. Fail faster to succeed sooner
6. The project as a "complex adaptive system"

Aspect 1: The Natural Gift of Some People to Create Rapport with Others (the Connectivity Skill)

> The most important single ingredient in the formula of success is knowing how to get along with people. Theodore Roosevelt.

You will almost certainly have had the experience that, sometimes, you feel comfortable talking with someone who you have just met and you cannot identify why this happens. It is very common. It is a "gift" that some people possess naturally. We could develop some ideas as to why this happens, for example, these people care about the feelings of others without any specific personal interest of their own, or that they are, in general, very positive and empathetic or even that they feel very authentic and confident. But as it is not the purpose of this chapter to develop this, we can try to simply summarize it as being a natural gift that some people have.

It is common to find people with this "gift" in activities and roles related to sales, business development, or any other responsibility that requires one to start commercial relationships, business engagements, etc. They are the door openers. They are also very good at connecting and aligning people for a common purpose.

The relevance of soft skills for working well with people tops the list for common skills and habits of highly successful people. Research done by the Carnegie Foundation and Harvard University showed that as much as 85% of your job and life success depends on your ability to get along with people. These studies also concluded that only 15% of employment and management success is due to technical training, while the other 85% is due to personality factors.

And here is when this "soft," and shall we say "natural," skill becomes very relevant, in the context of projects and how to promote and trigger people connectivity across teams and areas that share a common objective. When project teams are designed, this critical skill set is often not considered carefully, as in general it is not seen as a formal skill requirement. This applies, to give just one example, when it comes to the people who will oversee the interfacing between areas in tasks such as eliciting business requirements, change management, or tool rollouts. These are just some examples of responsibilities that have the need to connect people as an underlying requirement, in addition to the obvious technical skills that the people responsible also need to have.

We can refer to some real cases, where putting certain individuals in specific roles in a project, which required a strong interfacing between areas, teams, or locations, had a considerable positive impact on how the work evolved. We can also refer to cases where the individuals with the wrong set of "connectivity" skills destroyed the possibility of successful collaboration inside the project team, ultimately leading to the failure of the project. When this connectivity skill is insufficient or lacking, also in the project leadership, the project is certain to fail. It is simply a matter of time.

I was once given the responsibility of taking over an existing global program, and the journey started without knowing my internal customers and with almost no team in charge. What is more, the program was very strategic and highly relevant in the company, with a truly global footprint. There were many parallel workstreams that were not particularly under control. In short, I was soon in a difficult situation as, with no team in place yet, I was faced with more and more demands from a wide variety of stakeholders who were not prepared to wait for their needs to be addressed and not prepared to wait until I had the "ideal" team in place to cope with all their demands. They simply wanted their own demands attended to and solved, which was fair enough. After sorting out some crucial topics on my own, I immediately focused on filling the first customer-facing and management roles, under some time pressure of course. When it came to the first person I hired, I set great store by his technical skills and background, which seemed more than suitable for the requirements of the role. But because I was recruiting under time pressure and had not considered the "connectivity skill" carefully enough, I didn't get the results I expected. Very soon my "mistake" became clear, and the "noise" in the different project interfaces for this role started to rise considerably. This immediately gave me two issues to solve: firstly, to manage the original demand and then to decide what to do with the new hire. The real mistake would have been to not react quickly enough and allow the lack of people connectivity in that specific context to develop to such an extent that it became a real problem. The solution was to start a new recruitment process and this time to consider carefully the need for connectivity skills. Finally, I hired two good talents who, in addition to their technical skills, were very good at dealing with business partners. All the project interfaces started to evolve with a very positive dynamic, and, after some time, the person I had initially recruited decided to pursue other opportunities outside the project. He had realized by himself that the role was not an ideal match for his profile and skill set.

Aspect 2: The Trusted Advisor Curve

Trust is, in general, one of the key success and efficiency factors for organizations. In the project context, the trusted advisor curve is an especially important subfactor. It is not only about enabling or fostering the possibility to establish good connectivity

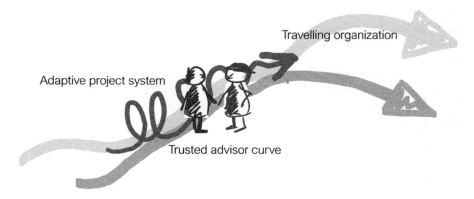

Fig. 1 Journeys of organization and advisor, closely connected in adaptive project systems (figure: Frank Kühn)

between parties, it is even more about how to make them sustainable and evolving with time in a value and virtuous circle.

There are many articles and essays that analyze and elaborate the concept that having a higher degree of trust between people in a population or corporate environment should result in greater cooperation (e.g., Putnam 1993, or La Porta et al. 1996). Another article develops a theoretical basis that aims to measure the link between trust and company performance, showing the relevance and link with which trust and performance can operate in organizations (Brown et al. 2015).

One much desired "soft skill," to foster the interaction between the parties in a project, is the capability to become a trusted advisor of your business partner. This is a skill that can be developed, but you need to make sure it is a priority for all the team members to develop it continuously. As in every interaction, you sometimes provide value and sometimes receive value; it is evident that every team member will have some counterpart to whom they need to become a trusted advisor, and this is the lens which needs to be always present, as a perspective to assess the project's health.

The basic rule to becoming a trusted advisor is to understand that this journey (Fig. 1) starts and evolves from the fact that you are able to add value to your business partner. So, to start the relationship, the first thing you need to ensure is that your first interaction is based on adding some concrete and tangible value, and then you continue in that manner. After you have successfully added value in the minimum required sustainable way, this is when your business partner might start asking you proactively for your point of view or, at a later stage, for your help on some specific problem they need to solve.

We refer here to the "trusted advisor curve" development, which defines a set of proceedings necessary to achieve this trusted advisor status. Once this trusted relation is achieved between parties receiving and providing some kind of service, everything becomes much more efficient, productive, and sustainable, with higher levels of innovation as well. One of the key proceedings in this trusted advisor curve development is for the service provider to focus on understanding the real needs of the party receiving their service (the service recipient). As part of this process, the service provider also helps the service recipient to define and detail better those objectives to be achieved.

Taking this concept to the extreme, for a moment, implies that the "technical skills" (in a very broad sense) are only secondary when it comes to developing trust-based relationships with business partners. Where possible, avoid putting technical discussions in the wrong order. In a project, this is one of the key sources of risk and damage for the overall objective to be achieved.

Once we received a call from a communications department, as they were in charge of the company intranet and they were having some issues to manage the content as they wanted, due to technical limitations. We quickly discovered that they were dealing with a small and local IT company that had reached its limits. The first interesting aspect was understanding why they were working directly with an external IT provider and not requesting this from their own internal IT department. But, as you can imagine from your own previous experiences with IT departments, they had various very valid reasons for not doing so up to that point.

We were quickly able to identify a suitable solution for them, as it was not really complex from a technical point of view. The challenge was more about starting the trusted advisor curve as, at that point, even we had a very clear solution to their problem, we just didn't anticipate their being willing to follow our guidance on those IT topics. Thus, we followed the basic rule of starting by adding value. We firstly managed to become the "interlocutors" between the company and the external IT provider. Then we reached an agreed exit of that "proprietary" and not scalable solution, on very good terms with that provider. Simply by doing this we started to show our genuine interest in becoming their trusted advisor, and we started by delivering, for them, concrete value-added. Just after this first value exchange, they were more prepared to listen to us in terms of the solution we had to provide. In the end, we ran a very successful project together, the capabilities of the communication team to manage internal content for the company were considerably extended, and we kept a strong relationship where they started to see us as trusted advisors, essentially counting on us to provide our point of view whenever they had new IT requirements.

I remember many other different concrete experiences in my professional career as an IT consultant and IT manager, when I was extremely frustrated because my business partner was not able to "see" and/or "perceive" clearly the relevant perspectives I was providing for a very concrete IT problem to be solved. Because not all of them were IT people and hence not able to identify those IT aspects by themselves, I thought I was in a clear position to help them, "technically" from the beginning. But the reason was that, even I was in a clear position to help them, they were not yet ready to listen to me. Because I was not yet a trusted counterpart at that stage of the relationship. This meant that, even though my advice or proposals were appropriate from a technical point of view, they were not yet ready to consider them. They were still not open to that fluent, efficient, productive, and even innovative relationship.

This means that we need to abandon the idea that, to be great technical people, with mastery of a specific area of knowledge, we are then ready to start providing guidance, input, or recommendations to business partners. Because this will not always be the case, we need more than just technical skills; we need the required soft skills to listen actively and identify as accurately as possible where we can delivery concrete value in order to start developing the relationship. To begin indicating to them how things should be done, or what their problem is, is definitely not the right way to go. One should listen actively, not talk too much, and come back to your new business partner with concrete value for their current reality. Once you have overcome the first threshold and your business partner starts to be ready to listen to your points of view, you should become a real fan of their needs, to fully understand them, and, on that shared journey, you can help them to better define the understanding of those problems. This comes before you are also able to start defining together the possible objectives to be pursued. To talk about possible solutions or even products comes right at the end of that journey.

This is a relevant perspective to the problem of people connectivity in the context of projects. The focus and active attitude to become a trusted advisor of your business partner is an essential element to success, fostering fluent collaboration between the different areas and parties in a project. This needs to be regarded as a curve: it is incremental and exists in all the relationships and interactions around the project if the relationship between and with the different parties is to be sustained.

Aspect 3: People First React and Think Emotionally Rather than Rationally as One Would Assume

As briefly developed above in the description of the trusted advisor curve, it could be a misconception and incorrect assumption that people connectivity will be sparked by an interaction that offers all the facts, perfectly structured, from a purely technical perspective. This could still easily fail after all that effort has been made. The reason is because this intended people connectivity could initially rely much more on the "how" than on the "what." It is about how we can spark and sustain that people connectivity.

Considering that the brain is divided into three parts with the first and deepest part driven mainly by raw emotion, we should assume that initial connectivity between people involves a lot of information that is filtered emotionally and instinctually. As developed by Oren Klaff in his book *Pitch Anything* (2011), how we initially present ideas to proceed with a solution is fundamentally different from how people receive them. To keep the connectivity between areas active and profitable, you must attract your business partner's attention and interest by making the most of the initial momentum created in that connectivity. To reach the decision-making part of your counterpart, you must first overcome the conditioning applied by the brain's first emotional filter.

People with the "gift" mentioned above in this chapter can prepare the scenario and their opposite numbers in a much better way to receive the new ideas (the change) that the project will bring. The reason? Only if you spark the people connectivity first will your counterpart be ready to receive the "more rational" information. So, if you start totally rationally and not consider the role of the initial connectivity factors, then you will not be able to make your ideas flow to the other person. This is perhaps why, as Maya Angelou said, people will forget what you said, people will forget what you did, but people will never forget how you made them feel.

When working in consultancy and business development, we ran many customer presentations for services and projects we were intending to engage on with those current customers or prospects. The results of those meetings and presentations were only successful if we had spent enough time and focus preparing the dynamic of the sessions rather than merely the content. Considering that those engagement processes were taking place in Latin America, that was also an additional cultural aspect to be regarded. Based on those experiences we can state that, only by applying different techniques for capturing attention, taking emotional aspects and mind-sets into consideration, did we have sufficient attention from those audiences to move onto through the more rational and technical topics. This needs to be regarded and monitored continuously and not only at the opening of the presentation or even relationship, as there will be always ups and downs in that more emotional or primitive connection.

Aspect 4: Storytelling: Impacting on People's Need to Identify

We know and understand that human beings follow some pattern behaviors. Let's say a set of behaviors that, one way or another, will always appear in a different context, cultures, and realities, as those that are related to the human being as a species. Just to give one very simple but representative example of pattern behaviors, everyone will take always a compliment positively. Even if one is aware that the compliment is not meant genuinely, or that it is being used to influence or even manipulate, a person cannot avoid feeling some kind of happiness and closeness to the person who gave the compliment because, deep down, that compliment is received positively. It goes without saying. Now, how can this happen? Perhaps because everything is directly connected to our ego, the ubiquitous and strong ego that every human being has. This needs to be carefully considered for communication across the project. Storytelling is one effective technique.

When it comes to storytelling, the natural effect that involves the other person is related to giving the audience or counterpart the possibility to somehow identify with the story being told. This again relates directly to our ego and is then inevitable. As social animals we always want to feel that we form part of something and we always want to feel identified with and understood. So any possibility to make us feel identified with, firstly (by affecting our ego) and also bringing that sense of belonging as social animals, will give us the opportunity to bring those individuals we are speaking to closer to the idea or concept we are trying to get across.

Considering the above as a possible valid reflection, it is always important to apply the storytelling technique to have more effective communications in specific project contexts and to achieve the required levels of engagement around the different topics involved. This concept needs to be considered when it comes to people connectivity in global programs with a varied set of nationalities and cultures.

One additional factor that is also essential to foster the correct use of storytelling in projects, as an enabler in different interactions, is the business acumen that every team member should already have and continue to develop. Sound business acumen on the part of every project team member, concerning the main topics of the project, is required to craft storytelling that can really reach other people. Every team member must develop this business acumen, thus making them able to use the storytelling technique to make project development safer in challenging business scenarios and complex organizations.

With my teams, we used to go through some critical sessions related to sponsor engagement, new business stakeholders' engagement, onboarding of new key team members, and budget planning discussions. As is normally the case in challenging and transformational programs and projects, the right team preparation and alignment on how to pitch the projects and solutions, with a great deal of business acumen (not just IT-related content) and carefully applying the storytelling technique, delivered excellent results in line with our expectations. So, this is a technique that I would highly recommend to teach, practice, and spread in teams so that it becomes a crucial part of the team's everyday work.

Aspect 5: Fail Faster to Succeed Sooner

How can we find the positive trend, the virtuous incremental iterations, in a timely manner and in a pragmatic way? And how can we continuously calibrate our direction accordingly? These are questions that need to be asked continuously and communicated to the whole team until the end of the project. The project leadership must play a very determined and consistent role, to ensure that these questions are focused on. This aims to find continuously those "forces" that will sustain the positive impact while progressing to the objective.

The concept of fail faster to succeed sooner has been frequently regarded as one of the positive side effects of agile methodologies. As described in different articles and blogs about agile software development, failing faster allows things to be fixed earlier in the process, as well as enabling the decision to proceed, improve, or cancel (Fig. 2).

In this chapter, we want to focus attention on project leadership and governance in terms of the relevance of people connectivity. In software development, agile methodologies involve releasing new versions of the product in shorter periods so that customers can check and validate the direction. Here we extrapolate that idea to the context of connecting through the different resources in projects with the aim of identifying faster those connections that are not going as expected so that they become transparent and can be corrected.

A
We have to adhere to our
decisions, or we will lose
our face.

B
Decisions are good until
we know better, or we
will lose our business

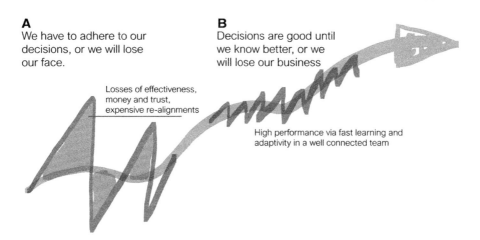

Losses of effectiveness,
money and trust,
expensive re-alignments

High performance via fast learning and
adaptivity in a well connected team

Fig. 2 Fail faster to succeed sooner is one of the most prominent features of agile organizations navigating the VUCA world. It assumes that leadership is understood as a task and not as a position (figure: Frank Kühn)

It is a sad fact of project management that wrong connections across team members and involved areas will arise. If these bad connections are not considered in a timely manner they will, over time, be very detrimental for the feasibility of the project, eventually resulting in a clear risky situation for the overall project objective. Managing these interferences to connectivity carefully in a timely manner means making them transparent in a proactive, prudential, and positive way as soon as possible. The next step is to promote a new way of reconnecting the parties. This is essential and needs to be based on the concrete experiences of the project, as there are no two teams or projects that behave in the same way. Each project represents a specific reality and needs a specific procedure that should be continuously developed based on active monitoring and constant realignment. As previously stated, it is inevitable in every project that people connectivity will not always flow as expected, so the issue is less about this issue per se but about how fast we can identify the "failing connections" and enable them to succeed sooner. It is about measuring and acting to change the trend actively and continuously. This is perhaps one of the key activities and responsibilities of the project management team. Remain agile, measure constantly so as to adjust if necessary. Maintain the virtuous iterative/incremental proceeding (I/I).

Try to remember cases where people connectivity did not work well and you didn't realize this or didn't act in time. What were the main issues or consequences? By reflecting on this, you can identify why it is so essential to tackle these kinds of issues in projects in a timely manner. But what is even more rewarding is to identify cases where you were able to manage such issues and fix them. In those cases, how did you proceed? What you can try next time based on these experiences? Focusing on value-driven interactions is a good way to manage such scenarios. In general, when there is no clear value contribution from each party in a specific project interaction, then this starts to become an increasingly serious issue that requires the management team to act as soon as possible to correct the undesirable dynamic. By reorganizing the work or roles, slightly or radically depending on the situation, you try to facilitate again interactions driven by clear value contributions. You need to consider that, in some cases, correcting this means changing roles or even removing certain people from the project. Always bear in mind the relevance of different cultures, mind-sets, backgrounds, and personal agendas. By approaching them in a positive and pragmatic way you, will be in a good position to rearrange the setups by reorganizing the work or roles as mentioned above.

Aspect 6: The Project as a "Complex Adaptive System"

It is essential to manage projects as a whole, organically, regardless of size, complexity, geographical scope, etc. The idea is to invest the required focus and effort to acquire the general view of the project. In this sense, it is fundamental, too, to manage all the "interfaces" and people connectivity involved, inside and outside.

Projects can be seen as a complex adaptive system, in which people connectivity plays a key role in that adaptability to different circumstances. As elaborated in the book *Aspects of Complexity* (Cooke-Davies et al. 2011), complex projects are known for nonlinearity, irreversibility, and general disconnection between cause and effect. As an analogy to help understand the nature of complex adaptive systems, think of the weather or human body, which both involve dynamic shifts, extreme internal interdependence, and high connectivity.

Try using this comparison and practice this perspective when running projects, understanding them also as "complex adaptive systems." Guided by general project management practices, you have to follow the plans, you have to tackle the outstanding and unexpected events that could jeopardize the plans, but you should also take a look at evidence of anomalies in people interfaces that are not even related to the mainstream or key activities. These anomalies could contain much more information about the project health than you would initially think. Even though they might appear minimal, you should keep an expert eye on them.

When leading projects, you are in charge of setting the context for the different parties involved. As projects keep moving forward and some workstreams are more predictable than others, by paying specific attention to as much "resource connectivity" as possible, you are managing the whole thing from a holistic point of view. Not having the right project leaders performing this role carefully is one of the main root causes of project failures or of the project not reaching its given objectives.

I remember one important regional project in Latin America, where all the indicators were apparently "green" and both sponsors and top management were very proud of the overall progress so far. The formal communications about the overall project progress were always very positive and that was, in general, the perception in the company too. I had some responsibility over one of the delivery teams, and we were also "on green" and on schedule. But suddenly I observed that some specific aspects of the test phase preparation and the interactions of the teams in those preparatory activities didn't look as they should have done. Surprisingly, when it came to preparing the schedules to have the business users prepare and execute the initial tests, together with the project team, the preparation activities didn't work as expected. This was particularly surprising for me, in such a well-performing project and with, apparently and based on ongoing formal communications, project deliverables that were so desired by the business representatives. This key touch point and poorly performing activity was, for me, a critical people connectivity issue, which showed something much more serious than just an anecdotal misunderstanding. There were strong root causes for the lack of coordination and readiness, and these facts provided me with important information for the whole context.

As I did not have responsibility for the whole project, I tried to highlight this finding to the overall project management, but unfortunately, this was not taken into consideration at that time; the project management were confident that the main key performance indicators (KPIs) were looking okay, for the main phase at that moment. To cut a longer story short, the project was cancelled just few months after going live. It became clear that, finally, the business was not so convinced about the value of the project. This is why, perhaps, at that more "lateral" stage of preparing the testing activities, the business users were not as ready as one could expect. Massive investment was more or less wasted, and blunt frustration overtook many of the professionals who had been involved in the project. All their effort, dedication, and delivery were suddenly, and unexpectedly, discarded, and they couldn't understand why. Some postmortem reviews finally brought a lot of clarity about the main reasons for that failure, and this confirmed a direct relation to the anomalies I had observed at a much earlier stage. Much of the failure was to do with wrong management of people connectivity and failing to observe the project as a complex adaptive system. Remember that projects sometimes provide key alerts from areas that we are not observing as the naturally relevant ones for that project stage.

Attempt for an Initial Overall Conclusion on People Connectivity in Projects

Through the development of this chapter, we have found that a first key factor and prerequisite for people connectivity is the "sustainable purpose." The teams require a context setting to find the "why" concerning what they are doing and need to feel that, to create meaning, there is a journey ahead, full of uncertainties and changes that will need to be faced together as a travelling organization. The sustainable purpose is thus a source of energy and ensures that project teams have the required resilience for very demanding journeys.

The sense of control and stability is an illusion in today's organizations. Unfortunately, or not, we cannot think any more like: "Oops! another change"; change is continuous, and we need self-driven and empowered teams. We need holistic approaches (behavior, systems, processes) to develop travelling organizations, understanding that the organization is continuously on a journey towards best possible results. We also tried to write with a view to the near future for organizations, where we still have top and middle management keeping the illusion of Taylorism in the context of complex global projects with lots of people connectivity involved. We are no longer in control; connections appear distributed and dynamic. No longer vertical or top-down. No longer one person who changes the reality of so many so simply. Any professional, taking a leading role in projects, must understand that this "VUCA"-driven world requires strong focus in setting the context for each and every team member, so they have the right environment and understanding to do their best. In this dynamic, our aim is to have reflexive and self-empowered teams. It is time to understand the real role of the leader.

To develop organizational knowledge, a key focus is connectivity. We focused on the "connecting resources" factor to avoid the compartmental thinking of the company's resources in terms of structural silos, boxed competencies, etc. The six aspects covered in this chapter, around people connectivity in projects, tried to trace a thread of related topics that can be regarded to achieve better executed projects, by developing people connectivity capabilities. Better people connectivity increases efficiencies and sparks more innovative environments. All this is due to the progressive confidence in all the professional relationships across the teams involved, and we need to regard this as essential in every project we embark in.

A project is a lot about personal relationships, building trust, acting consistently in different situations, etc. We have tried to highlight that it is not only about having the right technical skills, it is not even about developing perfect project plans, fully detailed requirements, or exhaustive risk management. These elements and good practices are of course very necessary, but if you don't have the right individuals who can generate and foster the required connections between team members and stakeholders, with the minimum required shared trust developed, the project will fail sooner or later (ideally sooner to prevent much higher investment being wasted). Aim to find professionals with the required technical skills for the role but place special focus on understanding how much this role would become relevant in building the required relationships in the project context, i.e., developing people connectivity. Once you identify that the role could have some influence or key responsibility in relationships between areas, team members, etc., then you need to consider carefully, and as a mandatory requirement, the "connectivity skills" of the professionals taking on those roles. They need to be able to build up engagement, good relationships, and trust between all parties involved.

We would really like to leave the reader to reflect on the above topics and try to reach some meaningful conclusions that could become tools for their own current or future challenges.

References

Brown, S., Gray, D., McHardy, J., & Taylor, K. (2015). Employee trust and workplace performance. *Journal of Economic Behavior and Organization, 116*, 361–378.

Cooke-Davies, T., Crawford, L., Patton, J., Stevens, C., & Williams, T. (2011). *Aspects of complexity: Managing projects in a complex world*. Newtown Square, PA: Project Management Institute.

Klaff, O. (2011). *Pitch anything: An innovative method for presenting, persuading, and winning the deal*. New York: McGraw-Hill.

La Porta, R., Lopez-de-Silanes, F., Shleifer, A., & Vishny, R. W. (1996). Trust in large organizations. *The American Economic Review, 87*(2), 333–338.

Putnam, R. D. (1993). What makes democracy work? *National Civic Review, 82*(2), 101–107.

How Established Companies Can Move to the Next Level by Using the Three Pillar Model

Reto Püringer

Abstract

After years of investment, companies' well-established workflows, systems, and management practices are now confronted with changing markets and customer needs. Three typical hurdles to transformation have been experienced: the global–local paradox, silo-orientation, and the risk of changing priorities due to changing management. The proposed design pillars help to overcome them by means of committing everyone to a distinct purpose, empowering teams to travel towards their purpose, and promoting the connectivity of resources across structural boundaries.

The editors of the book introduce **Reto Püringer** who has worked for more than 20 years in the banking and insurance industry. He has held various senior positions in global companies. His practical experience ranges from Strategy Development, Business Model Design, Product/Proposition Development/Management, Enterprise-wide Portfolio Management, Program/Project Management, Operations/IT Management, Large-Scale Change Program Delivery to Financial/Actuarial Management over different geographies and time zones, hierarchies and units, and cultures and systems.

R. Püringer (✉)
Zurich, Switzerland

© Springer Nature Switzerland AG 2020
P. Wollmann et al. (eds.), *Three Pillars of Organization and Leadership in Disruptive Times*, Future of Business and Finance,
https://doi.org/10.1007/978-3-030-23227-6_9

Introduction

Our world is changing. Every day we can read news of new technological innovation, consumers who are buying more and more online and start-ups that were bought by large companies for huge sums of money to secure special knowledge and/or technologies. There is no doubt that the way we buy and use products and services will look dramatically different 10 years from now. It has already changed in the last 10 years; in 2008, I could not have imagined buying my clothes via Zalando or booking my summer holiday completely online with no paperwork required. All this has happened, and, with it, new companies have been born, whereas other companies have died a painful death.

This changing world means big challenges for, in particular, established, large, and mainly global companies. During the last 10–20 years, they have invested in people and capabilities to serve their customer base, and many of these assets will soon be outdated, as customers will be asking for something different. Their organizational setup, systems, processes, roles, and incentive systems are set up according to an old mind-set that does not allow them to transform and make themselves ready to survive 10 years from now and may even hinder them from doing so. Why?

Firstly, large companies typically have rigid systems and decision-making processes in place—including political "games"—that require alignment across divisions and departments and that make them slow and sometimes ineffective when it comes to adopting change, whereas new companies can quickly react to market trends, and their business model is, in essence, geared towards change and attack.

Secondly, in many cases established companies still have good and ongoing revenue streams based on their existing business model—any change that would fundamentally affect this model is only done when it is really required. But this is the problem: when fundamental changes do have an impact on the market, then it is too late to change. When customers move to new competitors and buy different products and services, then revenue falls away, contribution margins start to disappear, and the existing business model can't be maintained any longer. In a short time, this model may collapse like a house of cards.

The Three Pillar Model as a Means to Transform from the Inside

In this chapter, I will share my view that the three pillar model can be a fundamental help for established organizations as a means to transform them from the inside. We have to acknowledge that change in any established organization is difficult and will, as a matter of course, meet with resistance. Resistance not only comes from employees at the bottom of the pyramid but much more from middle management who are afraid of losing power and influence. There are limited ideas as to how a new setting might impact day-to-day life in detail with all the good and bad it might entail; therefore the future appears threatening for a lot of people. Unfortunately, they forget that if they don't change, life could be even worse.

I have seen change programs that failed miserably, where external consultants created theoretical solutions that were not understood by the organization—with no relevant internal stakeholders included in the solution's design. They tried to impose change in a "top-down" timeline within 3 months, ignoring that the absorption of change takes time and needs belief that things will improve after the change has been implemented. But such timelines are designed to enable the project to be completed on time and within budget, and the consultant can declare success. But after the project is completed and the consultant is gone, everything will go back to the previous state: nobody can explain any longer what this change is really about and what would be better afterwards. So why bother changing at all?

My personal conclusion is that established organizations need a constant stream of small changes that are easy to absorb, driven by internal people, across all departments and divisions. What I mean by change is not just a project activity to prepare a change, but rather a constant and incremental deployment of change that is tangible for customers and reflects their changing behavior.

The three pillar model helps established organizations to connect the "old" and the "new" worlds, leveraging internal know-how and considering that nobody knows what the world will look like even 2 years from now. The model also helps to build a cultural foundation and to attract scarce talents in the future. These—very young—people require autonomy and are not willing to work within rigid structures offered by some of today's large companies.

How Does the Operating Model of an Established Organization Influence Its Adaptability to Market Changes?

But before we look how the three pillar model can be applied to established corporations, we need to look how they typically operate. What is preventing them from continuous change and what things could they leverage in order to be more adaptable? Obviously, there is no single way, and different companies and industries work in different ways. One common question to start with—at least for multinational companies—is the question of why they exist? Wouldn't it be better to just have local companies that don't have the complexity of coordination and burden of a Corporate Center or headquarters? And what is actually the purpose and concrete benefit of the global teams that manage and control the country organizations?

The reasons large corporations exist are—among other things—that they have the ability to create global brands that people consistently trust, to achieve scale and synergies that allow them to operate cheaper and more efficiently, to create processes and systems that are transferable into different markets, to diversify capital and revenue streams, and last but not least to attract talent and related knowledge by offering international and more interesting careers.

But the business itself is always done in a local market, where cultural differences of customer needs and market specifics (incl. regulatory, legal, tax, etc.) need to be considered. On that local level, where a customer ultimately buys a product or service, the only thing that matters is whether or not a company is making a difference in the eyes of customers.

What we can certainly say is that it is difficult to create an operating model for a large corporation considering and combining the reasons why they exist with the local aspects of each market. I have never seen a perfect solution; however you do it, there is some form of trade-off: if you create an operating model "by market" you have the risk that every market invents its own assets; if you create an operating model "by-product," then you may have standard products, but they may not fit every market, and it's unclear who is in charge, etc.

So, whatever is done there will be a trade-off, and, as a consequence, I have observed three specific aspects in the financial services industry that hinder large corporations from reinventing themselves as they focus, in the worst case, more internally on themselves rather than externally, i.e., on the customer.

The "Global–Local" Paradox

In multinational companies, there is always a so-called global layer that is responsible for the overarching strategy and the "reasons" multinationals exist (which I mentioned before). On the other hand, there is a "local layer" that is responsible for executing the business or selling the products and services to the customers and servicing them afterwards—this is basically where the money comes from (Fig. 1).

The Global layer has the advantage of having a comparably fresh view of things as they are not part of the "day-to-day" business: they can analyze industry trends, competitors' moves in different countries, and forthcoming technological innovation. They normally have a good view of what, in theory, should be done from a general business perspective, but they often lack knowledge of local realities. And, in most cases, the Global Layer has power over capital and performance goals.

The Local layer, on the other hand, has a good view of what needs to be done to deliver the targets set for the next performance period. They understand their markets and customers extremely well, but normally they have a shorter time frame in mind as they need to execute their plans. And what is more, they often lack capital to invest in change since capital is managed centrally.

What I unfortunately observed is that in many cases—despite everybody having good intentions—the "connection" between the Global Layer and the Local Layer fails, which results in a paradox as everybody wants to do good things, but the maximum is not achieved.

An example of this paradox is centrally driven IT platforms—more relevant than ever in the digital world—that aim to standardize products across markets to make the company faster in terms of product changes and thus create a cost advantage. Almost all of these projects I have seen had big challenges, or even failed, as the general global ideas concerning change and the more short-term view to cope with the "here and now" of local customers did not match. To overcome this, new governance layers were established that added unnecessary costs, made processes

Fig. 1 Local and/or global? (figure: Frank Kühn)

slower, and, overall, made everything more rigid and less agile—with the result that the initial aim of these projects was not achieved.

In essence, there is a "Global–Local" paradox in my view when everybody tries to create added value from their own perspective. But because contexts and incentive systems between global and local organizations are so different, capital is wasted on shared projects that, at the end of the day, have zero impact on customers.

Silo-Orientation

Whenever you organize a team of a certain size in a traditional way, you will end up with an organization that is mapped in a more or less rigid organizational chart. And then, when the organizational structure is clear, every "box" needs a head and team members. Performance goals will then be structured along the "boxes." To make a career, you move between boxes or upwards, etc. So primary organizational goals rather than outcomes/results from an end-to-end customer view are the focus of performance bonuses.

Normally large corporations have an organization in place that internal people are used to and that has been established over time. I have observed that people don't

Fig. 2 Vertical and horizontal silos, calling only for defined parts of humans (figure: Frank Kühn)

primarily think that they are part of a company connected to a shared corporate purpose, but they are part of Department A or Department B. They have specific roles and targets to meet that are related to those departments, and if they were asked by their family about their job, then they would explain what their job is in their specific department. Their everyday problems and what they talk about are related to those departments (Fig. 2).

This is not bad if you live in a world where markets do not change very much. The issue is when markets and/or customer demand and behavior change. It is then very difficult to respond to those changes as the organizational structure is very rigid—especially when you want to be quick. To change an organization, you need to change the meaning of each "box," you need to redefine roles and related grades, reconfigure who is working with whom, recalibrate performance objectives, and so on. This is a big task! But how will you know that what you are doing will solve the problem?

Everyone in their box is incentivized accordingly, and every change is a risk as the boss or the boss' boss might not like it (with potential consequences for year-end ratings and thus financial consequences). You can hire an external consultant who creates a top-down view of a future organization (i mentioned earlier why this can fail) or you can ask the people bottom-up with the risk that they might feel comfortable with the structure they are currently in. Whatever you do, it will be very difficult to change an existing organizational model fundamentally and quickly—there is no ideal solution unless your current organization includes a degree of flexibility. If it doesn't, then the three pillar model might be a good way to start.

The point I want to make is that established companies normally have a silo mentality that is difficult to overcome. I cannot claim to have academic proof here—but I believe that slow adaptation to market changes depends significantly on how "silo-ed" an established organization is.

Changes in Management Priorities

Based on what I mentioned before, you can already imagine that, in large corporations, priorities are often set by individual senior executives "top-down" (in the "silos" mentioned above). These are all very bright people, and I had the opportunity to meet really exceptional personalities, for which I am very grateful! But you need to consider that these individuals are exposed to a large group of internal and external stakeholders. Therefore, they are under enormous pressure to deliver something to these people. These executives have the power to allocate funds for change projects but also to remove them.

If a large corporation really wants to change fundamentally, it needs constancy and time. This is not merely a couple of months. It needs constant focus on the same key priorities over years to ensure that a change develops into something different perceived by the customer. The change I mean is not only a change to systems and processes but, much more, a cultural change that transforms a large corporation into an organization that is able to respond instantly to the needs of a changing customer base.

But usually when a new executive is appointed, he or she will start to think about their priorities. The goal will be to show success in terms of those priorities in 12–18 months. I have experienced one individual who actually planned priorities for 2–3 years with the expectation that, after that period, he or she would be gone. And this actually turned out to be the case.

The point in this regard is that, in large corporations, there is the risk that some executives are in their role for a comparably short period of time. They then define their priorities, and everything below them (people, funds, suppliers, etc.) will be adjusted to rigidly follow those priorities. The problem is that, after they are replaced, another executive will join the company and will again redefine priorities. Often these priorities are different to the previous ones, and again everything below them will be adjusted (Fig. 3).

Fig. 3 Changing priorities—changing motivations (figure: Frank Kühn)

In organizations where priorities are centered around those executives then obviously everybody reporting to them will follow those priorities stringently as well. Even if the priorities are wrong from their point of view, they seldom speak up—the risk of being fired or sidelined is too high. And everybody knows there will soon be a replacement anyway. So why bother?

The result is therefore that those companies will fix specific issues in the short-term, but they are rarely able to set priorities that translate into fundamental or transformational change.

If an industry is not facing fundamental challenges, then this is fine, and, with this setup, you can focus on specific things that incrementally improve the existing setup. The problem is more that if an industry is facing fundamental changes, then this behavior might not help to transform. The company might even do a lot of activities that fix the problem but unfortunately not those problems that will help it to survive in its industry!

There are some examples I have seen where, due to the above aspects, priorities changed by 180 degrees almost overnight—what was good one day was bad the day after. But I have also seen great examples where a strong management had unchanged priorities over a strategy cycle with perceptible results in terms of business transformation.

How the Three Pillar Model Can Help to Overcome the Challenges

Considering all these challenges, the question is what could be done better? In my opinion, there is no patent remedy, but I believe that the three pillar model is a good means of overcoming the challenges. In certain contexts, people speak about "agile organizations" as a response to the digital world, and I think our model could be a useful application of an agile concept.

How to apply the three pillar model in a practical way?

The application of such a model is a big change in itself. Owing to some of the arguments I mentioned earlier, a large corporation will only go through such a change if it's either driven top-down, e.g., by a board with a strategic vision or if a change is inevitable because of changes in customer behavior and/or revenue streams that are disappearing (although it might be too late then, etc.).

The beauty of the three pillar model is that it does not need to be applied radically. It can be applied in certain areas of the organization first and then, organically, spread gradually to other areas of the organization.

To apply the three pillar model, I have listed below considerations for each factor that might help large corporations to apply the principle of the model:

1. *Give everybody a relevant and distinct purpose with clearly defined results to be achieved—in all layers*

   One of the key mistakes in my opinion is that large organizations often organize themselves top-down in organizational "boxes." The issue is that these organizations are not very flexible, and if the internal or external context changes, then the initial "missions" of these boxes might become obsolete, which will ultimately lead to organizational inefficiencies!

An alternative would be to not create fixed organizational boxes at all. But instead think about which problems the organization needs to solve and then allocate people to specific teams that are tasked with solving these problems (which, of course, means that the organization needs to know the criteria to decide if a problem has been solved effectively, etc.). After a problem has been solved, the team is reallocated to the next problem on the list, etc. Now you might think: But what happens when all the organization's problems have been solved? What happens to the people? My answer to this question is that I have *never* come across an organization with no problems. It seems to me that there are always sufficient problems to be solved.

Some problems are more related to customer service processes (e.g., effectively answering all customer enquiries); other problems might be more change-oriented (e.g., creating a new "self-service" capability where customers can process some enquiries themselves). But this approach can only work if an organization has an agreed list of problems with a clear prioritization as to what is at the top of the list and what is at the bottom. And, as mentioned before, there must be a clear definition of a problem being "solved," etc.

The problems facing organizations on a day-to-day basis are a mix of short-term issues to be resolved (e.g., a current customer is not happy) and fixed problems with a longer time frame (e.g., investment is required to move to a new business model). The prerequisite for success is therefore to blend these short-term problems, which are more related to the existing business model and revenues, with longer-term problems that are crucial if the organization is to stay in business or survive in the industry.

And voilà! Now we also have a clear purpose for management! The task of management is to ensure that the organization has an aligned and documented list of problems, which every relevant problem has a team working on finding a solution within an expected time frame, and the underlying resource base is developed in a way that the appropriate resources are motivated and available. If something is not a problem, then it does not need to be solved!

It would then also be clear which problems are solved in a local market (e.g., making the customer happy) and which problems are solved "above" the local markets. As management is now responsible for managing the list of problems, then no team should be working on the same problems! And if they were doing so, they could go back to management and tell them that something needs to be adjusted; otherwise they will not be able to fulfill their purpose.

Think about how engaging this is for an organization where everybody knows that his work is related to a dedicated purpose and they are fully in charge of solving it! If done intelligently, nobody in a market or in the Corporate Center would be working on irrelevant problems!

After an organization has decided which problems need to be solved and which teams are working on them, it's now up to the team to travel towards the solution to those problems. This requires complete empowerment.

2. *Fully empower teams and individuals to travel towards their purpose and to solve their particular problems.*

Once all problems have been sorted out, then they can be assigned to a dedicated team or to individuals. The people assigned to those teams are either selected because they have specific knowledge that they can contribute to solving the problem or because they really want to solve the problem and learn on the way (even if they are not yet an expert!). The team should decide who they want in the team and who not—which requires a culture of open dialogue and respectful "straight talk!"

The role of management is then to coach the teams and help them. By way of comparison, consider a football coach: the football coach does not play on the field (although he might have played when he was younger, etc.); his task is to coach and motivate the team, keep them fit, ensure consistent tactics, and so on. If this principle is applied in a large organization, it will not require a lot of management layers. The only layers required will be teams who solve problems, management who coach the teams, and management who ensure the availability of a consistent list of problems to be solved. Not much else will be required.

It is also not necessary for teams that are working on the problems to have to present a detailed plan upfront; they should provide a high-level journey in which direction they want to travel and transparency about progress to the management layers I mentioned above, including the funding they need. They can then organize their tasks, and, if they need to change the way they have chosen, they can do so as they are fully empowered. The only imperative is that they demonstrate progress and confidence that they will be able to solve the assigned problems on time.

This concept might also need a much stronger HR function that is able to provide an internal market to supply the people who are able to solve the problems in both the short-term and the long-term as well as managing a capability portfolio in a strategic way using career and/or development paths with no silos. The focus of Senior Management is then to understand much better which teams are playing well, which individuals are developing, what skills are required, and so on.

The travelling organization moves away from detailed plans that are outdated the day after they have been produced (which requires a lot of work), to teams that are empowered to travel step-by-step to solve a well-defined problem. If they need to do something that is not required, they will not do it as the main incentive they have is to be successful in their mission.

3. *Promote connectivity and eliminate all barriers to it*

You may well object and say, "Wait a minute! This will create chaos in the organization, we need top-down coordination that will ensure no overlaps, coordination and so on!" I believe this is old thinking! Instead of creating extensive roles that coordinate the organization, I believe that the teams that are travelling towards their purpose or are on the way to solving their problems need to be empowered to connect to other teams and/or other parts of the organization.

Because these teams are empowered, they know what they need. They might be missing some specific knowledge for a certain task, they might need to understand some underlying data that is not available, etc.

To enable the team to obtain that knowledge, the organization has to be persuaded that connecting with other parts of the organization is not bad but, conversely, is actually rather useful. It might take time to connect upfront, but it will reap dividends afterwards.

To facilitate connectivity, we first of all need transparency. But, as discussed, we already have a list of problems to be solved; we only need to make this list generally available, including who is working on what! This does not need to be anything sophisticated, just something to identify who can help.

To make connectivity happen, the following are required: a culture that supports transparency, trust, and openness and a consistent modern set of tools that enables people to get in touch easily and helps them work virtually across countries.

Moreover, modern office setups that enable people to get in touch easily and give them the opportunity to have a chat at the coffee machine or around the watercooler are also crucial.

Summary/Conclusions

I have tried to present the three pillar model as a solution for large corporations that are stuck in their existing business models, currently optimizing it well but unable to transform themselves and respond to changing customer behavior—especially in the digital world.

The model helps to overcome the:

- "Global–local paradox" by, e.g., giving everybody a purpose or a unique problem to solve locally and globally instead of having inflexible organizational structures.
- "Silo-orientation" by allocating work in a more flexible way to people and by being transparent as to who is doing what and by promoting the related connectivity.
- Risk of changing priorities due to new management by giving leaders dedicated tasks to maintain and nurture an aligned set of problems that need solving or to coach teams on their journey to solving a problem.

I am aware that it might sound unrealistic to attempt to apply this approach in some of today's large organizations, but I am convinced that, if an organization starts to do so, then they can learn, explore, and adapt the approach on their way to responding to the challenges brought about by the new digitalized world.

The Art of Travelling in Films: The Road Movie 303

Peter Wollmann

Abstract

The article is about how a road movie can help to teach the art of travelling for an organization on the basis of strong and valid analogies and of supporting out-of-the-box thinking. This is shown with 303, a film about a journey in various dimensions—3000 km through great landscapes in Europe, through fundamental questions about manhood and what has to be changed, through personal crises and the self-perception of the protagonists, through the slow development of a relationship, through the development of a new view of one's potential personal future. After watching the film, people are ready to openly embrace new experiences. What could better support the mindset of a travelling organization!

The editors of the book introduce **Peter Wollmann** who is now acting as a senior mentor, sparring partner, trusted advisor and catalyst for leaders in new roles and responsibilities and for organizations. Previously, he had diverse senior positions over nearly 40 years in the Finance Industry, with last years as programme director for global transformations within Zurich Insurance Company (ZIC). He is the author and publisher of a range of books and articles on strategy, leadership and project and project portfolio management.

P. Wollmann (✉)
Consulting Partner, Bonn, Germany
e-mail: pw@peterwollmann.com

© Springer Nature Switzerland AG 2020
P. Wollmann et al. (eds.), *Three Pillars of Organization and Leadership in Disruptive Times*, Future of Business and Finance,
https://doi.org/10.1007/978-3-030-23227-6_10

Introduction and Link to the Three Pillar Model

Organizations—and here especially leaders, managers and other key players—can significantly benefit from different perspectives coming from other walks of life such as, among other things, the arts and culture as well as through reframing in alien contexts or analogies. Reframing in fresh and/or alien contexts is in general a profound concept to create new insights by framing things in significantly different contexts like, e.g., from art.

In our case, films about travelling or with significant travelling aspects help to emotionally adapt to a travelling mindset and to change normal, more inflexible, thinking, at least for the 2 h in front of the screen. The combination of stimulated senses—visual and auditory—combined with the imagination being stimulated by identifying with actors and/or situations touches you emotionally and takes the audience—at least temporarily—to another world. Road movies in particular have some strong magic and stimulate the yearning to get away and be somebody else in a new world.

Especially, this magic and the associated curiosity to explore something new, combined with the decision to set off, is crucial for moving from the 'old business world', which is going to die, to a new one which cannot yet be described in detail but which will be completely different in terms of hierarchy, top-down decisions, Taylorism, silos, micromanagement, analogue processes, short-term thinking, focus on career, ways of working and cooperation, etc.

We stressed at the beginning of the book that the new business world—if it were ideal—would be designed according to the trio of pillars which, interestingly, can be very well connected with travelling in films.

Sustainable Purpose

The sustainable purpose of travelling in films is usually to explore and experience something new and unknown, different from, and more attractive than, one's normal life. Very often—especially in road movies—the journey is the aim, not a special destination, as the potential destination is unknown, and so no decisions can be made. Taking the journey as the purpose also means the conscious decision to consistently leave something behind and to rely on the faith that something better will be found at the end of the road.

Travelling Organization

It is obvious that the people in a road movie or a film with at least a strong travelling context have to have the appropriate mindset (otherwise, the film would not make sense). In general, there are special personalities described who start their trips for various but often strong emotional reasons (e.g. searching for a better life or love, escaping, visiting partners or friends, despair, revenge). There might be defined targets for the journey or a random mindset—in many cases, targets are often re-calibrated or re-defined on the road. And the mindset is to be on the move, with a portion of curiosity and openness and often also fortitude thrown in to the mix as well. Usually, a lot happens in these films, and the characters guess that they will be different at the end of their journey (of the film). This atmosphere—amplified by the sound track—is standard for these films. Incidentally, the number of characters is not relevant for our analogy with business, but normally, these are smaller groups of individuals—which helps the audience to identify emotionally with them.

Connecting Resources

It is also obvious that the touchpoints and interfaces of the travellers with world surrounding them are key; the way they cope with this is a central theme of the film and a significant factor for the whole story. In hostile environments, travellers might fail (see Easy Rider) or at least have to overcome considerable challenges; in positive environments they achieve their 'transition'. The art of managing connectivity is, in any case, crucial.

First General Insights

The category of road movies—or films with significant travelling aspects—seems to apply the three pillar model comprehensively, as shown in the initial thoughts described above. And these films have the advantage of creating strong—positive—emotions, so this means that they fit very well for analogies, stimulation and also reframing in alien contexts if needed.

Following on from this thought, it might be a good idea to design workshops with the transition programme team and its stakeholders accordingly, which means, for example, developing a screenplay for the film about the transition journey. In this case, strong narratives and pictures are needed.

Conversely, it may be interesting to look at road movies in the transition team and the wider community, to capture the personally stimulating aspects and to discuss how these can be transferred to the (context of the) organization. In this case, multiple mechanisms of reframing in alien contexts, stimulation and creative framing would be used.

Last but not least, let's have a closer look at the very successful road movie 303 and take it as an example.

The Road Movie 303 and Its Perception

Description based partly on https://de.wikipedia.org/wiki/303_(Film)
303 is a 'dialogue film', a combination of road movie, philosophy and love story. The director was an assistant to Richard Linklater (whose famous dialogue films

Fig. 1 Purpose, travelling and connectivity from different perceptions as individuals or team, as acting people or from a distant observer's view (figure: Frank Kühn)

'Before Sunrise', 'Before Sunset' and 'Before Midnight' were, however, static from a travelling aspect).

303 tells the story of two students on a trip from Berlin to Portugal, driving 3000 km in a camper (Fig. 1). We have, on the one hand, the 24-year-old biology student, Jule, who has just failed her final exams before the end of the summer semester and who, in addition, is unintentionally pregnant. Her mother urges her to have a termination, but Jule hesitates and firstly wants to involve the child's father—Alex, who is writing his doctoral thesis in Portugal. She sets off in her Mercedes Hymer 303 camper, which had previously belonged to her brother, who took his own life. Shortly after Berlin, she picks up the politics student Jan, who is of a similar age and who wants to hitchhike to Cologne and from there travel by bus to northern Spain to meet his biological father. Coincidentally, the two protagonists quickly end up talking about the sensitive topic of suicide, which leads to a serious argument and a temporary falling-out. After a strong intervention—Jan prevents Jule from being harassed—they re-unite for the trip—firstly planning to drop Jan in Cologne.

Soon a new dispute unfolds, this time concerning the theory of evolution, capitalism and key questions of manhood, e.g. what naturally best develops manhood—competition (Jan) or cooperation (Jule)? They continue the fundamental discussion during a long walk through a forest and their first meal together. In Cologne, Jule asks Jan to accompany her for another 500 km and Jan gladly accepts. Arriving in France, they only drive on country roads and decelerate further, always continuing their conversations on ethical questions, the necessity of worldwide cooperation, the role of biological conditioning for people's preferences, etc. They journey through picturesque landscapes and enjoy quiet places and hidden resting places, as well as they enjoy everything, which arises around the food intake at a common routine. Their conversations become more and more personal and concrete but not less controversial. After the great questions of humanity, they now turn to the relationship between men and women—including what is crucial for these relationships to form and survive, the role of drugs to escape one's inner voice reflecting and commenting on all activities.

But they cannot escape reality forever; on one of her occasional phone calls to Alex, Jule tells him about her pregnancy—and is deeply disappointed by his restrained reaction. Jan tries to console her with an exquisite sweet, a tarte aux pommes and a first, yet very timid, tender touch in order to alleviate her stress.

It becomes clear that both are about to fall in love—but very slowly and very decently.

Before they can confess their love for one another, they have reached Jan's destination in northern Spain. In Jule's presence, he sees his biological father from a distance, but cannot bring himself to approach him, and continues with Jule on her way to Portugal. After a hike in the Picos de Europa, from which both return completely soaked and cold, they finally give in to their feelings. In the morning, Jule confesses to Jan that she is pregnant and, a little later, that she has decided to have the child. He picks up both messages. In Porto, she starts bleeding, consults a gynaecologist and discovers that she has lost the baby. She ends up dropping Jan in the middle of the village in Portugal, before she drives on to Alex—with a completely uncertain outcome. Jan is waiting. Firstly, he falls asleep in the café and then on the steps of the market place. In the middle of the night, Jule returns in her 303; both hug and kiss each other passionately.

Perception and Comments

The general perception of the film was very positive. It was stressed that the film—despite being over 140 min long and focusing on dialogues—was never boring but exciting and moving.

A key comment is that it is an 'anti-Tinder film' giving broad time for relations and persons to develop in fast-moving times. It is deceleration pure. And it is a real road movie, in which the director is said to define new standards, understanding that travelling is a form of existence that opens the heart and consciousness.

The dialogues between Jule and Jan are so vivid because the screenplay was developed from around 200 recent video interviews with young people.

303 was, according to one critic, the unexpected summer adventure of 2018. 'A film like the second before the kiss, just auspiciously spread out over 145 min. A film in which one has the feeling that all the supposedly aimless talk about the world, about people, about society could lead somewhere. A film in which one feels compelled to shout out: Just get on with it and kiss each other, for goodness sake!'

So, it is a film about a journey in various dimensions—3000 km through great landscapes in Europe, through fundamental questions of manhood and what has to be changed, through personal crises and the self-perception of the protagonists, through the slow development of a relationship and through the development of a new view of one's potential personal future. And this journey is underlaid by sublime landscapes, the steady feeling of travelling, a great soundtrack—pure emotion but embedded in intellectual and fundamental reflection. After watching the film, you are ready to have new experiences. What could better support the mindset of a travelling organization!

Learning Items for Organization and Transformation

On a meta-level, we have, in general, two categories of organizational learnings:

- From history: what do we learn from the history of organizations for the future?
- From alternative approaches: what do we learn for organizations from alternative and alienated approaches such as watching a film or creating a film about the concrete organization?

In this article, we will obviously concentrate on the latter approach.

The learning items for organizations, and especially the transformation of organizations, might be formulated like this:

Transformation of an organization—especially if it is significant and leads to the unknown—needs a significant mass of energy which has to come from the convincing purpose (NB: energy based only on 'economic necessities' is not enough), and this reflects that, in road movies, the energy mirrored in the images of consistent motion is based on the purpose for the journey. This is complemented by the energy that comes from the deep and growing connectivity between the humans who are travelling.

It is always obvious from the films that starting the journey and moving to a new constellation or condition needs the right timing and also a lot of fortunate coincidences (one has to accept that not everything can be planned and steered in detail) and determination (people who are deep down strong and resilient). In general, the concept of resilience has to be reflected on different levels, personal ones (are there enough resilient actors in the transformation team?) and organizational ones (mirrored in the mindset of the current organization).

It has to be clear that—as in the film—everyone brings their personal history (or baggage) and sensibilities that have to be accepted and respected and that it makes sense to have personal conversations that touch precisely on this. Long journeys especially need trust, and trust grows from personal exchange, which might also mean touching on sore points and controversial fundamental beliefs. If it is possible to open up to others with very intimate biographic details, strong confessions, fears, etc. and if this always handled in a fair way, trust for the shared journey will be established. When it comes to organization transformation, road movies can teach us that a suitable true exchange has to be started—which happens by itself in the film but needs a vehicle in the organizational transformation. It is one of the most important tasks for transformation leaders to create opportunities for trustful exchange of opinions and mindsets, experiences and expectations going far beyond the 'limited' transformation targets.

And last but not least, one gets from the films that connectivity doesn't imply equality from the beginning but openness to interact, exchange and synchronize on an equal footing.

Summary of Learnings

Based on the information described above, we can summarize as follows:

- You can learn a lot from a good road movie about the three pillars of organization design and especially about the necessary mindset for travelling organizations.
- It is obvious that reframing in alien contexts, or better still analogies from arts and culture, is very helpful to understand organizational needs.
- These reflections are helpful for interventions with transformation programme teams and stakeholders concerning direction and motivation.
- The feeling of being on the move does not need speed but continuity.

Further Reading

Breuer, F. (2009). *Reflexive grounded theory: eine Einführung für die Forschungspraxis.* Wiesbaden: VS Verlag.

Hirschauer, S., & Amann, K. (Eds.). (1997). *Die Befremdung der eigenen Kultur. Zur ethnographischen Herausforderung soziologischer Empirie.* Frankfurt: Suhrkamp.

Hitzler, R. (1986). Die Attitüde der künstlichen Dummheit. *Sozialwissenschaftliche Informationen (SOWI), 3,* 53–59.

Kruse, J. (2009). Indexikalität und Fremdverstehen: Problemfelder kommunikativer Verstehensprozesse. In B. Rehbein & G. Saalmann (Eds.), *Verstehen* (pp. 133–150). Konstanz: UVK.

Kühn, F., & Wollmann, P. (2012). Interaktion als Organisationsstrategie. In F. Kühn & P. Wollmann (Eds.), *Interaktion als organisationsstrategie* (pp. 10–11). Berlin: ICG.

Reuter, C., & Wollmann, P. (2012). Rapid project planning with interaction. In F. Kühn & P. Wollmann (Eds.), *Interaktion als Organisationsstrategie* (pp. 188–194). Berlin: ICG.

Strauss, A., & Corbin, J. (1996). *Grounded theory: Grundlagen qualitativer Sozialforschung.* Weinheim: Psychologische Verlags Union.

Wikipedia (2018): *303 (Film),* Handlung. Retrieved from https://de.wikipedia.org/wiki/303_(Film)

Wollmann, P. (2012). Wirksamkeit und effizienz in China und im Westen. In F. Kühn & P. Wollmann (Eds.), *Interaktion als Organisationsstrategie* (pp. 22–28). Berlin: ICG.

Modern Architecture Supporting Organization Design

Peter Wollmann and Mersida Ndrevataj

Abstract

The article reflects the reasons why organization design and leadership for enterprises in whatever industry and of whichever, size and maturity state, have to include the very real, tangible and concrete aspect of architecture now more so than ever. Architecture provides orientation and reflects the company's DNA with the described three pillars. Architecture is a main factor in transformations— not merely a negligible or onerous task to be considered but rather a high-priority long-term important one. Beyond the interests of the pure enterprise, some major topics facing mankind were tackled such as how to save the environment, how to promote health and well-being and how to support education. Architecture is a key science and profession that gives answers to the question of how we want to live tomorrow in general, not only in our working environment.

The editors of the book introduce:

Peter Wollmann who is now acting as a senior mentor, sparring partner, trusted advisor and catalyst for leaders in new roles and responsibilities and for organizations. Previously, he had diverse senior positions over nearly 40 years in the Finance Industry, with last years as programme director for global transformations within Zurich Insurance Company (ZIC). He is the author

(continued)

P. Wollmann (✉)
Consulting Partner, Bonn, Germany
e-mail: pw@peterwollmann.com

M. Ndrevataj (✉)
University of Venice, Venezia, Italy

© Springer Nature Switzerland AG 2020
P. Wollmann et al. (eds.), *Three Pillars of Organization and Leadership in Disruptive Times*, Future of Business and Finance,
https://doi.org/10.1007/978-3-030-23227-6_11

89

and publisher of a range of books and articles on strategy, leadership and project portfolio management.

Mersida Ndrevataj who is an architect and urban planner based in Venice. Her professional objective is to help better shape the built environment through a multidisciplinary research-based and human-centred design process. To this end, she is currently working and learning, immersing herself in the field of Environmental Psychology. For the last 3 years, she has been working as a Cultural Mediator and Project Manager for the Venice Biennale.

Architectural Answers on the Three-Pillar Model Requirements

In 2018, the Biennale Architettura in Venice had one focus on 'Freespace' or 'Public Space', how to create settings for—planned or random—encounters, interaction and cooperation in our days. The public free space topic was applied to cities, villages, enterprises, etc.—which means in different perspectives and contexts. The importance of an architecture providing the ideal public spaces in which context ever is overwhelming, the architecture is, therefore, a key success factor for an organization's efficacy, performance, stability and resilience. In this context, the Danish pavilion exemplarily showed the new BLOX building at the harbour of Copenhagen.

The official statements stressed the following[1]:

- 'Natalie Mossin has chosen to tell a Danish story of pursuing a joint approach to holistic sustainable development through interdisciplinary alliances and across sectors and communities. This theme is particularly topical in Denmark this year where the non-profit Realdania society is generously handing over the keys to BLOX—a newbuild designed by OMA to house the new Danish Architecture Center, BLOXHUB and a wide variety of other creative entities', said Kent Martinussen, CEO, Danish Architecture Center.
- 'BLOX is much more than a building. BLOX is a new space on the Copenhagen harbor and a hub for activities, proposals and meetings between people, from visitors attending the Danish Architecture Center's exhibitions and families with children at the playground to professionals working daily with sustainable urban solutions. The aim is for BLOX to promote awareness of, and work on, architecture and urban development as key ingredients in creating a sustainable society that enjoys enhanced quality of life', said CEO of Realdania Jesper Nygård.
- Freespace—generous architecture. The thematic framework was created by Yvonne Farrell and Shelley McNamara, Curators of the 16th International

[1]https://www.dac.dk/en/press/pavilion-of-denmark-at-the-16th-international-architecture-exhibition-

Architecture Exhibition. Under the caption 'Freespace', the two lead curators will be focusing on the primary focus of architecture: the space in itself and its potential for generosity.

- The exhibition in the Danish pavilion responds to the overarching theme by homing in on the scope of opportunities that arises when we—faced as we are by a large number of sustainability challenges—embark on the transition from bright ideas to the rigors of implementing new practices. This scope of opportunities can foster generosity—a Free-space—where architecture's particular contribution can give built form to our needs and ideas. The title of the exhibition in the Danish pavilion sums up this approach in 'Possible Spaces— Sustainable Development through Collaborative Innovations'. The title refers to the new opportunities that must be pursued in order to drive sustainable development, and the scope that arises when architects collaborating with professionals from other disciplines push the limits of what is possible to implement novel solutions.

Those quoted official statements cover already some key insights for our article:

- The importance of architecture to cover the diverse urban needs in contexts of work and leisure, transport, mobility and contemplation.
- The importance of architecture to ensure and enable encounters, cooperation and interaction—and at the end surprising innovation.
- The importance of cross-profession cooperation in a diverse and complex world.
- Architecture has a strong symbolic meaning and influences mindsets.

Coming from this, it is easy to describe a connection to our design building blocks or pillars.

Link to Our Three-Pillar Model and Some Initial Fundamental Practical Thoughts

As already mentioned in the general introduction to the book, it is irreversible that the 'old business world' is going to die. Old world means—only to take some buzz words—hierarchy, top-down decisions, Taylorism, silos, micromanagement, analogue processes, short-term thinking, focus on career, etc. So, transformation is indispensable and with this a new culture and mindset. Architecture might and must represent this change very well. We know the philosophy and concepts behind the new headquarters of companies like Google and Apple, and we have seen videos and photos about them. Nevertheless, we have to reflect that, on the one hand, architecture has a more abstract and general ambition than only to fit for Silicon Valley companies, so we have to understand the operational principles behind interesting examples from which part of the world ever and connect these principles with our three building blocks or pillars of organization and leadership. On the other hand, architecture has to be very concrete that means it has to fit to a very concrete setting best (Fig. 1).

Fig. 1 Different approaches to architecture aligned to the organizational setup, e.g., hierarchical or collaborative, giving adaptive space for connectivity and travelling around a shared purpose (figure: Frank Kühn)

Sustainable Purpose

Enterprises with a well-described, convincing, motivating sustainable purpose, which is giving orientation to the leaders and employees, always need a concrete representation of the purpose in something tangible for the employee and the stakeholders. Since centuries, buildings present the self-understanding and sustainable direction of leaders of country or institutions and their culture. The building as a demonstration of hierarchical power top-down has to be substituted by a network-oriented structure, which supports very flexible interaction and cooperation in general. Additionally, to this general characteristic, attributes have to be integrated which link with the (business) specific parts of the purpose.

In any way, it is important that there is no contradiction: an enterprise with a special customer-orientated purpose must, for example, be perceived as open for customers.

One of the key requirements today, in general, is the demonstration of transparence and work–life balance in order to convince young professionals to work for an organization—a challenging task also for the architects.

Travelling Organization

The whole organization will have be transformed to have the 'travelling mindset', that means in terms of architecture that flexible groups of people need flexible and creative and animating free spaces to meet, interact, cooperate, interact with the environments open for quick changes if needed (this means adding more participants, running presentations, having undisturbed workshops over days, having access to all technical devices and all media, offering documentation options over longer periods, allowing picnics, etc.). People have to feel like on a trip in these contexts.

Connecting Resources

The necessity to allow—or better to proactively offer, to force or to automatically make happen—that people from all over the organization and beyond meet by accident, get in touch for interaction while having a coffee and cooperate in relaxed environments was already mentioned. Architecture has to connect and not to separate in these days. A high percentage of innovation, good ideas, commitments and plans are made unplanned when people meet by accident. The example of the BLOX building in Copenhagen shows how this can be achieved today, best in a place where different paths of mobility meet stationary professional hubs which provide open space areas for uncomplicated, convenient meetings.

On the other hand, architecture itself links more and more with other sciences and professions like technology, environment care, sociology, policy, etc.—so designing enterprise buildings in linkage with (public) open spaces got an interdisciplinary task.

How Architecture Today Is Meeting the Described Key Challenges

The success of an organization strongly depends on the types of building they occupy, the site they select and the workspace design they choose. In relation to this statement, the architectural reflection goes more specifically on:

- The architectural role on creating and promoting a sustainable enterprise and quality of life.
- The architecture role on creating the optimal working space and improving productivity.
- The implementation of a built form of our needs and ideas in a constantly changing environment and interdisciplinary context.

In support of the defined key challenges of the future, architecture has developed the following concepts and forms.

1. *SMART Enterprise Buildings*
   To face the challenges of network, fast evolving and user requirements, the next generation of buildings must be highly adaptable to different environments. All buildings and organizations must modernize to operate in today's world. The future requires becoming smarter. Smart buildings will transform work, the workplace and the urban landscape in the next years. Smartness means being sustainable, flexible and healthy. Smart buildings have a sustainable

consumerism and an efficient space use; they are functionally flexible and can accommodate agile, dynamic and creative ways of working; they contribute to a healthy working experience and to the workforce well-being (The EDGE in Amsterdam, Le Hive in Paris, Majunga Tower in Paris).

Enterprises can play a leading role in the creation of smart cities, as they run in an urban infrastructure. Creating smart enterprise buildings and linking them together, the urban landscape can be redefined and the urban life can be improved (Jurong Lake District in Singapore, Songdo city in Seoul).

In the future cities will continue playing an important role. Becoming smart, their public spaces will be used as support for the community to meet and collaborate. In this context, it is worth mentioning that according to the concept of the BLOX building in Copenhagen, mentioned in the beginning of this article, it is impossible to simply pass it without interacting with the building even though it is a major traffic hub between several destinations. You have to go up and down and pass several parts of the building which invite you to stay for a drink, to meet people or to view at something. This is best explained in a video with Ellen van Loon, often called 'the Dutch design duchess' of the world-renowned Office for Metropolitan Architecture (OMA). She talks in the video about the ideas and 'architectural contamination' that went into creating the new multifunctional BLOX building in the heart of Copenhagen.[2]

It's also important for city planners and entrepreneurs to collaborate with each other on creating new models of entrepreneurship. This way, they can drive placemaking and regeneration of disadvantaged spaces, instead of building new office buildings.

2. SMART Workspace

In the smart age, the work style and workspace change and give rise to a more connected and complex work environment.

The workplace is not anymore only a physical location. It is both a physical space and a virtual space. At the same time, there is a demand for an agile workspace—a transformable and adaptable working environment. The agile workspace layout is composed by a variety of working areas, and it allows employers to work wherever they feel more inspired and energized.

The workplace is a network structure formed by mobile, remote and virtual workers. Therefore, technology, connectivity and communication will be a survival need.

The future workplace is more human; it ensures comfort (air quality, lighting, heating, etc.), health and well-being to the workers. There is an increasing focus on the well-being who has led to the development of a WELL Building Standard certification.[3] Creating ideal work environment enterprises boost productivity and attract employers.

---

[2]Video on youtube: https://www.youtube.com/watch?v=ZEF8D8t7tTA
[3]https://www.wellcertified.com

The workplace is community oriented; the work is flexible and responds to work–life balance and quality. The workplace is based around social activities, services and common workspaces.

3. *Entrepreneurial Workspaces*

Architecture is a container of physical and human resources. Entire buildings are being designed to encourage the encounters and the collaboration between employers and disciplines. The workplace evolves in an infrastructure of social interaction zone and innovation and creativity. As a result, the workplace becomes more flexible; it has no more physical boundaries and offers a fluid interaction. This way people with a common interest meet and collaborate.

Here, below are some workplace design approaches and their characteristics:

- Activity-based working or the non-assigned seating is a workspace design approach where employees are not tied to a particular space, traditionally a desk, but they transit between different settings according to the task they are doing. These ways they have more opportunities to interact in between them.[4]
- Co-location or innovation hubs, it is a workplace approach where multiple organizations share the same building. This is considered as an important infrastructure in a multidisciplinary context, and it is usually engaged with innovative projects. This workplace encourages a new form of collaboration between disciplines who generates innovative thinking. It's also a shared infrastructure that merges global and local resources to create innovation.[5]
- Co-working or the membership-based workspaces, where flexible workers share flexible workspaces. The space is flexible, and it can be configured according to the different needs. The co-working members work for different organizations. They have different skills that they can provide to the community. They are usually engaged in a social mission, and this makes the members feel part of a community. They organize networking events, training programmes and social events.[6]

Nowadays, the role of architecture and urban development is to create and promote a sustainable environment and quality of life. So, the longevity of future buildings depends on their ability to adapt themselves to a quick social and technological evolving landscape. That's why enterprises have to combine their strategy and structure to the next smart generation.

Moreover, architecture and enterprises must be both 'everything at once', and their collective knowledge will become more powerful.

---

[4]https:// www.iofficecorp.com/blog/favorite-examples-of-activity-based-workplace-design

[5]https://www.forbes.com/sites/michellegreenwald/2018/04/02/a-new-wave-ofinnovation-hubs-sweeping-the-world/#50d91fe51265

[6]https://www.dezeen.com/2018/10/27/seven-shared-offices-co-working-interiorsroundups/

Conclusion and Lessons Learnt

We think we gave some convincing reasons why organization and leadership for enterprises of which industry, size and maturity state ever, has to include the very real, tangible and concrete aspect of architecture with a lot more focus than in the past. Architecture gives orientation and reflects the company DNA with the described three pillars. Architecture is a main factor in transformations—not a more or less neglectable or onerous task to think through but a high-priority long-term and important one.

The ideas of international architects at the Biennale last year were animating, stunning and very real. And beyond the interests of the pure enterprise, some big topics of mankind were additionally tackled like how to save environment, how to create health and how to support education. Architecture is a key science and profession to give answers to the question how we want to live tomorrow in general, not only in our working environment.

Further Reading

Alessandro, T. (2012). *Progettare gli uffici: Qualità e comfort nelle diverse soluzioni spaziali del luogo di lavoro*. Maggioli: Santarcangelo di Romagna.

Banda, P., Sosnowchick, K., & Berto, A. (2010). *Interni biosostenibili: Spazi commerciali, uffici, servizi: Criteri di scelta per la progettazione di aree lavorative: Guida ai prodotti e ai materiali*. Napoli: Gruppo editoriale Esselibri-Simone.

Brivio, E. (2015): *Now we work: Progettare gli uffici dell'innovazione*. Milano: Il prisma.

Casciani, S., Fiorenza, O., Roj, M., & Caruso, C. (2000). *Workspace/Workscape: I nuovi scenari dell'ufficio*. Milano: Skira.

Klanten, R., Ehmann, S., & Borges, S. (2013). *Work scape: New spaces for new work*. Berlin: Gestalten.

Kuo, J. (2013). *A-typical plan: Projects and essays on identity, flexibility, and atmosphere in the office building*. Zurich: Park Books.

Memoori—Smart Building Research under. Retrieved from https://www.memoori.com

Menzel, L. (2009). *Office: Architecture + design*. Salenstein: Braun.

Piardi, S., Natile, V., & Tieghi, S. (2012). *Office design: Smart organization & layout: dall'analisi al progetto*. Milano: Angeli.

Stewart, M. (2004). *The other office: Creative workplace design*. Amsterdam: Birkhäuser.

Uffelen, C. V. (2014). *Corporate architecture*. Salenstein: Braun.

Part III

Practice Cluster: Projects and Interventions

The exciting question is how—in the current context of disruption—projects, especially large transformations and change initiatives, can be designed, led, and realized. Peter Wollmann tackles this question in a more strategic manner at a project portfolio level and then at a more tactical level, focusing on interventions in disillusioned organizations. Then, Frank Kühn sums up the story of a successful enterprise project, and Alfred Mevissen describes the challenging aspects of an international art project

Project Portfolio Management of Global Enterprises

Peter Wollmann

Abstract

It can be predicted that, in the future, on average, more than 50% of the value creation of enterprises will be created in projects. This means that budget, resources and expertise will become even more scare compared with the volume of the demand. Thus, it is crucial to develop a suitable management model for the project portfolio that really works—in comparison to the many existing concepts that are intellectually brilliant but do not work in practice. The article will make some of the current key contradictions and inconsistencies transparent and propose ways to fix them pragmatically in the world of volatile, uncertain, complex and ambiguous (VUCA) enterprises.

The editors of the book introduce **Peter Wollmann**, who is now acting as a senior mentor, sparring partner, trusted advisor and catalyst for leaders in new roles and responsibilities and for organizations. Previously, he had diverse senior positions over nearly 40 years in the Finance Industry, with last years as programme director for global transformations within Zurich Insurance Company (ZIC). He is the author and publisher of a range of books and articles on strategy, leadership and project and project portfolio management.

P. Wollmann (✉)
Consulting Partner, Bonn, Germany
e-mail: pw@peterwollmann.com

© Springer Nature Switzerland AG 2020
P. Wollmann et al. (eds.), *Three Pillars of Organization and Leadership in Disruptive Times*, Future of Business and Finance,
https://doi.org/10.1007/978-3-030-23227-6_12

Introduction

As already mentioned in the general introduction of the book, it is already some sort of 'common—at least often shared—knowledge and understanding' that the 'old business world' is going to die. Old world means—only to take some buzz words—hierarchy, top-down decisions, Taylorism, silos, micromanagement, analogue processes, short-term thinking, focus on career, etc.

If this was true for the organization in general, it is even more striking in the world of projects and project portfolios which is especially sensitive for fundamental changes. And building on the observations that enterprises get more and more project driven, this means that it is crucial to find solid and sustainable solutions to run projects and project portfolios under the new preconditions and environmental frames.

In our latest book on *Leading International Projects*, an impressive range of very diverse cases and insights from the cases' analysis was presented—which showed that management concepts have to base on shared acting and mindset, based on fundamental building blocks and operational principles, but have to be very flexibly tailorable to a concrete situation in the more detailed operations perspective and that especially the idea of having the famous 'Ten Tools To Use For Success' might give readers a good feeling but would not work.

It is obvious that—if we already have such a challenge in the single-project perspective—the project portfolio management is even more demanding. The author of this article had had responsibility for steering project portfolios over some decades and also diligently written articles and even books on this topic—but it is transparent for him that the contradiction between good theoretical concepts and tools, on the one hand, and enterprise practice, on the other hand, never was larger than in these days. This is surprising as the scientific research and concept development is quite consistently driven by universities (like TU Berlin and University Hannover, to name some German universities) and institutions (like PMI or DGPM).

In this article, the author will try to develop some ideas about a successful future project portfolio management for enterprises in the VUCA world. It is not the ambition to add a new theoretical concept to the impressive number of existing ones but interpret the three-pillar model in a project portfolio context as a base for enterprises to develop/adjust their existing concepts accordingly. Cases of existing concrete project portfolio management are not described in detail as this does not seem to be necessary for the considerations about concept adjustments—and especially needed cultural changes.

As it can be predicted that in the future, on average more than 50% of the value creation of enterprises will be created in projects, that, on the other hand, budget, resources and expertise will become even more scare compared with the volume of the demand it is crucial to develop a suitable management model. The article will make some of the key contradiction and inconsistencies transparent and propose ways to fix them in volatile, uncertain, complex and ambiguous (VUCA) enterprises' world, which means among others to develop how project portfolio management needs to be organized and managed in the future in a more dynamic way, nevertheless showing clear direction and belief in covering the strategic direction of the enterprise.

Link to the Three-Pillar Model

So, we firstly should try to explore the case for project portfolio management in the new business world more intensively analysing concrete issues in applying the key leading building blocks or pillars for 'good organization' developed as a hypothesis in the beginning of the book.

Sustainable Purpose

It is obvious that the sustainable purpose of the project portfolio is to best cover the sustainable purpose of the enterprise, and 'best' means in the most effective and efficient way short, mid and long term.

This statement contains two key challenges: on the one hand, the purpose of the enterprise has to be sustainably, transparently—and operationalizability—formulated, accepted and shared. On the other hand, the coverage of the different timely and content-orientated dimensions of the enterprise's purpose by projects is quite difficult, especially if the tactical and fundamental environment is changing fast—we will come to this point in detail below in the next bullet point.

The perception in many companies is that the top management have real problems to take sufficient time on the fundamental purpose discussion and making the outcomes operationalizable as it is absorbed by troubleshooting and tactical issues.

So the right level clear and convincing orientation that aligns and inspires the people for a joint endeavour is (partly) lacking, and the communicated visions are either reduced to trivial statements ('we have to serve our clients') or reduced to figures and financial goals so that the distinctive success factor of the enterprise and its resulting competitive advantage is not transparent.

Travelling Organization

Understanding is needed that the organization and its projects and the project portfolio are continuously on a journey towards best possible results and joint success under partly unforeseeable influences.

This statement also contains some key challenges: in most enterprises, more or less inflexible financial systems and tools require solid and fixed project and project portfolio information. The enterprise wants to have a solid and sustainable financial plan (e.g. budget) over a longer period to be prevent surprises for the investors and keep the share price solid. Flexible budgeting is not very common so far. This is difficult in disruptive situations where transformation projects have to be started, which cannot be finally planned in the beginning over the whole life cycle. It makes life not easier that the bonus/reward systems are complex and not flexible—so project sponsors and leaders as well as project portfolio managers suffer from some rigid preconditions which do not fit to the character of projects and project portfolios in these days. This means that the concept of a 'travelling organization' fundamentally contradicts to the current management practice in most enterprises, to change this, a 'cultural revolution' and a real 'system change' will be necessary.

How far this 'revolution' has to go and how the mindsets have to be changed can be shown in the attitude against entrepreneurial risk—which is naturally high in projects and project portfolios. Even though there is an intensive discussion about leaders and employees to be more entrepreneurial, the risk aversion did increase tremendously as organizations try to prevent all risks. The level of risk acceptance even in the context of projects—and so the project portfolio—is quite low. And the risk aversion is—naturally—the higher, the more budget is dedicated to an initiative.

Another environmental challenge, which should be mentioned, is that especially complex projects often need external providers which have to be booked via enterprise procurement. Often, the most flexible and scalable providers are more expensive than those, which base on mid- to long-term fixed contracts with fixed resources. The impact is obvious: to change/modify those contracts in situations which require this, is demanding, takes a lot of energy and time which would be needed somewhere else. This is—of course—valid for all re-planning in rigid, inflexible systems.

So it would be necessary that enterprises accept the 'Travelling Project Model' or 'Travelling Project Portfolio Concept' which means that even if you don't know what you have to face after the next bend in the road and what the best result will be then, you strongly believe in your motivation and capabilities to manage it. This makes a fundamental difference to the illusion of business consistence, strategic stability and structural continuity in disruptive times as presented in classical sometimes promised to the people after having completed a transformation.

Travelling project and project portfolio organizations need holistic agility in their mindset and DNA covering agile mentality, self-reflection, change readiness and delivery orientation—and the support of the enterprise, especially from the top management.

People in a travelling project and project portfolio organization are curious, open and impartial, self-reflected, experimental and well coping with uncertainty, stress, special challenges and unforeseen obstacles. And they are able to find fascinating solutions in all difficult situations and to develop the right narrative for the communication into the enterprise. If this works well over a certain timeline, the trust in the organizations and the acting people will be developed—and justified trust is one of the best success factors of organizations and secures effectiveness and efficiency.

Connecting Resources

It is obvious that projects need an overwhelming amount of interaction inside but also at the diverse interfaces to the line management, other projects and the providers chosen. Project portfolio management is to a certain degree interface management and connectivity management. It has to be aware that impact, value and efficiency of the project portfolio need the connectivity between individuals, between people and organization, between ways of working and project customer needs, and between strategy and skills. This means managing connectivity, avoiding development of unconnected strategies and processes, and re-arranging connectivity on the company's journey continuously. This makes a fundamental difference to compartmentalization of the company's resources in terms of structural silos, boxed competencies, individual incentives and behaviours.

The key issue in this context is the pure mass of potentially relevant connections to be covered. A lot of tools are available to support—and they are helpful in the detailed technical and financial perspective but not a substitute for personal contact and discussion. Situations which are strategically complex—e.g. as a lot of different interests and perceptions have to be managed—cannot be fixed by a technical tool. The tool supports as a provider of data and basic information which is relevant but not sufficient for a comprehensive solution.

Summary of the Key Challenges

The three-pillar model shows that project portfolio management design is crucial for general organization design for enterprises in the new business world. But the obstacles to have a reasonable concept implemented and well working in practice are tremendous:

- A clear enterprise purpose and strategic direction are necessary—in an operationalizable format, well communicated and well shared.
- A 'Travelling Project Organization Model' and 'Travelling Project Portfolio Organization Concept' have to be embedded in the enterprise DNA and culturally accepted.
- The finance systems for projects/the project portfolio have to be made flexible enough and modifications/changes so easily digestible.
- The project portfolio needs a 'sponsor' in the top management on upper board level with an entrepreneurial mindset and connectivity skills to moderate interest reconciliation on top management level.

Project portfolio management needs to be regarded as a strategic, highly value adding unit, not as a poor 'technical service'. The staffing of the unit has to regard this demand.

- The project portfolio organization has to have the issue/troubleshooting skills on the journey being able to cope with unexpected situations and with the ability to develop honest and helpful narratives for the top management and the surrounding organization.
- The project portfolio organization has to have strong connectivity skills.
- There should be solid tools for basic data and information collection and storage for the project portfolio in place to provide connecting conversations with the needed details.

A Well-Working Case from the Nineties

A local champion with still quite old-fashioned business operating model and structure was bought by a modern global player in the finance industry which wanted to diversify in these lines of finance business. To be able to cope with challenging situation, the local champion started immediately a broad organization development programme which covered among others development of a tailored project and project portfolio management concept inclusive implementation which also covered all educational and cultural aspects.

The purpose of the organization development programme, and also the to-be situation strived for by it, was so very transparent: the local champion was intended to become an appreciated and well-respected, integrated part of the Global Player with the chance of mutual support in a joint development. It should not vanish in absorption without making a clear contribution to the Global Player.

The sponsor of the organization development programme was the very ambitious CEO of the local champion who wanted to make 'his' company as soon as possible from a structural and systemic perspective at least as modern as the Global Player.

The organization development programme contained the development and implementation of a strategic management concept and so among others the definition of an enterprise purpose and strategy based on capabilities in strategic success factors to gain sustainable competitive advantages. To achieve this, a bundle of strategic key projects was developed and decided to reach the key targets in a defined timeframe. To run the projects and the project portfolio, the developed tailored respective concepts were developed and implemented.

The responsible manager for the development of those concepts and their implementation but also for the following maintenance—strategic management, project and project portfolio management—was a direct report to the CEO who was supported by a body/committee of high-level board member representing the unit of 'his or her' board member with the 'license' to take decisions.

This committee acted as empowered steering committee—or partly also on a high level as the development team—of the mentioned management systems, respectively, and afterwards took over the joint steering of the strategy realization and the connected key projects or the project portfolio, respectively.

There were four very lucky preconditions guaranteeing for the success of the proceeding:

- The absolute loyalty and support of the CEO to his organization development initiatives and the people running it, which included frequent, very open and productive official meetings and unofficial exchanges.
- In this context, the regular involvement of the whole board in design and status meetings on a regular base—and from this the understanding of a journey with some flexibility.
- The trustful and respectful cooperation of the members in the committee who achieved, on the one hand, to present the interests of their board members and their units but, on the other hand, were open for a reasonable compromise/shared solution reconciling the contradictive perspectives.
- The excitement of the whole enterprise stuff to build up something valuable in the context of the Global Player. People were really very proud and extremely engaged.

In terms of the three-pillar model, an ideal setting was reached:

- A sponsor on highest level with sustainable support and a clear purpose and direction message which everybody understood.
- A reasonable understanding of the necessity of a flexible journey or to be a travelling organization.
- An underlying concept of cooperation and structure (committees, broad involvement of all parties, entrepreneurial mindsets, clear and honest status reporting, etc.) which produced trust which made at the end the acceptance of being a travelling organization possible in spite of all reserved attitudes.
- A build-up connectivity across the whole organization basing on responsible people with the necessary skills—e.g. to be critical, challenging, able to compromise and able to trust. A deciding factor was the moderation/facilitation of the development initiatives and the committee work.

So, one of the key insight is about the special setting basing on people, their personalities, mindsets and skills and on the needed systems gives the base for the connecting of the people in their daily work.

That is, on the one hand, good news—as always with a positive case, where challenging concepts work well. The bad news, on the other hand, is that firstly the high flexibility of the established solution got lost later and the organization fell back on a lower maturity level for several reasons. Secondly, in general, the complexity of the environment (market, regulation, political factors, and globalization impacts) and complexity—and size—of the organizations increased significantly since then. A setting as described will not be found or generated easily in these days—even though this is missed (see Joe Kaeser's desire to make Siemens be transformed from a large supertanker to a fleet of flexible speedboats—in a speedboat, the described setting would be possible).

So the fundamental lessons learnt is that—to reach the preconditions for the favourable setting—a very large organization has to be clustered, virtually divided, etc. to come to a manageable sublayer of it. But that will not be enough. The culture of flexibility, a pragmatism in solving of issues and conflicts, the absence of a mainly risk-avoiding attitude, the ability of key persons with different interests to find reasonable compromises, the respect for those who explore other business opportunities in another way than the personal preference looks like, all this has to accompany and complete the purely legal and organizational setting to become successful.

Summary of Solution Proposals for the Project Portfolio Management to Be Applied in the Favourable Setting

As already mentioned, it is not the ambition to develop a completely new project portfolio management concept for enterprises in the VUCA world but to present adjustment proposals for existing concepts and routines.

The solution ideas follow the described key challenges which were developed following the three-pillar model:

- Build up and maintain a strong connection with top management and enterprise strategy to make sure that there is clearly and transparently fixed and communicated enterprise purpose and strategic direction and that it is in an operationalizable format.
- This will very often be an explorative journey in close cooperation during which the needs from project portfolio management can challenge the purpose formulation during the try to prove that can be well applied to shape the project portfolio.
- Build up and maintain a strong connection with top management and enterprise HR/culture department to make sure that 'Travelling Organization' cultural model is embedded into the organization with diverse measures and that a 'Travelling Project Organization Model' and 'Travelling Project Portfolio Organization Concept' are accepted in the enterprise.
- Make clear with Finance how the finance systems for projects/the project portfolio can be made have flexible enough for the needs of project and project portfolio management and what the concept for the continuously necessary modifications/changes could look like. This covers key corporate processes like budgeting, reporting, etc.
- Establish the project portfolio management in the enterprise orgchart at a 'sponsor' in the top management on upper board level with an entrepreneurial mindset and connectivity skills to moderate interest reconciliation on top management level. This also should make clear that project portfolio management is regarded as a strategic, highly value adding unit, not as a poor 'technical service'. The staffing of the unit has to be made accordingly with strategically minded people with business knowledge and systemic understanding.

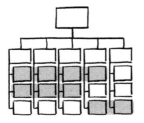 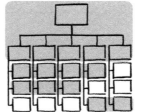 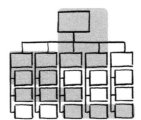

1. The initial state of a rigid project landscape to be managed by the lines	*2. More flexibility and cross-silo project portfolio management is possible in the next development state*	*3. The future agile success model might be the 'Project Portfolio Management as a Moderated Platform of Projects'*
• Fix budgets allocated in yearly budgeting process • Departmental interests & influences dominating • Realization mostly in organizational silos • Project Managers with the additional task to coordinate cross-departmental collaboration individually • Cross-departmental decisions dealt between line managers	• Top Management-Committee coordinating and aligning departmental interests flexibly • Budgeting process in place but non-bureaucratic budget adaptions possible if needed • Priorities, interdependencies and resource allocation centrally planned and managed • Projects apply organizational guidelines • Strong focus on knowledge development/lessons learnt in defined events	• Direction given via transparent corporate purpose and strategy of whole enterprise and its layers • Customer needs are decisive • Self-organized enterprise layers defining their projects, flexibly coordinating and connecting resources via a vivid platform • Focus on agile and explorative proceeding with fast entrepreneurial decision making • Project community for sharing knowledge and solutions in continuous exchanges

green	Centrally steered with mostly line management perspective and whole enterprise view
orange	De-centrally steered by agile layers with mostly project perspective

Fig. 1 Potential maturity development path of project portfolio management, starting from a level with deserves the term 'managed project portfolio' (figure: Frank Kühn)

- Train and develop the project portfolio unit in issue/troubleshooting skills and the ability to cope with unexpected situations and to develop honest and helpful narratives for the top management and the surrounding organization. This also includes the continuous development of connectivity capabilities. The development measures should be run involving key interface units of the enterprise.
- Establish regular interactions on diverse levels with all involved parties to develop solutions and proceedings with all relevant parties in a tailored way, fitting to the concrete situation. This includes as well fixed committees in project portfolio clusters as well as spontaneous meetings in the case of special demands.

- Make sure that there are solid tools for basic data and information collection and storage for the project portfolio in place to provide connecting conversations with the needed details.
- Exploit the opportunities from digital factors like real-time transparency, virtual cooperation, flexible building of communities to handle interfaces, knowledge sharing/lessons learnt, etc.
- Connect the project and project portfolio processes to other management processes (such as knowledge management, strategic HR development, organization development, budgeting, etc.).
- Connect the project journey with the corporate journey in terms of good practices you want to experiment with. Do they fit in terms of competencies and culture? Where do you want to make a step beyond? Are the approaches you want to try in the projects or project portfolio too 'extravagant'?

Perhaps, the potential positive maturity development path of project portfolio management could look like the graphs in Fig. 1, starting from a level with deserves the term 'managed project portfolio' (as there are more or less 'prehistoric' and rudimentary states before this possible and not such rare).

Further Reading

Berg, F., Kühn, F., Reuter, C., & Wollmann, P. (2012). Experimentelles Projektdesign. In F. Kühn & P. Wollmann (Eds.), *Interaktion als Organisationsstrategie* (pp. 195–206). Berlin: ICG.

Dignen, B., Pleuger, G., Kühn, F., & Wollmann, P. (2012). Starting an international project. In F. Kühn & P. Wollmann (Eds.), *Interaktion als Organisationsstrategie* (pp. 176–181). Berlin: ICG.

Kühn, F. (2001). Facetten des Multiprojektmanagements. In M. Hirzel, F. Kühn, & P. Wollmann (Eds.), *Multiprojektmanagement* (pp. 35–51). Frankfurt am Main: FAZ Buch.

Kühn, F., Reuter, C., & Wollmann, P. (2012). Risk & control system interaktiv implementieren. In F. Kühn & P. Wollmann (Eds.), *Interaktion als Organisationsstrategie* (pp. 207–211). Berlin: ICG.

Kühn, F., & Wollmann, P. (2012). Interaktion als Organisationsstrategie. In F. Kühn & P. Wollmann (Eds.), *Interaktion als Organisationsstrategie* (pp. 10–11). Berlin: ICG.

Reuter, C., & Wollmann, P. (2012). Rapid project planning with interaction. In F. Kühn & P. Wollmann (Eds.), *Interaktion als Organisationsstrategie* (pp. 188–194). Berlin: ICG.

Willke, H. (2001). Projektübergreifendes Wissensmanagement. In M. Hirzel, F. Kühn, & P. Wollmann (Eds.), *Multiprojektmanagement* (pp. 117–130). Frankfurt am Main: FAZ Buch.

Wollmann, P. (2001). Multiprojektmanagement im Kontext der Strategischen Planung. In M. Hirzel, F. Kühn, & P. Wollmann (Eds.), *Multiprojektmanagement* (pp. 22–36). Frankfurt am Main: FAZ Buch.

Wollmann, P., & Berg, F. (2007). Building a project portfolio management system in a complex matrix organization. In M. Hirzel, W. Alter, P. Wollmann, F. Kühn, G. Pleuger, V. Carlbaum, F. Berg, B. Dignen, & H. Jonasson (Eds.), *Workbook future organization* (pp. 28–36). Frankfurt am Main: HLP Management Connex.

Design and Impact of Interventions in Change Processes

Peter Wollmann

Abstract

The Anthropocene is marked by technological development and enthusiasm as well as global crises fostering fear and distrust, alienation and singularization of people. Managers running change processes have to be aware of such influences from the world around them, designing and facilitating powerful interventions, transferring the three pillars of organization and leadership into valuable experiences: Credible and inspiring purpose, travelling organization as shared endeavour, connecting resources and experiencing joint success. The article gives examples for corresponding events and behaviours.

The editors of the book introduce **Peter Wollmann** who is now acting as a senior mentor, sparring partner, trusted advisor and catalyst for leaders in new roles and responsibilities and for organizations. Previously, he had diverse senior positions over nearly 40 years in the Finance Industry, with last years as programme director for global transformations within Zurich Insurance Company (ZIC). He is the author and publisher of a range of books and articles on strategy, leadership and project portfolio management.

P. Wollmann (✉)
Consulting Partner, Bonn, Germany
e-mail: pw@peterwollmann.com

Introduction

Recently, there was a very interesting article by Bernd Scherer, Director of The House Of the Cultures Of the World, Berlin, about the Anthropocene in my favourite newspaper *Süddeutsche Zeitung* (12 June 2018, page 13).

Bernd Scherer describes some of the most important shades of disruption caused by the new (geologic) era or the so-called Great Acceleration of the 'Manhood-Earth-System' ('Great Acceleration' means, for example, acceleration of population increase, of increase in gross national product, in carbon dioxide production, of decrease in rain forests, etc., which means a planetary transformation. This transformation was mainly made possible by transforming planetary time into manhood time by exploiting fossil raw materials accumulated over millions of years into energy and mobility for some few centuries.

In this context, the understanding of knowledge is fundamentally changing, says Bernd Scherer: so far, the natural and cultural sciences have strived to create an understanding of 'nature' and 'culture'; now knowledge is mostly focused on creating new worlds and steering and controlling them as well as possible. This becomes obvious when one considers knowledge-driven worlds of machines that create new realities and where people communicate with those machines. The ideal case is that machines run process from state A to state B without needing people to think about the how (e.g. the underlying algorithm).

Further, Bernd Scherer stresses that, in parallel to this technology sphere, which creates new planetary infrastructures, the economization of society is taking place by means of which human behaviour is becoming commodified, that is, is becoming an item of merchandise that can be bought and sold.

Bernd Scherer mentions a drugstore chain which uses the interest of women in special articles to draw the conclusion whether or not they are pregnant and afterwards sends them individually tailored offers—a special phase of life is reduced to the correlation with a part of the product portfolio of a drugstore chain, with the information coming from the algorithm. Cyberspace is not a world parallel to the real world but interacts with it, penetrating deeper and deeper layers of our social and psychological lives.

Developing and steering these infrastructures are achieved by a few experts, a majority of people lose proactive roles in a driver's seat and feel like an object, only indirectly providing the infrastructure by feeding it with their knowledge and data. The consequences are obvious on different stages—in political life, in companies, etc.—says the author. In one sentence: the Anthropocene is specially marked by an excess of technological production of new worlds in parallel with a deficit of sense—and the feeling of severe defamiliarization. And this is also—this is now my conclusion—a key factor to be regarded in the transformation from the old to the new business world (and it is good to know that the business world is part of the 'overall world' and influenced by it).

There is another key factor to be considered—the perception of status of the world in general and how people can cope with it. There is a broadly shared feeling that the number of catastrophes and amount of bad news in the world today are increasing—which means the decline of democratic political systems worldwide, the various wars in Syria or Yemen, the unsolvable Middle East conflict, the refugee crisis in the EU, the presidency of Donald Trump, the potential trade war, climate change, etc. People have to cope with bad news, with disrespect and hate, etc. every day, which feeds the feeling of that the end of the world is nigh or at least those parts of the world that people would love to live in. This means that we are not living in a world in the spirit of optimism and the belief that the world is becoming significantly better. This might be caused by social media (and the situation could be partly better than perceived), but there are some unpleasant facts that bear out this scepticism. For the article, the general perception is important—not the facts. The current feeling of being in a general decline, the lack of hope and belief in the chance for a better world has reached a degree which is special, according to Philipp Blom, an important historian and writer, who states that is quite unique in the history of mankind that societies live totally without optimism or a vision for the future.

But beyond such potentially overly negative perception, there are some very old and traditional enterprises that were managed so poorly over years that a dwindling spiral cannot be overlooked and nor can the failure of desperate attempts to stop this (very often from new management teams every 1 or 2 years). The unbelievable could come true: that these enterprises, which seemed so invulnerable ('too big to fail'), might vanish—and nearly everybody has some examples. This magnifies people's pessimism.

This general mental state is not helpful if it affects the enterprise for whom people work. General sensitivity, based on the condition of the wider world outside, meets the concrete sensitivity created by a crisis at one's concrete employer. It is understood that, in general, positive and optimistic people are better able to cope with a concrete issue. Managers running significant transformations in enterprises have to take into account that there is an additional impact from the surrounding world which is not necessarily based on content but on mentality.

So, the exciting question is: What do you do to make a transformational change in some sort of 'desperate, distrusting and pessimistic environment' successful? And how do you manage a suitable intervention 'to open the door to cultural change' and afterwards building up systemic institutions, attitudes and skills 'to keep the door sustainably open'? It is—to underline this clearly—not a focus on 'heroic management', where the strong leader intervenes and everything works fine afterwards. It is a tandem: the intervention opens the door and the minds so that the much-needed institutional or systemic long-term concepts can be started and further developed.

The hypothesis of this article—as an answer to the fundamental question in the paragraph above—is that, from the aforementioned reasons, it is necessary to draft a creative combination of a powerful intervention with short-term effect to open the door to a potential change in attitude by the people involved and a consistent setup of systemic long-term institutions to support transition and make it successful. The focus of this article is on the intervention part.

Link to Our Three-Pillar Model and Some Initial Fundamental Practical Thoughts

As already mentioned in the general introduction to the book and now highlighted in a larger context in the introduction to this article, it is irreversible that the 'old business world' is going to die. Old world means—only to take some buzz words—hierarchy, top-down decisions, Taylorism, silos, micromanagement, analogue processes, short-term thinking, focus on career, etc. So, transformation is indispensable.

But—to follow the introductory word—transformation is a lot more difficult from a content-based and cultural aspect than ever before. But nevertheless, the new business world—if it were ideal—would be designed according to the trio of pillars for organization and leadership, developed and described at the beginning of the book, which all offer solutions to the 'transformation dilemma'.

Sustainable Purpose

Enterprises would have a well-described, convincing and motivating sustainable purpose giving orientation to the leaders and teams. This sustainable purpose would give a real sense to the stakeholders on the basis of individual value systems. With top management constantly embodying this sustainable purpose as role models, the described loss of trust and lack of optimism might be—partly—overcome. Therefore, it is crucial that top management take sufficient time to consider the fundamental purpose discussion and make the outcomes operationalizable—and do not get bogged down in troubleshooting and tactical issues.

Since a lack of trust, belief and positive thinking, and therefore motivation, is a significant obstacle for the joint acceptance of a sustainable purpose, a strong intervention with following continuous systemic activities is necessary to start convincing people.

Travelling Organization

The whole organization would be transformed to have the 'travelling mindset', which means it would be conscious of being on a permanent journey through a fast-changing landscape with unforeseeable obstacles and new preconditions, but confident enough to be able to flexibly cope with it. If a chosen path turns out to be not very successful, another more promising one can be easily and quickly taken. This also means that the governance and steering concepts are adequate and supportive. This 'travelling' experience would create a straight, non-artificial active experience for the people involved and provide them with the feeling of influence. But this means that both modern, adequate leadership and personnel policy, on the one hand, and the culture of autonomous teams, on the other hand, have to be a top priority. Leaders and managers who don't live these fundamentals have to leave the enterprise. Personal development has to focus on building the required attitudes and skills.

It is absolutely crucial to sustainably create a positive experience with becoming a travelling organization as fear, distrust, previous bad experiences, etc. have to be overcompensated for. Intervention in this context means to be very clear and consistent with those not following the culture and concrete principles of a travelling organization, especially if at higher management levels.

It is crucial to carefully and transparently communicate success on the journey on a regular basis and to have events with all leaders and employees to go through progress, discuss it and make sure that perceptions converge.

Connecting Resources

The organization has a solid overview of contexts, interfaces and resources and is able to take the best benefits of flexibly connecting, cooperating and coordinating across the enterprise and its stakeholders. Interaction always creates new stages where new aspects of the world under consideration are proactively produced.

Large-scale transformations very often fail because, among other reasons, the demand for interaction in a multilateral enterprise world is underestimated (and hence not considered in the activity, time and resources schedules of the transformation).

The key issue in this context is the pure mass of potentially relevant connections to be covered. A lot of support tools are available—and they are helpful from the detailed technical and financial perspective but not as a substitute for personal contact and discussion. Situations that are strategically complex—for example, because a lot of different interests and perceptions have to be managed—cannot be fixed by means of a technical tool. The tool might give support as a provider of data and basic information that is relevant, but it is never sufficient to deliver a comprehensive solution (no new template changes the world).

It is important to support the pursuit of connecting resources across the organization by intelligent interventions (e.g. bringing people in alienated environments together across silos in order to build up relationships and mutual understanding and informally exchange views and information) and systemic institutions (cross-silo bodies and committees with a clear task). Both these will support the setup of strong, vivid, formal and informal networks which have stronger impact than the official organization as laid down in the organizational chart.

Further general important aspects of the challenge to achieve this are covered in the first chapters and articles in the book with examples from various different industries.

Summary of the Key Challenges

The three-pillar model and the additional fundamental thoughts described above show that transitions of demotivated or even desolate organizations need an intelligent balance of interventions and systemic institutions to be followed very

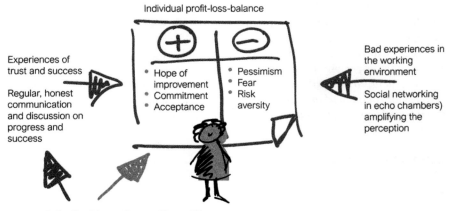

Fig. 1 Addressing the personal profit–loss balance: Positive experiences must compensate negative experiences and the loss of trust—which is much more challenging than the other way around (figure: Frank Kühn)

consistently. This all has to be reflected in the general organizational design for enterprises in the new business world and the steps involved in realizing this design. But in practice, the obstacles are significant:

- The general situation of the world and the way it is perceived coupled with bad experiences in their working environment make people tendentially pessimistic, passive, risk averse, fearful and demotivated. Their motto is 'Don't trust anybody! Everything that superiors say is a lie, selfish, manipulation. Things will never get better'.
- Social networks are intensifying the feeling of a fundamental demise with no way out.
- Personally, the hope of improvement has often been disappointed. After having experienced, for example, top management changes with four '100-day programmes' four times in 6 years and four times the promise 'I came to stay to change something sustainably' and having experienced a lack of success every time I no longer have any realistic capacity for hope left.
- It needs a lot of positive experiences to compensate for one negative experience and the loss of trust that this involves. Changing attitudes from positive to negative is a lot easier than the other way around (Fig. 1).
- Therefore, positive interventions have to be convincingly different from the normal and also be credible, which is a real challenge. There are no standard concepts, and everything has to be tailored.
- Interventions will only be successful in the long term if accompanied by systemic and institutional changes—but the timeframe this entails might overwhelm an enterprise whose outlook and orientation is more short term.

- Successful transformation is, therefore, only possible with a powerful, competent and patient sponsor who has a strong belief and strong will, can creatively and credibly draft interventions and systemic and institutional changes and can think in 3- to 5-year timeframes and feels responsible over the whole cycle (and lets people feel that this is serious). This is rare.
- And finally, successful transformation needs regular, honest communication and discussion about what progress has been made and what success achieved.

Some Ideas on Potential Interventions

In order to be 'a door opener', the chosen intervention has to:

- Be new and creative.
- Be unexpected and surprising.
- Involve some reframing in alien contexts.
- Bring credibility.
- Be interactive and provide communication based on trust.
- Be totally different from other typical '100-day programmes'.
- Have a certain degree of openness for the content-based outcome (not fixed from A to Z in advance).
- Be run by the transformation sponsor in person with much involvement and timely commitment.
- Be accompanied by high-level role models with a clear cultural message.
- Be supported by good communication experts (no spin doctors).
- Have the highest possible involvement of a large representative group of employees.
- Deliver a rough view of planned sustainable follow-ups in the form of systemic and institutional changes.

After the last financial and economic crisis associated with a significant lack of trust in policy and politicians, Ireland started a spirited democratic attempt: a body called the 'Citizens' Assembly' was setup with the task to develop ideas and concepts for the further development of the Irish constitution as a recommendation for the Irish parliament. A total of 100 members were selected: 66 citizens representing all social strata, walks of life and professions and occupations of the people of Ireland, 33 members of the parliament and 1 facilitator. The body met for one weekend once a month for 1 year to discuss important topics. The aim was to give the chance for solid information, to have really good debates, to appease the angry citizens, to build up respect for political work and to provide insights that would be a basis for respect. Especially, it brought people together for private conversations in breaks or at the bar. People who would be expected to disrespect each other found a way to mutually understand and tolerate different positions—across the different subgroups 'ordinary citizens' and 'Politicians'.

The results are well-known and encouraging. The latest one, the referendum in Ireland on abortion, got a clear result, did not split society as such topics had done before and triggered debate on a respectful level. The overall perception is that this courageous democratic experiment changed attitudes in a quite desolate state—which is a more complex organization than an enterprise.

In summary: There was a powerful sponsor—the Irish government, a serious political will expressed in an appropriate and trustworthy way, excellent facilitation and patience (preparation, accomplishment, a follow-up over more than 2 years). This may be common sense but it is, sadly, not applied all that often.

What could this mean for an enterprise? The perfect fit has to be tailored individually, so the following proposals are only to provide food for thought. Let's take an enterprise which had had this permanent change at top management level over the last couple of years, a lot of '100-day programmes', a lot of new strategies and, connected with this, short-term growth, profit, staff cuts, targets, a lot of organizational changes which meant new organizational charts, etc. Despite this, the enterprise did not develop as management had hoped. The employee surveys showed a significant lack of trust, motivation, etc. Now the new (next) CEO steps in. It would go without saying that he is in it for the long haul and will take responsibility. He has a strong modern entrepreneurial belief and the political will to do something different. He is willing to take risks. He has convictions about the target culture and he has made it clear that he is not going to accept exceptions, especially at higher management levels, even in the case of 'high performers'.

So, a promising initial setting is in place and the 'door-opener interventions' have to be scheduled. To reach people, the focus has to be on real interaction and communication (avoiding all purely formal statements and actions) in an environment that allows professional and personal networking and relationship building. This should be accompanied by strong and honestly meant gestures of top management.

In more concrete terms: imagine if the new CEO does not occupy an office of his own for the first 6 months but sits every day, for x hours a day, in the office together with people representing all hierarchical levels in the company and alternates every 3 days! The schedule is fixed in advance and is not changed significantly to show the priority that these conversations with and listening to the employees and leaders has. Or a desk is placed close to the main entrance and the CEO sits there for 2 hours a day, with a vacant chair, and works and also asks people coming in to join him for a conversation (on a random topic). In parallel, all office doors of C-Level and C-Level direct reports could be removed to show the lack of barriers (for those enterprises where not everybody sits in open plan offices). In both cases, it would be helpful if an assistant were on hand, among other things to take notes so that key parts of the conversation outcomes could be documented, and a task force be installed to fix 'easily solvable issues' within 3 days.

These individual interactions could be complemented by workshops with alienated perspectives (e.g. with an artist who supports some mixed teams of employees to paint the desired target situation of the company). The paintings are hung, with some focused explanation, on the walls of reception, company restaurant, largest meeting room, etc. and the CEO and his/her team go quarterly/every half year along the paintings together with the painters and evaluate the progress.

The number of potential actions is infinite. It is important that the key attributes are covered (encouraging interaction and conversation, surprising and creative, going from formal to concrete, etc.). In any way, the door should be opened a little and people prepared for sustainable improvement.

This is crucial: it has to be clear all the time that these activities have high priority, that they are taken very seriously by the sponsor and that they will not be postponed or constantly modified if something new arises.

Some Ideas on Starting Systemic Institutional Changes

As already mentioned, the focus of this article is on the intervention part. But as we have already stated that an intervention (as a door opener) only makes sense if, at the same time, long-term systemic institutional changes are started (to keep the door open), we will now outline some high-level thoughts:

- Consistent personnel policy (hiring and only retaining leaders and employees who fit the cultural profile—independently of their performance, content-wise). This personnel policy also has to reflect diversity aspects.
- Cross-organizational cooperation and interaction needs—in addition to informal touchpoints (the famous chat at the coffee machine or water cooler), which have to be supported by appropriate architectural and building measures—'formal bodies' with high appreciation in the enterprise (this might be committees to steer the project portfolio or the value chain in a special business field). The bodies might need to be composed of different members such as subject-matter experts or senior management for different targets and purposes. They are, however, essential (also described in various other articles of the book).
- Platforms for cross-organizational exchange of experience and learning such as regular workshops or similar events.
- Regular 'transformation status events' where the status of completion compared with the target statements, etc. is evaluated and discussed. In these events, the progress made and the success achieved to date can be described, discussed, evaluated and perceptions of them shared.

In those institutional bodies, the transformation agenda can be regularly reflected on (as an official agenda topic and with the involvement of the transformation sponsors). This ensures that a vivid enterprise practice is in place with the chance of sustainably taking the leaders and employees, with an atmosphere of complete trust, conviction and motivation, on the enterprise journey.

Summary of Solution Proposals

This summary can be kept as a tightly focused overview since the details were described in detail above:

- A demotivated or desolate organization needs a combination of a creative, powerful intervention with short-term effect to open the door for a potential change in attitude among the involved people as well as a consistent setup of systemic long-term institutions to support transition and make it successful— coupled with a suitable organization setting.
- The organizational setting especially means a powerful top manager (CEO) with strong beliefs, convictions and skills, ready to take entrepreneurial responsibility and risk and committed to staying for a reasonable timeframe.
- The intervention has to be particularly new and creative, unexpected and surprising, with some reframing in alien contexts or environments, bringing credibility, interactive and providing communication based on trust and totally different from other typical '100-day programmes'.
- Such interventions can be even very successful on a large scale (see the example of Ireland).
- The systemic and institutional changes cover, especially, informal and official cross-silo interaction, cooperation and communication.
- Regular, honest status evaluation and discussion about the transformation progress on a regular basis and discussion about successes achieved.

Further Reading

Berg, F., Kühn, F., Reuter, C., & Wollmann, P. (2012). Experimentellesprojektdesign. In F. Kühn & P. Wollmann (Eds.), *Interaktion als Organisationsstrategie* (pp. 195–206). Berlin: ICG.

Dignen, B., Pleuger, G., Kühn, F., & Wollmann, P. (2012). Starting an international project. In F. Kühn & P. Wollmann (Eds.), *Interaktion als Organisationsstrategie* (pp. 176–181). Berlin: ICG.

Kühn, F., & Wollmann, P. (2012). Interaktion als Organisationsstrategie. In F. Kühn & P. Wollmann (Eds.), *Interaktion als Organisationsstrategie* (pp. 10–11). Berlin: ICG.

Reuter, C., & Wollmann, P. (2012). Interaktion durch Verfremdung. In F. Kühn & P. Wollmann (Eds.), *Interaktion als Organisationsstrategie* (pp. 182–186). Berlin: ICG.

Willke, H., & Wollmann, P. (2012). Multi-level interaction resilience and cross-cultural learning. In F. Kühn & P. Wollmann (Eds.), *Interaktion als Organisationsstrategie* (pp. 57–74). Berlin: ICG.

Wollmann, P., & Berg, F. (2007). Building a project portfolio management system in a complex matrix organization. In M. Hirzel, W. Alter, P. Wollmann, F. Kühn, G. Pleuger, V. Carlbaum, F. Berg, B. Dignen, & H. Jonasson (Eds.), *Workbook future organization* (pp. 28–36). Frankfurt am Main: HLP Management Connex.

From Well-Engineered Products to Customer-Centred Solutions

Frank Kühn

Abstract

The article describes the travel of an electronics company. The purpose of its transformation was to become a flexible solution partner for its demanding customers and to remain an attractive employer for talented people. Travelling meant developing organizational competencies supporting the continuous synchronization with market dynamics and customer requirements. Strengthening its connectivity was crucial: interlinking the competencies distributed in the global organization and developing joint agile practices and shared shop-floor processes.

The editors of the book introduce **Frank Kühn** who has been facilitating projects on transformation, organization and leadership for over 25 years. Frank graduated in engineering and received his doctorate in work science. After gaining leadership experience in research and industry, he became a partner at HLP in Frankfurt and ICG (Integrated Consulting Group) in Berlin and Graz. Today he is a self-employed consultant, business partner of ICG and is associated with further development and project partners. He has published a wide range of publications and teaches courses at universities.

F. Kühn (✉)
Consulting Partner, Dortmund, Germany
e-mail: fk@kuehn-cp.com

© Springer Nature Switzerland AG 2020
P. Wollmann et al. (eds.), *Three Pillars of Organization and Leadership in Disruptive Times*, Future of Business and Finance,
https://doi.org/10.1007/978-3-030-23227-6_14

Pillars of Organization and Transformation

The case is about the journey of an electronics company, a mid-sized global player, that started its transformation from a solid product supplier to an agile solution provider, learning how to continuously adapt the company to dynamic markets. This meant in terms of our pillars:

- Formulating and sharing the commitment on the transformation purpose—to become both a flexible solution partner to their customers and an attractive employer to their people
- Linking this development with the paradigm of travelling organization that allows continuous synchronization with the dynamics and disruption in markets and technology
- Developing connectivity between ambitions and competencies distributed in the global organization, sound experience and new creativity, agile management practices and robust shop-floor processes

In technical and organizational terms, the transformation implied a change from standardized offers and established workflows towards customer-centred solutions and adaptive development processes synchronized with the customers' business journeys.

In terms of competencies, it meant creating the motivation and structures to flexibly connect the employees' expertise and creativity across the global organization and collaborating in changing teams.

In terms of leadership, it meant taking the people on this expedition through uncertain territory with rapid reflecting, learning and re-alignment loops—and to understand that this would be a continuous process in the future.

Urgent Situation and Need for Sustainable Transformation

For decades, the company had produced high-tech electrical components for manufacturing plants. The engineers and development teams had felt very involved with the place that allowed them to use all their knowledge, ambition and pride in realizing brilliant products.

But in the last 2 or 3 years, the signals had become stronger and stronger that technical expertise and enthusiasm were not enough. They had to accept that their customers were looking for reasonable and specific solutions for their complex systems rather than highly sophisticated off-the-peg products.

Thus, the executive team decided to realign their tried and tested product development process (PDP) towards a Solution Creation Process (SCP) that should enable them:

- To re-orientate and re-understand their business and organization towards radical customer orientation

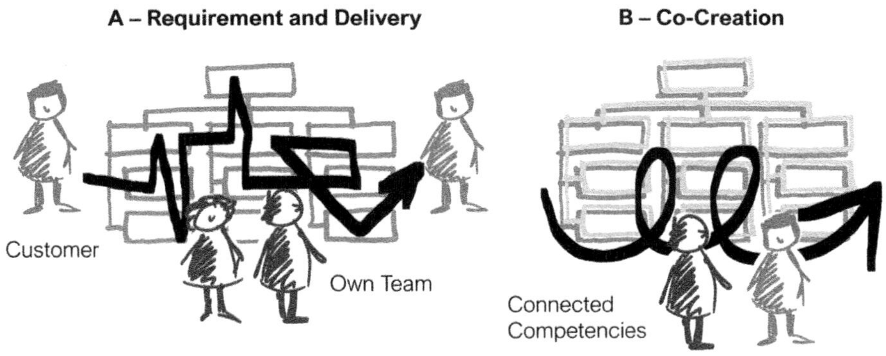

A – Requirement and Delivery   **B – Co-Creation**

Customer

Own Team

Connected
Competencies

Fig. 1 From (**a**) a complicated process for realizing the customer's demands and delivering appropriate products towards (**b**) a co-created solution linked with the customer's journey and connecting the resources (author's own figure)

- To expand their development, engineering and sales competencies towards solutions and systems, suiting the customers' true needs
- To become the preferred partner of their customers as a role model for collaboration based on trust
- To develop appropriate leadership and build teams in order to connect skills, knowledge and functions (such as sales, R&D, production, supply chain) distributed in the global organization

To date, the company structure had been focused on selling standard products, and each extra solution had to be specifically organized in development projects that had to overcome structural hurdles and struggle for limited resources. Figure 1 shows the necessary transition towards an organization that is built around a collaborative process designed to co-create the optimum solution together with the customer.

Figure 2 displays exemplary circles of connectivity. This was another visualization to explain the relevance of interlinking crucial resources. For instance, customer needs: they are relevant if they are connected with the corporate purpose and strategy (for understanding opportunities and needs of future-proof business) as well as with the peoples' motivation and capabilities (as a pre-condition for co-creating powerful solutions and success).

Thus, the need for transformation was explored and, as an 'entry to the future organization', a first change project was started around a new solution creation process (SCP) covering the following steps:

- Sharing the mindset and enthusiasm for becoming a solution provider in the global organization

Fig. 2 Circles of connectivity—How to connect relevant resources and develop crucial interactions (author's own figure). The better the crucial areas fit together, the higher the value and impact of organization and leadership

- Developing a progressive solution creation process including a framework of operational agile principles, as a driver for the further cultural and structural change
- Setting up a core team (driving the project) and a champion team (carrying the change into the organization)
- Making the employees a community which stands for the SCP concept and is committed to the transition as a whole
- Prototyping SCP cross-functional collaboration workshops and development projects involving key customers

Therefore, the executive team started to work together with the international management teams and the employees on the corporate purpose as a guiding concept for the future solution creation process, on the organizational journey that was to start with the new process and on the resources to be connected to make it a success story. It should become a two-level experience for management and employees: First, learning new technical and organizational capabilities to face future challenges, and second, learning how to create and maintain the joint momentum that would be needed on a continuous journey.

Connect Strategic, Structural and Cultural Challenges

The challenges were manifold: setting up the core team and the champions, taking the employees on board and turning them into a change community, overcoming organizational silos and barriers, releasing managerial responsibilities and introducing new decision-making procedures, further developing a true collaborative mindset within the organization and with business partners, being a role model and walking the talk. Finally, the joint work on processes as effective vehicles of any transformation is underlined. The following paragraphs describe these challenges in more detail and give examples how they were solved.

Setting Up the SCP Core Team and Champions

To date, there had been some experience of being member in a core team of technical projects. But there wasn't much shared experience in the organization as to how to involve people in that bigger dimension of transformation. This finding led to the question: How to staff the core team and the champions?

At first, the requirements expected of such key people were defined together with the executive team: belief in the purpose and the success factors of the transition; a will to take responsibility, to learn and develop themselves; both systemic and systematic thinking; credibility and acceptance among managers and employees; commitment to overcoming intercultural and cross-functional borders. HR business partners, heads of departments and key players were involved in the research, and a number of individuals from all over the global organization were identified.

The next question was how to get them on board? Via top-down instruction, as usually? And wouldn't this be a contradiction to the vision of an agile organization carried by self-responsibility, autonomy and connectivity of motivated humans? How to address their passion and how to overcome any doubts that the project would work?

Thus, the second step—and real breakthrough—was a joint workshop with the executive team, the future core team and the champions. They met on an equal footing, discussed the aims and set-up of the project and co-created their tasks in the project: the executive team as sponsor and 'highest instance' to be involved in decision making; the core team as driver of the project, coordinating people involvement, process development, internal and external communication; the change champions as ambassadors of the transformation and the new solution creation process, as role models in applying the process, as contacts to everyone interested in the organization. This initial workshop—as a piece of joint organization development—created a huge commitment to the project and enthusiasm to be part of the transformation. Resources were connected across the hierarchical structures, the travel group had formed and found their initial set-up.

Getting the Employees on Board and Turning Them into a Change Community

The next question arising was about the employees as a whole. How to involve them? Change projects and organizational transitions have to face various unforeseeable developments, uncertainties, barriers and resistance. In a certain way, they are the prototype of the future travelling organization, providing the travellers with valuable experiences and learning opportunities. At the same time, change projects often suffer from bad experiences that employees have had in the past; thus, many of them had developed survival strategies and behavioural patterns that wouldn't make the project easier.

The key idea was to let grow a real change community. Not in terms of establishing a community as a new silo for selected people (as practiced in the past), but as a common movement, open to all employees. Taking this way was a fundamental decision, and it worked step by step. Change galleries displayed the project's progress, project news was published, employees were invited to download a project app and contact the change champions, the core team and executive team involved themselves in discussions. One effect was that—besides an expanding change community—further colleagues joined the circle of the change champions who were interested in taking a more active role in the development. This possibility was fundamental because it stood for an open organization with permeable borders and changing roles, as needed for realizing adaptive and travelling organizations.

One issue was to onboard the managers and key players of the international units. Recent experience had shown explicit reluctance to subscribe to a governance concept elaborated and presented by the central controlling function. Remembering this event, the procedure now followed the principle: First discuss then develop. Ask before answering. One of the key questions was: To what aspects should we pay attention to make our journey a joint success? Even if some answers were different from the ones that the executive team had expected, the outcome had the advantage of being co-created and committed to by all parties.

A groundbreaking event was a management retreat to work with the international leaders on a prototype of a common vision. Further events followed in order to involve the employees, using so-called vertical communication (Fig. 3), i.e. a market place format with small groups, each staffed vertically with representatives from the executive team, core team, champions, local headquarters, middle management, works council and operational teams.

There was a double intention: To win over the people for the change and to further exercise open organization. The intensive cross-level discussion on this market place led to shared understanding of the purpose, and it connected the people and their concerns with the journey they were being invited to join. One question proved useful in terms of lessons learned: What have been your good or bad experiences with change, as drivers or as affected persons?

The good experiences in past projects were: we understood the urgency of the goal, we were involved, we felt well informed, we felt acceptance of our concerns, we could bring in our ideas and experiences, we experienced success, etc. The bad

Fig. 3 Vertical discussion—
Encouraging and exercising
direct communication,
connecting information, views
and opinions in one place
(author's own figure)

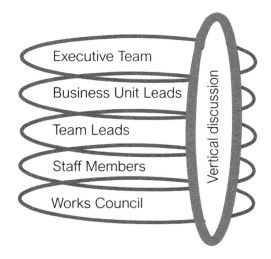

experiences were: the reason for a change project wasn't properly explained to us, we didn't have any background information, we didn't know how things were connected, we didn't know who was involved in which way, etc.

The answers in these workshops corresponded very closely with the answers to the question: to what aspects do we have to pay attention if we want to make our journey a success story? Most statements were about communicating the purpose, creating a joint journey together with the people, respecting and connecting the resources they were willing to bring in.

Overcoming Organizational Silos and Barriers

As a main hurdle the participants of the workshops addressed bad collaboration across structural, functional and local borders. The differences between functions (e.g. classical conflict between sales and R&D) seemed even bigger than those between regional cultures. This was addressed as a huge barrier in a process that was intended to blend all competencies.

Key to success was the communication of the purpose and urgency of the development, emphasized again and again by the executive team who involved themselves in many discussions. One of the most effective interventions was the absolutely clear statement that there was no alternative to overcoming organizational and cultural barriers towards future collaboration as a cultural key for competitive advantage.

Therefore, one exercise in the collaboration workshops on the new solution creation process addressed mutual understanding in cross-functional teams: What are our individual perceptions, mental maps and behavioural patterns? What do we see and feel, how do we categorize and interpret it, how do we typically react to it? How is our perception and behaviour influenced by professional patterns and expectations? Without openness for this quality of exchange, there wouldn't be real connectivity between people that were being asked to follow a shared purpose and start a joint expedition.

The reflection and discussion on the current product development process and the future solution creation process turned out to be effective drivers of the transformation. The PDP for one product had taken 1 or 2 years due to the sequential process model with all the well-known conflicts built in: Marketing informed R&D about trends and demands, R&D developed a product, Purchasing tried more or less successfully to buy the material, Production was angry due to manufacturability problems, and Sales complained about late market entry. The SCP should stand for an integrated, collaborative process from the beginning: all functions connected to understand the challenge, bringing in their ideas and concerns, supporting and reflecting the process end to end. The process was to be managed by a process team, caring for collaboration and progress. (There was a certain intended similarity with the transformation process: the core team caring for the process, the champions taking an active part in carrying the process.)

Releasing Managerial Responsibilities

An additional barrier was the hierarchical management practice that had been in place for many years: superiors instructed employees, and employees did as they were told; employees asked superiors for instructions, and employees received them. To be a superior, leader or head was understood as a position, not as a task, and the guiding management principle was command and control. Some managers who didn't share this principle had to leave the company. Former attempts at business process re-engineering had failed because they had questioned the top-down management approach.

But during recent years, managers had suffered more and more from work overload, struggling with increasing business requirements, experiencing more uncertainty and complexity, conflicting with decentralized units looking for more autonomy and facing a younger generation with different expectations of leadership.

Now, they were expected to support the core team, champions and a growing change community, to align their functions to a solution creation process, following process teams and their decisions made in favour of a customer-oriented process across the classical structure. The principle was to serve the customer instead of the superior. In terms of connectivity, this meant releasing individual managerial responsibilities and distributing their land.

Some of the managers were very open minded, well understanding the need to shed classical management practices that no longer worked effectively. Others seemed reluctant and even sabotaged the development via explicit hierarchical behavior: instruction (instead of purpose), fixing (instead of travelling) and dividing (instead of connecting). In such cases, the core team and executive team learned how to differentiate between will and skill and how to cope with conflicts quickly and sustainably. In the end, each manager had to make his or her individual decision whether to join the expedition or to leave it, whether to stand behind the purpose and vision or not and whether to be open to trustful connectivity or not.

Rapid Conflict Solving and Decision-Making Procedures

There were typical situations that slowed down the product development process as well as the management processes in general. The speed of product development suffered from so-called decision meetings involving a number of functions. Each participant used the opportunity to contribute his or her opinion or concern or any statement. In addition, the workshops were badly prepared, moderated and followed up. This showed two bigger cultural issues: personal staging and weak conflict management. A lot of conflicts were hidden beneath superficial harmony and came up in all meetings and discussions, preventing the participants from joint problem solving. Even decisions, once taken, were misused for ignoring new findings or refusing others' opinions.

New conflict management and decision-making practices seemed necessary, firstly, as a general prerequisite for an agile and travelling organization, and secondly, to empower and speed up the future solution creation process.

In a first step, the managers learned how to differentiate between making so-called 'ballistic' decisions (believing in a stable target and predictable course, keeping to taken decisions) and making smaller, quicker and time-limited decisions (allowing a procedure iteratively connected with changing conditions). For instance, they didn't invest much time in developing a perfect solution creation template valid for the future but made a rapid double decision: firstly, to apply a template prototype (which the core team designed within 2 h) and, secondly, to review it after 6 months and then to modify it, if necessary.

In a next step, they agreed how to prepare decisions (three options and one proposal, with pros and cons, discussed in advance with experts) and how to apply sociocratical practices such as 'consent'—in simple terms: after a proposal is presented and explained, it is regarded as agreed if there isn't any valid objection, without further discussion.

A further breakthrough was conflict management workshops, where all parties involved in the product development process and future solution creation process were invited to work on their contradictory views and interests. Alternating pairs of participants were asked to identify their relevant conflicts and solve them; if they felt unable to do so, they were asked to involve a third person who could help them. The solutions were presented, received feedback and became part of the project. Thus, a lot of main conflicts were solved and the participants experienced agile conflict management.

Such decision-making procedures confirmed the identified pillars: shared purpose as guidance for effective decisions and conflict management, connectivity for integrating experiences, interests and creativity, speed as key to managing travelling organizations in an uncertain environment.

Collaborative Mindset: Internal and External

To stress the difference between current management practice in a hierarchical structure and future needs in a travelling organization, a leadership and collaboration programme was set up. It had two goals: firstly, developing a new collaborative mindset and behavior and, secondly, applying it to re-designing key processes, starting with the solution creation process.

In this context, the project tackled a further uncertainty: true cooperation and co-creation with customers which hadn't been practiced systematically thus far. Pending projects and current customer relationships were discussed, collaboration scenarios developed and next steps agreed. For instance, one action was to design and carry out cooperation workshops that included participants from marketing, sales, R&D and production as well as participants from customers (starting with friendly ones). The workshops were designed as vivid platforms for connecting experiences, needs and ideas for future solutions and shared processes. They set the next milestones for the organization's journey.

Be a Role Model and Walk the Talk

Beside all these activities, some doubt was perceived among the employees; some of them didn't really believe in their manager's capability and motivation to change and to be true role models for the future organization and, especially, for the solution creation process.

Additional measures were agreed to tackle this challenge: managers were offered coaching when taking on their new roles, critical meetings were facilitated by the champions, specific workshops provided the participants with knowledge and tools for managing a travelling organization and connectivity, peer consulting sessions supported exchange of experience and good practice.

In addition, both managers and employees were involved in communication circles (following the initial vertical communication) where they were invited to discuss critical issues concerning the transformation and the process development. Thus, they experienced a different kind of connectivity: a new place, a new format, a new quality of communication and a new cross-structural openness—each connected to each other.

Common Work on Processes as Effective Vehicles of Any Transformation

As already mentioned, core processes such as the SCP are optimal vehicles to drive any transformation, not only in structural but also in cultural terms. People are not only told that a sustainable purpose is a need in travelling organizations, giving the direction and keeping everything together, and connecting internal and external resources is necessary to deliver progressive solutions and to prevent scarce capacities being wasted. They will believe it or not.

Instead, people were involved and practiced the transformation and its advantages from the beginning. They experienced a new quality of collaborative process design. They connected their interests and knowledge, co-created solutions, solved conflicts, made rapid decision, got customer feedback and integrated it effectively—driven by a committed purpose and experience of connectivity. They experienced the process as a key driver, end to end, from customer needs for solutions to customer success. And it is all about daily practices to be applied, peer to peer: how to tackle issues, solve conflicts and take decisions.

Some Further Takeaways for the Travel Group

There have been a lot of lessons learned in re-defining the solution creation process as an entry project for a future-proof organization and an agile working culture. The most fundamental learning points are the following.

Arrangement: Organizations move—always—whether we like it or not. The employees have experienced little adaptations or fundamental transformations. Ask them: What has happened to date, what is the current situation, what expectations and ideas do they have about the future? And facing the transformation towards a travelling organization: What should we do differently or less or more? What in our culture could prevent us from succeeding? You will get relevant insights for an effective travel arrangement.

Communication and involvement: Clarity is a prerequisite of trust, which you will need for the transformation. Communicate a clear purpose and reason, involve your teams in planning the joint endeavour and connect the people across the organization, again and again. Value their feedback, views and questions. Maintain their energy and be present. Be always aware: resistance is often based on scepticism, fear or if people feel badly treated. Human beings are ready to change but resistant to be changed.

Balancing advantages and disadvantages: The purpose has to be consistent and credible, convincing and connected to the employees' concerns and the organization's capacities. Strike a balance between what the people will lose and what they will gain when joining the journey. What is the outcome of the balance? Do you need to strengthen the purpose? Do you need more trust from your travel group? Do people need more connectivity between the strategy and their work, between the purpose and the urgency of change and between employees? Do you all need quick results or exciting experiences as soon as possible?

Taking new roles: Support and coach your managers and team leads in taking on their new role in the travelling organization (which might be disruptive for many of them). They have to be role models. And they will be continuously observed by their teams in terms of how they accept and succeed in their new role. Discuss with them what their new roles mean. Discuss typical interactions that are part of the new role: conveying the purpose in conversations, meetings, goal definitions, even with challenging audiences; taking people on the journey via involvement, empower-ment, encouragement, feedback; connecting all available resources in order to avoid wasting time and energy, integrate expertise and creativity, create quality and acceptance.

Social connectivity: The purpose of organization is to make people cooperate in order to solve a problem in the world. Create events that clearly demonstrate your understanding of connecting your most valuable resources: offer vivid platforms to make the people interact with each other and with your providers and customers, discuss connectivity deficits in the organization and develop joint solutions. Install social hubs as key elements of your travelling organization and your new solution creation process.

Structural connectivity: Check that all organizational resources are connected to the intended transformation and its prototype, in this case the solution creation process. What does this mean for other processes, functions, projects, technologies, skills in terms of innovation and development? Learn together how to connect all these threads.

Open organization: Open the organization, otherwise it can't travel. Strategies, teams and functions, roles and tasks, processes and practices may change. Internal and external resources may migrate through the organization, wherever they can contribute benefit. This is not arbitrary but agile, based on agreed rules. The purpose will guide you. Connectivity keeps it all together. Prototype it, e.g. by means of a core process, as exemplified in this article.

An International Art Project on Freedom

Alfred Mevissen

Abstract

The author shares his experience acquired in the international project 'Pillars of Freedom' on the topic of freedom outside the organization; some concepts appropriate for organizations can be deduced from these experiences. Radical rethinking is needed—from organizations characterized by safety considerations and strictly target-oriented behaviour towards cooperative approaches governed by possibilities that open up with project-oriented working and various connectivities. Mobile units with maximum decision-making power will be established and use the possibilities of digital cross-border cooperation with alternating partners. Compliance issues and health and safety training will be replaced by self-regulating mechanisms governed by transparency in action. Thus, organizations will be better prepared to keep pace with the speed of information explosion and changing starting positions.

The editors of the book introduce **Alfred Mevissen** who has been working as a European project manager at Novartis Pharma for the last 8 years. Prior to this, he worked as head of sales in two other companies after a classic career in sales and marketing. Following his passion for sculpting, he is the initiator of the international art projects www.pillars-of-freedom.com and www.art-moves-europe.eu.

A. Mevissen (✉)
Novartis Pharma, Basel, Switzerland

© Springer Nature Switzerland AG 2020
P. Wollmann et al. (eds.), *Three Pillars of Organization and Leadership in Disruptive Times*, Future of Business and Finance,
https://doi.org/10.1007/978-3-030-23227-6_15

131

Pillars of Freedom

Thoughts about ways out of the dilemma of large organizations in the age of compliance in a digital world demonstrated by the example of 'Pillars of Freedom—an international art project on the topic of freedom'.

When I started my sabbatical on 1 August 2016, I looked back on 31 years of experience in marketing and distribution in the pharmaceutical industry, gained in three group companies structured very differently. The first 12 years were spent working in the sales force of a strongly marketing-oriented group. After that, I worked in a group company governed by finances where I held a national management position in sales, and, in the last 6 years, I acquired experience in diverse international projects in the areas of change management and strategic skills—projects that I was given the chance to support or even lead. Especially the last few years were marked by massive organizational changes within the group, accompanied by the increasing impact of compliance issues. This, in turn, had an important effect on the structure of the organization, bringing about new departments and new ways of internal networking.

But these were not the only changes to be faced—in addition, there was the digital world, with its new possibilities which people in this industry were perhaps afraid of or, shall we say, which were seen by them with a certain degree of respect. Looking back, one can say that, here, two completely contrary developments coincide. On the one hand, there is the subject of compliance with the requirements of ensuring ethically correct and legally secure behaviour within a large organization; for this, a structure and some control mechanisms must be implemented; on the other hand, there are mechanisms and dynamics in the digital world that are impossible to monitor or control.

Of course, the chances and possibilities of this world are fascinating, but its risks are also to be feared to the same extent. If you look at this situation, it soon becomes obvious that organizations face extreme challenges.

Thus, one can rightly talk of a dilemma. But what is, in fact, the dilemma? Or rather, the actual question is how can it be overcome? But first, let us look at the essential factors of the dilemma. On the one hand, there is the necessity to create a system which cannot easily be compromised or attacked neither ethically nor legally. Such a system is necessary to keep at bay very expensive claims of competitors and authorities. And this may affect, perhaps, thousands of employees because the wrongdoing of one single employee can trigger such events. Therefore, structures must be built into the company that ensure adequate employee training, but, at the same time, protect the company. As a consequence, control systems are created and networking among departments is enhanced. Thus, decision-making processes are slowed down and made more complicated.

On the other hand, there is the new digital world which seems to be uncontrollable and which must allow risks and incalculable outside influences. A new digital world which, however, also brings about undreamt-of possibilities—not only with regard to communication, but also to the development of new products and processes. It is here where the problems for the organizations arise.

The organization's departments that are responsible for ensuring risk prevention and that are controlled from the top become increasingly powerful in the company. As a result, these departments try to make communication controllable and, in fact, to control it in order to avert potential damage. The power of these departments starts to affect the whole network of the international organization, particularly as in different countries, there are legal or social regulations that are applied with differing degrees of stringency. But if the organization wants to make sure that standards are being met at the international level, the strictest regulation will set the pace and influence the whole network even if, in some countries, more possibilities are granted than in others. That is because colleagues work together on joint projects under different national conditions and because all members of the network are forced to meet their national standards.

In the digital world, work is very much influenced by impulses, open communication is encouraged, and exchange with customers is desired. But the problem is that this way of communication is only controllable via those impulses that the company releases to this autonomous world or by how the company reacts to external impulses. Now, it ultimately becomes clear that traditional mechanisms of networking and of network management do not work anymore. The dilemma is inevitable. How is the employee who has completed various trainings on risks, regulations, compliance and law to find their way independently and adequately in an impartial media and digital world. Each action means walking on a knife edge. And the companies find it difficult to give proper support and to make available the necessary means that will enable employees to manage this balancing act.

But Why Is It So Difficult? Or Might It Not Even Be Possible?

Even if it seems to be a discontinuity, in the following, I want to talk about my project 'Pillars of Freedom' that I mentioned above and share my experiences acquired in this international project on the topic of freedom outside the organization. Perhaps, some concepts that may be appropriate for organizations can be deduced from these project experiences.

Having in mind the impressions described above, I started my sabbatical; I simply wanted to live for the moment and wait and see what would happen. I wanted to pursue my passion—sculpture—with great determination. Moreover, I also had the idea to take my newly gained time to take a stronger position on social issues. In this respect, the topic of freedom is particularly close to my heart. During a stay on the Lofoten Islands in 2014, the idea emerged to have a Pillar of Freedom created by an artist in each of the countries bordering the Baltic Sea. The Baltic Sea in particular seemed to me to be a good example of freedom, because there old and new democracies are located adjacent to each other.

With the impressions gained from working in corporate organizations over many years and with the thoughts in my mind what I could do during 1 year of freedom, I first went to Laas in South Tyrol at the end of July. On the first weekend of August of each year, there is a wonderful festival in this village, called 'Marmor und Marillen' (marble and apricots), which includes a sculpture symposium. Talking to the artists, I presented them my idea of the 'Pillars of Freedom' project. I was surprised to discover that four artists were immediately interested in taking part in such a project. The only problem for me was that those artists were not residents of any country bordering the Baltic Sea. Thus, they did not fit into my scheme. Over a glass of wine, however, I asked myself, 'Why not?' Because this was a chance to start a network and to create connections to other artists about whom I did not know much, apart from the fact that they supported my idea to design the topic of freedom in the form of works of art and thus to send a message to society to show more active commitment to the cause of freedom. Regardless of the Baltic Sea issue, we agreed to stay in touch. Shortly afterwards, I met a power-saw artist. I talked to him, too. He was also interested in the project. But he was not a stone sculptor and, thus, did not fit into my scheme either. But why not involve him too? At least, he supported my idea. Well, I did not know anything about power-saw sculpture. But did I have to?

Back home at an exhibition, I met an artist who worked with felt. She was enthusiastic about the idea of the project and said that she was keen to take part—also not in the scheme. Over the following days, with all these impressions in my mind, I thought about what I should do about it. Then on a long walk, I decided to modify my project idea and put it in concrete terms.

Several questions came to mind:

- Must there be stone sculptures only?
- Why should the sculptures be created only around the Baltic Sea?
- What kind of material should I 'allow'?
- How can I get in touch with artists?
- Which media can I use to do this? How can I use the media?
- Which networks can I tap into?
- How can I create and manage a website?
- Where is the money to be raised?
- Do I need money at all and if so, what for?
- Or am I able to win people over to the project just by using my persuasive efforts and presenting a project idea?
- What do I really want to do in my sabbatical?
- Do I want to invest time in a project?
- What commitment am I entering into with such a project?
- Which conditions are not up for discussion? Which conditions are indispensable?
- How can I protect myself against potential problems?
- How can I guarantee the quality of the participants?
- Do I need a project plan? Should I set any goals for myself?

Many more questions came to my mind.

If I was to apply the standards that I used to apply in my previous projects, this project would have died at this point, because the effort to consider in advance all these questions in one project plan would have jeopardized my newly gained freedom.

In short, despite these concerns, I decided to define four conditions:

1. I am going to create a pillar of freedom myself on the topic of freedom of speech.
2. Potential participants in the project will have to create a pillar of freedom, which is at least 2 m high, by 9 November 2017.
3. The topic must convey a positive message of how freedom can be realized in our society.
4. From 9 to 12 November 2017, the pillar will have to be made accessible to the public at the place where it will stand and during this period, it will be part of a virtual 'Gesamtkunstwerk', a synthesis of many individual pieces of art.

These conditions form the indisputable basis of the project.

For the other questions, I decided to allow a maximum of flexibility and openness in the creative process. No target, but an ambition. Thinking in terms of possibilities, not in terms of solutions; not having to do anything, but being allowed to do everything; providing impulses and waiting calmly for reactions, deriving new impulses from these reactions; finding new ways, not searching for them; advancing the project enthusiastically, being always open to accept new ideas except, of course, regarding the indisputable conditions imposed by me. In particular, the clarity in the message and the simplicity of diction would certainly help to easily distinguish between supporters and sceptics and thus to create a basis in order to quickly build a network upon which you could promote the common cause very quickly, focused on the topic and without a lot of discussion.

Well, why have I told you all of this?

At this point, I want to return to the dilemma of large organizations. What makes steering the company so difficult is to control the diverse networks inside and outside the company. What is extremely difficult for organizations is to analyze and differentiate what exactly, and which flows of communication, must be controlled, to give exact specifications for them and to have the courage to leave the rest to a floating system in order to benefit from diversity and to enhance efficiency. Power and traditional structures play as great a role in this as safety considerations driven by fear and as the division of the company into departments that are not linked effectively.

The targets must be reduced to the core of the entrepreneurial aims, which must be formulated clearly, simply and unambiguously.

The complexity of the modern world and the speed with which situations change require faster and more open ways of communication as well as a drastic shift of the areas of responsibility. On the one hand, the essential and undisputable preconditions need to be simplified and reduced, and accordingly, this process must be communicated in a clear, simple and authoritative manner. Then, in addition, these areas of responsibility need to adopt a holistic approach and to work cross-functionally. On the other hand, locally oriented thinking, targeted on the individual, and trust in the skills of the employees are necessary to an extent not required so far, in order to utilize the possibilities of the new digital world, but also to let networks based on 'Sharing Best Practice' emerge. For wherever people who pursue a common idea meet, a momentum arises that has to be exploited. Then it does not matter whether the connection or the communication takes place via the topic itself or via the successful method. This momentum can then be utilized productively. In organizations, however, this kind of trust and composure regarding the duration is often hard to imagine.

Communication Becomes Connectivity Through Freedom and Common Prospects of Success

In the course of my project 'Pillars of Freedom', I began to discover the world of social media, which was new to me. I carefully created various accounts and tried to make the security settings as restrictive as possible. But I soon realized that this was not very helpful given my target of building a network. That is why I published my profiles and decided to control the spectrum of reaction via my way of Web posting. Even in this respect, acting consistently makes sense. It is certainly advisable to avoid assessments that may offend others and to focus on positive formulations of one's own message.

Controlling your connections is made via *your presentation and not* via *security mechanisms.*

However, another decisive, or perhaps the decisive, factor for successful connectivity between individuals or systems is the home base, the dialogue platform, the documentation platform and the possibility to connect to other participants of the project. This is the point where everything comes together. But even at this point, there are significant obstacles to overcome. How easy is it to access? How attractive is the presentation? Can each participant identify with it? Does the platform have a cooperative design? Can dialogues be facilitated and initiated invitingly? These are decisive success factors. But even if all this is realized, there is at least one more factor to be considered in order to allow connectivity to arise from a network. This is to say someone is needed who keeps the platform up to date and manages the traffic on it. Here it is important to find the right balance for the respective group. In many organizations, there are standard procedures involving newsletters. Where connectivity emerges from a network, there is someone who closely watches the traffic on the platform and develops a sense of when communication should be fluent and when connectivity is to be enhanced with new impulses in order to initiate new discussions or actions. Equally important is the continuous growth of the platform or at least a dynamic that is recognizable from the outside.

Connectivity Needs Fresh Impetus and Opportunities to Develop

In this way, I advanced my project 'Pillars of Freedom' (www.pillars-of-freedom. com) during the last 7 months and was delighted to get to know many interesting people, getting impulses, learning new aspects and experiencing how much you can achieve by just implementing one idea and unconditionally using the various digital media-related possibilities. Deliberate, but rapid, decisions have certainly played an important role in this as enthusiasm, an open mind and courageously discovering new ways have been important for success so far. Now, after just 10 months, 76 artists from 17 countries are participating in this project and every one of them will create and design at least one pillar of freedom and make it accessible to the public. When all pillars of freedom are united into a Gesamtkunstwerk on 9 November, this will be a loud and impressive message to society, calling for more active commitment to living in freedom and respect. Perhaps there is still another aspect to be mentioned. Since all pillars convey a positive message of how freedom can be realized, there will be no room for sceptics and critics who are quick to exactly identify potential problems but have no idea of how to solve them.

Thus, I was able to gather useful experience in this project and learn how to be able to build networks involving the much discussed and always admired social media. A defined, but open, temporary connectivity can emerge from these networks—just by working with a common idea, an open platform and regular communication. This way, an important common issue could succeed simply on the basis of the personal and financial efforts of each participant. Upon completion of the project, this connectivity will dissolve because its goal will have been achieved. What remains, however, is a network that is accessible in whole or in part to every single member to address other issues and from which new projects will emerge. And all of this without an organization with defined structures. Of course, I am well aware that such an approach is not really comparable to everyday work and the requirements of large organizations driven by financial issues. Yet, I am convinced that large organizations will have to get used to such or similar procedures and will have to show much more ambition and willingness if they want to survive.

Conclusion

Considering all these aspects of a very rapidly changing world in which organizations have to face change processes as constant companions, the question arises as to how organizations can position themselves anew for the future to be able to function successfully in the digital reality. Traditional organizational structures will certainly become less significant and will be replaced by the growing importance of 'networks in the sense of connectivity', which form temporary communities based on a shared interest in certain topics and which cooperate to be able to achieve common topic-related objectives.

In this respect, radical rethinking is needed—from a philosophy that is typical of the specific organization and characterized by safety considerations and strictly target-oriented behaviour that is always in the interest of shareholders, and towards a cooperative approach that is governed by the possibilities that open up with various alternating partners.

To reach this goal, safety structures must be reconsidered so that, based on simple and clearly defined strategies, open cooperation with partners with shared interests can be realized effectively with openness and flexibility and focused on the project in question.

The involved loss of power and control in favour of diversity and partnership will certainly not run smoothly. There is no doubt that new start-up companies easily find their way in this new world of connective networks and have the chance to outperform the established companies. In future, change processes must no longer be treated by companies as exceptional situations, but have to become an integral part of the company's strategy since they will be one of the keys to the company's success. Departmental thinking will be replaced by project-oriented working in alternating connectivities by way of integrated project units formed for a certain period of time. This will lead to a loss of importance, for example, of the classical marketing departments. The central steering and managing of the company will be reduced to financial and strategic issues. In addition, mobile units with maximum decision-making power to implement the financial targets will be established and use the possibilities of digital cross-border cooperation with alternating partners. In such a working world, compliance issues and safety trainings, today requiring a great deal of time and effort, will be replaced by self-regulating mechanisms governed by transparency in action. This leads to new chances and a possible reduction of costs. Above all, such a world will be in a better position to keep pace with the over-whelming speed of information explosion and the changing starting positions.

After all, who still believes in 5-year plans these days?

Part IV

Practice Cluster: Humans and Enterprises

Hannspeter Schmidt first explores the fundamental psychological disposition for connectivity, followed by Bernadette Cass contributing cases of leadership development for organizational change. Afterward, we are led through concrete enterprise environments: Alberto Casagrande introduces us to the start-up scene, and Marie Schmidt explains the relevance of the pillars for organization and leadership in the pharmaceutical industry. Nicole Hönig de Locamini looks at large global consultancies, and finally Sharon Lalla gives an example of how the three-pillar model applies to a case of an American university.

Connectivity and Personality

Hannspeter Schmidt

Abstract

This article explores the coverage of the special psychological preconditions for connectivity capabilities and mindsets. Connectivity is a challenge for international, innovative organizations and their employees. International companies are challenged to develop consistent strategies for highly complex and interdependent markets; employees working in such complex structures require the personal abilities and psychological characteristics to successfully implement and achieve company goals. This article aims to illustrate an employee's necessary psychological abilities and highlights the psychological demands of successfully managing connectivity for individual employees.

The editors of the book introduce **Hannspeter Schmidt** who has been working as a psychotherapist for nearly 20 years. Additionally, he lectured at diverse universities and acted as assistant professor, trainer, and supervisor for psychotherapists and psychoanalysts. He was head of the psychological counsel in Cologne and has worked as an independent management consultant in the field of human resources management focusing on coaching and team development.

H. Schmidt (✉)
HPS Consulting, Bonn, Germany
e-mail: mail@hps-bonn.de

© Springer Nature Switzerland AG 2020   141
P. Wollmann et al. (eds.), *Three Pillars of Organization and Leadership in Disruptive Times*, Future of Business and Finance,
https://doi.org/10.1007/978-3-030-23227-6_16

Introduction

In the introduction chapter of the book, the three pillar model for organization and leadership was developed (shared sustainable purpose within the organization, ability to act as a "traveling organization" with high content-based and mental flexibility in an appropriate moving environment and a huge connectivity-oriented mindset and skills). It is more than evident that the sustainable purpose as the general direction and the traveling organization as the necessary explorative and creative flexibility and ability for connectivity are certainly a necessary precondition to be successful as an organization.

This article explores the coverage of these special psychological preconditions for connectivity capabilities and mindsets. It was originally written as the second part of Marie Schmidt's article on "Connectivity: A core element of European Market Access for Pharmaceuticals" but removed because of its overarching importance for other articles, too. However, it will refer to the case study in Marie Schmidt's article in several sections to provide real world examples for the psychological theory discussed.

Summary

Connectivity is a challenge for international, innovative organizations and their employees: International companies are challenged to develop consistent strategies for highly complex and interdependent markets; employees working in such complex structures require the personal abilities and psychological characteristics to successfully implement and achieve company goals.

This article aims to illustrate employee's necessary psychological abilities and highlights the psychological demands of successfully managing connectivity for individual employees.

Connectivity: Not a Centerpiece of Psychological Research But Still a Central Psychological Construct

The concept of connectivity is virtually unknown in psychological literature and research. It most likely appears as a secondary issue in publications on attachment theory, when the topic of neurophysiological correspondence is broached. For example, specific parts of the brain might show high levels of connectivity after experiencing certain learnings or treatments. In neurophysiological literature, this is discussed as evidence of double-loop learning and for successful learnings on a neuronal level. In the context of psychological aspects (e.g., in psychosocial psychology or in personality psychology), connectivity most likely means attachment, communication skills, and intra- and interpersonal interconnectedness. Therefore, one might wonder which personal characteristics, abilities, and strengths should a company employee hold in order to meet the connectivity requirements of the company and the marketplace as outlined in the case study of Marie Schmidt's article on connectivity in pharmaceutical market access. Which talents and qualities can be expected to cope with success-critical situations within the framework of the required connectivity? In the context of sociopsychological aspects, what questions arise for the suitability of an employee in a company with high connectivity requirements?

Connectivity of Challenges and Complexity of Requirements

If we assume that the ability to regulate affective emotional states serves the function of meeting demands regarding connectivity at work, a successful employee needs to have good communication skills. This enables them to cope with complex communication in complex social settings, with systems, with contacts, and with negotiators from diverse sectors as well as with team members. As stated in the case study on pharmaceutical market access, high connectivity in the field of work demands the ability to align oneself with diverse conversational partners and negotiating partners from diverging sectors with very specialized professional orientations, as well as, to take one example, working on the launch of a new product. The employee needs to be able to talk to developers, medical scientists, and biologists (who do not have a business background). They must be able to achieve goals and progress with budget management. They have to have specific knowledge of international and global markets. They must meet the requirements of R&D. They need knowledge about current politics governing national and international markets. At the same time, they must handle high demands on cross-functional connectivity with internal and external stakeholders. Furthermore, cultural diversities in national, and especially in international, markets have to be considered when launching a new product. Corresponding to various stakeholders and their interests, different criteria have to be met when bringing a new pharmaceutical product onto the market. The employee working on market access must consider the internal expectations of the company as well as the external expectations of political and commercial partners and manage those expectations while conforming to the focused and goal-oriented launch of the new product. They have to be familiar with external and internal interests of involved parties and to coordinate them as well as gaining transparency despite high complexity to convince all people involved (at the table or in the network) and achieve success. They have to meet expectations from the regulatory and political spectrum. They need to conduct standardizations when launching a product that will be appreciated across all markets and will induce everyone involved to support, facilitate, and promote the launch and to convince all the parties involved.

Connectivity and Personality

This brief outline illustrates the complex demands on connectivity when a new product is brought to market (according to the case study above). The technical expertise an employee needs to have are well covered in the case study. Now we'll discuss psychological aptitude.

My view of the psychological aspects of connectivity, regarding the demands an employee needs to meet, incorporates meta-psychological concepts of psychodynamics. Findings from infant research, attachment theory, motivational training, and from the theory of mentalizing led to concepts that help to understand psychological maturing processes which can be used to derive competencies for coping with complex connectivity. The self comprises the central inner-psychological construct of meta-psychological examination. The construct of the self (historically known as "psychic apparatus") is extremely complex in its construction and functioning. It is neither physically nor anatomically tangible but rather an emergent phenomenon of the central nervous system's activity, without being identical to it. Qualitative contents are representations of the relational experiences gained in life that give structure to the self along with the following substantial mental functions:

The ability to regulate is crucial in all psychologically significant areas, for example, the ability to communicate, the ability to manage conflict, tolerance for conflict, and general tolerance for pressure, to name but a few. The abilities to communicate, to build attachment, to perceive, to be imaginative and creative, to mentalize, to think, to defend, and to be autonomous play a central role. In psychodynamics, these abilities of the self are considered ego functions that are part of the self. The self can be thought of as a complex-structured center of the individual that undergoes lifelong development. It has the internal structure of a complex system with high connectivity, containing representations, the ego, and further entities such as the conscience, idealizations of the self, and one's own personality as well as the pool of instincts and emotions.

Within this intrapsychic connectivity of the self, attachment is one of the central motivational needs of the self. Maturity and development of the self depend on primary and secondary experiences of relationships to important persons. Secure attachment is only achieved by fundamental early childhood experiences that are confirmed in the course of a lifetime. Trauma can prevent and destroy attachment abilities and competency in relationships. Both are critical for managing connective demands. Relationships between parents and children that are emotionally intimate and sophisticated are building blocks for the development of future authenticity. Safe relationships in early childhood years and secure attachment to the most important people in our lives are central prerequisites for successful maturity and development of the self.

In order to work successfully, high-performance teams need their members to have this kind of self-concept. The individual intrapsychic connectivity of each team member enables interactive social connectivity inside the team. The team's connective capabilities are greater than the sum of the individual's abilities. The collective of such a team is able to access the aforementioned capabilities of the self and the functions of the ego of each team member. Team members recognize those capabilities in themselves and others. Increasing combined capacities motivates team members to work together, to solve forthcoming tasks, and to develop more connective competence and efficiency in the process of working together. According to individual psychological consideration of the existing level of development of an employee's structural level, a high-performance team needs more structural leadership the less the structural levels of the individual members are developed in order to use their connective capabilities. Structural leadership means motivating and developing structural connective capabilities. It also means fostering the belief that individual potential increases the team's capabilities and potential for success at solving tasks that demand a high level of connectivity.

Part of meeting collective requirements in social networks (e.g., in highly complex social situations involving partners when a new product is being launched in international and global markets) is the ability to perceive instincts, emotions, and thus, motivational intentions. This develops as a function of the emotional availability of persons accompanying their infantile, pubertal, and adolescent development and their ability to react communicatively and resonantly. This is the basic requirement to enable individuals to develop resonant communicational skills within themselves and their functions. Therefore, diverse instincts and emotions must be integrated into the self. Additionally, stable and resilient internal representations must be formed from the substrate of object relations, i.e., internalized experiences of interaction. These internalizations support an individual's ability to comply with sophisticated—we would say connective—requirement patterns at work and in the company. Above all, the plurality of requirements and the plurality of people involved (offering a multitude of affective, emotional, and communicative abilities) need to be managed. This can lead to success in negotiations and can help large cultural differences to succeed. As a child, the attachment figure (the "object") secures a communicative exchange about instincts and motivational impulses and helps to regulate the intensity of instincts. Later on, at the workplace, the individual and their psychical systems and functions must cope with that task. The self of the individual must regulate instincts and impulses to provide sufficient tolerance of frustration, pressure, and fear. Those traits are needed to persist and to thrive in the face of the changing demands that expectations of social environments, international and global partners, and negotiation parties as well as corresponding company departments exert on the individual. One very important notion of current metaphysical concepts is mentalizing. Mentalizing is synonymous with the growth toward mentalization and with future ability to mentalize. This means that an employee in Marie Schmidt's case study needs the ability to reflect on, and to understand, their own motives as well as the motives of others and to anticipate possible solutions in order to manage the demands of connectivity. In concrete terms, this means being able to partially and temporarily identify oneself with the motives of negotiation parties, to gain access to motives of negotiation parties, to create "resonant" offers, to convey understanding, and the attempt to accept different motivations of others. Motives of external stakeholders, departments in the company, of supervisors, of employees, and of partners in the process of gaining market access need to be understood, although, ultimately, they can only be used for reflection with the goal of finding consensus and of solving critical situations to satisfy all of the parties concerned. Only then can successful connectivity exist and be secured.

Discussion: Connectivity From a Psychological Perspective

Thus, it can be said that connectivity in the personality structure of a successful employee means using highly complex skills and abilities of the self as the central psychic structure of personality. It depends on their development whether connective communication, empathy, insight, reflection, and introspection can succeed in negotiations. Considering the interests of others always presupposes tolerance in one's own self. This enables negotiations to be conducted flexibly and with tolerance. Combined with taking company interests into account, this increases the probability of success. Connectivity from a psychological perspective and as a personality trait will most likely succeed if the personality (and the associating self as an inner-psychical network) is able to react to demands in flexible and tolerant ways. In addition to professional skills, this requires psychological competencies and a collectively connected inner-psychical functioning in which demands on connectivity are represented. Connectivity as a demand for an employee working on market access requires connectivity in the psychodynamic inner network of the self of the personality. Given the connectivity and the demands of the markets, only then can market access for the product be successful.

Further Reading

Bateman, A., & Fonagy, P. (2016). *Mentalization-based treatment for personality disorders: A practical guide*. Oxford: Oxford University Press.

Deris, N., Montag, C., Reuter, M., Weber, B., & Markett, S. (2017). Functional connectivity in the resting brain as biological correlate of the Affective Neuroscience Personality Scales. *NeuroImage, 147*, 423–431.

Fonagy, P., et al. (2002). *Affect regulation, mentalization and the development of the self*. New York: Other Press.

Mertens, W., Butz, U., & Lenz, G. (Eds.). (1991). *Die Seele im Unternehmen*. Berlin, Heidelberg: Springer.

Developing Connectivity, Leadership, and Effective Team Working Using the Working Styles Model

Bernadette Cass

Abstract

Connectivity is better enabled if it is accompanied by knowledge of Working Styles. This article shares live examples of consultancy assignments in the area of Working Styles that support leaders, teams, and organizations to maintain effective communication and awareness of choice within the context of fast moving volatile environments. The Working Styles model enables people to create and sustain powerful working relationships even when under stress, appreciating the value of different styles and collaborating for mutual benefit. Teams containing different Working Styles are creative and potent and can develop more options.

Bernadette Cass is an organizational change consultant and executive coach. She works with people who wish to change their patterns of behavior and improve communications and relationships. Much of her work today is accompanying leaders in their thinking as they grow and develop their organizations.

Bernadette's commitment to creating sustainable change developed in her previous career when she designed IT strategy for a number of blue-chip organizations and was responsible for the development and delivery of complex global technology programs. She has a track record of supporting teams and organizations to meet the challenge and develop new ways of thinking, working, and behaving, to achieve improved business outcomes.

(continued)

B. Cass (✉)
Heworth Associates Limited, York, UK
e-mail: cass@heworthassociates.co.uk

© Springer Nature Switzerland AG 2020
P. Wollmann et al. (eds.), *Three Pillars of Organization and Leadership in Disruptive Times*, Future of Business and Finance,
https://doi.org/10.1007/978-3-030-23227-6_17

Bernadette is a practitioner of Organisational Transactional Analysis, a member of the European Association for Transactional Analysis, and an International Coach Federation accredited coach. She leads professional education groups in York, UK.

Publications include contributions to "Leading International Projects," Kogan Page, and various case studies for specialist professional journals.

Introduction

Organizations with a culture of connectivity sustain powerful effective working relationships between individuals, managers, teams, customers and suppliers, creating opportunities to engage the full potential of all parties, and delivering substantive business benefit.

This article shares live examples of consultancy assignments that support leaders, teams, and organizations to maintain effective communication and awareness of choice within the context of fast moving volatile environments. Readers will gain valuable insights and practical approaches to creating and maintaining effective working relationships, including a "how to" guide to apply the Working Styles model to develop and maintain high performing teams.

The Working Styles model enables people to create and sustain powerful working relationships even when under stress, appreciating the value of different styles and collaborating for mutual benefit. Teams containing different Working Styles are creative and potent and can develop more options.

Connectivity is more fully enabled with a knowledge of Working Styles, in her books 'Working it out at Work', and Transactional Analysis for Trainers, based on the work of Taibi Kahler who developed the concept of Drivers, and Hedges Capers who identified Allowers (Hedges and Capers article, 'The Miniscript' Transactional Analysis Journal).

Leaders have a critical role in creating a culture which values different ways of thinking and problem-solving. In choosing how to communicate and behave toward others, they model what is acceptable behavior, and what is not. Leaders can be found in all parts of every organization, and can use Working Styles theory to deepen their own communication skills and to interact well with those around them. Providing teams with a knowledge of Working Styles can support people to be at their best and to sustain good team performance even when under pressure. In a Traveling Organization, leaders can create environments based on shared sustainable purpose, updating team awareness of changing organizational circumstances.

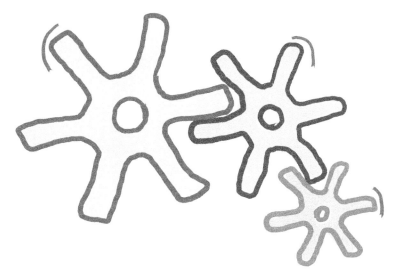

Fig. 1 Experiencing working with similar or complementary Working Styles, when the gears mesh together seamlessly and everything runs smoothly (author's own figure)

Working Styles

Have you noticed that other people may take a different approach to getting things done? Perhaps, you find this helpful in creating new options. Maybe it can be frustrating as you wonder why someone else doesn't see it your way. The chances are that you and your colleague are using different Working Styles to get things done, and when you're not aware of this it can lead to lack of understanding and confusion.

On the other hand, you may have experienced that it's easy to work with some individuals. You seem to have a natural understanding and rapport, and get on well. You find it easy to understand each other and work together effectively without too much effort. You may be experiencing working with similar or complementary Working Styles (Fig. 1).

Working Styles theory provides an insight into preferred ways of thinking feeling and behaving. There are five core Working Styles, and what may seem obvious to you is not necessarily going to be understood by someone with a different preference. Having an awareness of our own working style is invaluable as we consider how to communicate and collaborate effectively with team members, business partners, clients—and friends and family too. Research indicates that everyone unconsciously uses one, sometimes two, preferred Working Styles.

The Five Working Styles

There are no "right or wrong" Working Styles. Each Working Style has clear strengths and also some limiting behaviors, which often become more apparent when we're under pressure (Fig. 2).

Fig. 2 Five Working Styles
(Figure: based on Napper and
Newton 2014)

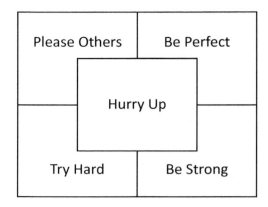

Please Others

These people are lovely to be around in teams! They encourage harmony, and are considerate of others feelings. They are tolerant and understanding, nurturing, and caring. However, their aim is to please others without asking for clarity on what is needed. They avoid conflict so may fail to speak out and ask for what they want, find it hard to say no, or to challenge others in case people are upset by what they say.

Be Perfect

They are known for accuracy and attention to detail, and work with thoroughness and few errors. They think things through and are well organized and efficient. However, they can be late with producing work as they want it to be completely correct, sometimes including too much detailed information which makes it complicated and confusing for others to understand.

Be Strong

These people remain calm under pressure and are great in a crisis. They have a strong sense of duty and will work logically and steadily even at unpleasant tasks. They are consistent, reliable, and steady. However, they find it difficult to ask for help or admit vulnerability and so can struggle unnecessarily alone. They don't easily show their feelings, which can be uncomfortable for others.

Try Hard

They tackle things enthusiastically, following up on all possibilities and aspects of the task. They are great at getting things started, often volunteering to take on work and getting new ideas and projects off the ground. However, they can leave tasks incomplete as they don't pay attention to all of the detail and can be more attracted by moving on to new activities.

Hurry Up

This Working Style is usually seen alongside one of the other Styles, not by itself.

These people get things done quickly. They respond well to short deadlines and urgency and produce speedy results. However, they can miss deadlines as they delay starting work until it becomes urgent. They often speak quickly and appear impatient, interrupting others which leads to unnecessary misunderstandings.

What Happens When Working Styles Come Under Pressure

Usually, we all have access to all styles, although we will have a natural pattern or preferred way of working that we default to. However, when under pressure we stay in our preferred Style, and lose our ability to choose an appropriate response. When this happens we're no longer in Working Style, we have shifted to being in Driver behavior. We are being unconsciously "driven" to think, behave, or feel in a certain way (Fig. 3).

When in Driver, we find it hard to see other ways of doing things. Our Working Style becomes the "only" way to get the task completed, and we can become convinced that "my way is the right way" and reject other ways of working. We can become rigid and inflexible, and increase our Driver behavior. In response, other people will move into their Driver. This can lead to misunderstanding, difficulty in maintaining communication, and frustration. Each of us becomes harder to work with.

Fig. 3 Working Styles coming under pressure when the gears break or lock together leading to disruption (author's own figure)

When this happens, we can use Allowers to invite ourselves and others back into Working Style.

Allowers

Each Driver has an Allower which provides a way to move out of Driver. When we are in Driver, we don't communicate effectively with other people, as we want other people to take the same Driver approach as us. Asking ourselves Allower questions is a helpful way to notice if we're in Driver, and each Allower invites us to move back into Working Style.

- Be Perfect—Keep it simple. Is it good enough? The 80/20 rule is helpful.
- Please Others—Please yourself. What do *you* want?
- Try Hard—Do It! Choose one task and complete it.
- Be Strong—Can others help? You don't have to do it by yourself.
- Hurry Up—Take your time (Fig. 1).

How Working Styles Support Effective Team Working

In my experience, team members find it helpful to know their personal Working Style. It provides insight and self-awareness of natural strengths and ways of approaching tasks. It also allows us to be aware of the pitfalls associated with our Working Style and how to avoid them. We can start to notice when we move into Driver, over-using our Working Style and reducing our productivity.

When people share their Working Styles others have the opportunity to recognize and appreciate different approaches to tasks, and to collaborate with those with a different Working Style. We learn to understand more about other people's behavior, and how to communicate more effectively with each other. Consciously choosing to invite a variety of Working Styles into discussions creates more options and produces richer outcomes.

Working Styles in Action: Be Perfect, Try Hard, and Hurry Up

Monique was working as a senior manager in a UK organization. She had responsibility for client facing services, liaison with external stakeholders and partners, and some income generation. She led the customer services team which prided itself on rapid response and finding effective customer solutions. Customer and business partner feedback was extremely positive.

Monique reported to Michael, the Finance Director. He was dissatisfied with Monique's performance. He criticized some of the less successful projects she had run with clients. He felt that she didn't pay sufficient attention to following agreed business processes, and she didn't complete monthly financial reporting on time, despite many reminders. Michael said Monique was ignoring his requests and not being efficient.

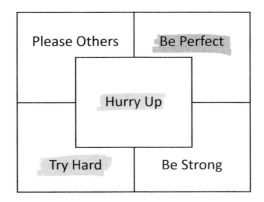

Monique and Michael were operating from different Working Styles. Being in Try Hard, Monique's natural response was to move to action and experiment with different customer solutions until they found an effective outcome. Her Hurry Up helped her to thrive and respond well to pressure. Michael was in Be Perfect. He preferred to think things through in more detail before moving to action, assessing options, and rejecting those that were less likely to be satisfactory.

Monique and Michael were taking different approaches to problem-solving. Each felt their skills, methods, and successes were unappreciated by the other. They became frustrated with the perceived lack of response and spent a lot of their time together in Driver behavior. Their working relationship was breaking down.

Once Monique and Michael realized they had different Working Styles they were able to take account of the fact that they would have naturally different preferences. Monique learnt to appreciate that Michael was good at anticipating issues, and consulting with him could save time energy and money. Michael recognized that Monique could get new projects off the ground quickly with good results, and was skilled at collaborative working. Together they formed an effective partnership.

Working Styles in Action: Please Others and Be Strong

Marc was a member of the Senior Leadership Team, reporting to the Managing Director, Rashad. Marc was popular and well-liked by his colleagues. Some months previously he had taken some time off sick, and in his absence other managers had willingly rallied round to cover his responsibilities.

Rashad believed that Marc was failing to deliver on two business critical projects, which would involve collaboration with his coworkers. He said Marc was not asserting his authority to get the job done. "We've supported him through his illness, and he's back now. Why doesn't he just get on with it?" He said he was completely backing Marc and was becoming irritated by Marc's hesitation and lack of results. "He comes into my office and wants to spend time in small talk". He couldn't understand why Marc was so concerned about asking other people to participate in the project work.

Marc was feeling intimidated by Rashad's brusqueness and desire for immediate project delivery. He felt uncomfortable about asking colleagues to give their time to the projects, and felt there were many reasons why they might not want to do this. The organization had previously run on traditional hierarchical reporting lines, and people weren't used to working in matrix teams. He wanted to take time to explore this and check it out with his peers.

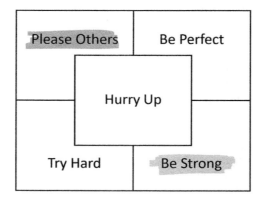

Rashad and Marc were spending a lot of time in Driver behavior. In Please Others, it was important to Marc that he took other people's feelings into account before he could move on to plan and deliver the project work. He wanted to hear Rashad acknowledge his concerns and recognize that the feelings on the team were important. Marc was also worried that his colleagues might not cooperate, or say no to his requests.

Rashad was in Be Strong, focused on structuring the projects and task delivery. He didn't see the relevance of discussing feelings, as the decisions had been made and communicated. He wanted to see project activity taking place and "get the job done."

When they learnt about their Working Styles Marc and Rashad realized that they could learn how to adjust their communication with each other and benefit from their different preferences. Rashad recognized that Marc was skillful at understanding the mood and attitudes within the team and that it was important to account for other people's feelings. He also learnt that it was important to make personal contact with Marc before the conversation could move to activity, for example, by asking how he was today or what he'd done at the weekend.

Marc was able to benefit from Rashad's ability to plan and make consistent progress with tasks. He learnt not to make assumptions about what others wanted, and appreciated Rashad's ability to be calm and unemotional about facts. With

Rashad's help, he recognized that what he was perceiving as possible confrontation about project work was a reasonable request. When they worked together and used elements of both their Working Styles Marc and Rashad made a more rounded powerful team.

Impact of Drivers Within Organizations

Teams and organizations have preferred Working Styles too, and sometimes different parts of the business use different Styles. This has potential to be creative and highly productive, or Driver behavior can lead to conflict.

Initial Conflict

Shelagh was a senior manager in a multinational organization. Her Research team were noted for the high standards and accuracy of their work. The team had strong track record of supporting customers through chemical regulation processes to achieve usage certification.

The customer base was growing and changing. The growth of biosecurity meant that new clients were approaching the company with different requests. This was recognized by the creation of a new Technical Enquiry team, who were recruited for their customer facing skills, and who did not report to Shelagh.

Shelagh and her team were unhappy with the new structure. There was confusion that the Technical Enquiry team didn't have scientific backgrounds or qualifications, and so couldn't provide accurate technical information.

The Research team frequently returned customer request documentation to the Technical Enquiry team because some details were incomplete. The Technical Enquiry team found it challenging to get effective support and replies from the Research team. They didn't understand why Research colleagues couldn't give them initial estimates so that they could respond to customers in a timely manner. There was a high degree of friction between teams, and business opportunities were lost as customers went to competitors who responded more quickly to initial enquiries.

Consultancy and Leadership Resolution

Shelagh recognized that the teams were at an impasse, and that resolution was required. Our consultancy focused on the following key questions:

1. What is current reality for the organization?
2. What is the sustainable purpose for both teams?
3. What Working Styles are evident?
4. What changes are required to maintain good connectivity and customer service?

Findings and Next Steps

1. After our initial consultation, Shelagh realized that she and the Research team hadn't recognized the importance and needs of the new customer base nor the changing commercial direction of the organization. The change in circumstances and Organization Travel had developed out of her awareness, and team beliefs and behavior about how to be successful were based on past achievements. We agreed a workshop format to share this information and bring the two teams together for a problem-solving session.

   It was critical to the success of the workshop that Shelagh fully embraced her leadership role. Shelagh shared the new context, which was critical for the engagement and commitment of the Research team. Shelagh also stated her personal commitment to find equitable ways of working to meet the needs of both teams.

2. The workshop invited both teams to share their values and purpose. They discovered many common principles, including the value of biosecurity, the desire to deliver good solutions to customers, and to support the commercial and ethical success of the organization.

3. Working Styles information was shared with the teams, and everyone completed the questionnaire.[1] I designed exercises for people to explore their preferred Style, and to learn more from people with different preferences. There were opportunities to work on real issues and experiment with using Allowers to create new ways of working.

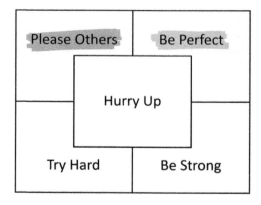

Both teams recognized that they had moved into Driver behavior. The Research team had criticized the Technical Enquiry team for inaccuracy and unreasonable requests from their Be Perfect driver. The Please Others driver of the Technical Enquiry team was frustrated by demands for what they saw as

---

[1]If you want to access the Working Styles questionnaire you can use the information in Julie Hay's book *Transactional Analysis for Trainers*. The questionnaire and information on purchasing additional copies can be found in the appendix of *Transactional Analysis for Trainers*.

unimportant detail, and the ongoing conflict with Research colleagues. They were also upset by their inability to respond to customer requests.

4. During the workshop, the teams were able to move out of Driver and recognize that all team members were working with the intent of delivering the best possible service. With awareness of their Working Styles, they gained a greater understanding of how to communicate effectively with their counterpart on the other team. They identified a series of changes and new processes to put in place.

How Leaders Can Use Working Styles to Develop High Performing Teams

Here are some tips on the process of sharing the Working Styles model, to support teams to deliver effective business results.

1. *Set the Context*
   You might find it helpful to consider some of these questions:
   (a) What is current reality for the organization and the team?
   (b) What changes are happening that will impact team members?
   (c) What are the challenges?
   (d) What relationships are changing, or what new relationships are to be created?
   (e) What previously successful activities will become less relevant?
   (f) What new behaviors are required?
   (g) What are current objectives and measures of success? Should these be updated?
2. *Share the Working Styles Model*
   (a) Working Styles are a useful resource for individuals to develop awareness of their own natural preferences, and for teams to maintain effective communication and connectivity, both within the team and with others.
   (b) Share the five Working Styles and the descriptions of their strengths and limiting behaviors.
   (c) Give team members the Working Styles questionnaire (see footnote 1) to complete, so that they discover their personal preferences.
3. *Familiarization*
   Invite people to work in pairs or small groups to share their Styles. Create pairs or groups consisting of different Working Styles.
   Questions to consider:
   (a) What do individuals recognize as their strengths, and how does that relate to their Working Style?
   (b) What do I most enjoy about this Working Style?
   (c) How does it support me to be effective?
   (d) What do I notice happens when I'm under pressure?
   (e) How does my style become limiting?
   As this information is shared, people with another Working Style will notice different ways of thinking, feeling and approaching tasks. Individuals can share

questions and insights about working effectively with a different Style, leading to group learning.

4. *Drivers and Allowers*

Under pressure, we move from Working Style into Driver behavior. This can be counterproductive when we interact with others. Using Allowers we can invite ourselves and the people around us to return to Working Style and create more options to achieve results.

Describe the Allowers and again in small groups invite people to share:

(a) What do I notice that appeals to me?
(b) What might I find difficult about the Allower for my Style?
(c) What help could I ask from others?
(d) How will I use the Allower for my Style in my current work?

5. *Using Working Styles to Support Day to Day Work*

Now that everyone knows about Working Styles, the team can consider how to get benefit from it by considering a live task:

(a) Consider a new or changed objective, or a current task.
(b) What is required for me to achieve this objective?
(c) What benefits will my Working Style bring?
(d) Am I noticing any driver response or limiting behavior?
(e) What Allowers do I want to remind myself about?
(f) What relationships are important to achieve this?
(g) How can I collaborate effectively with others to achieve this objective using my knowledge of Working Styles?

6. *Create a Team Working Agreement*

Where team members are working together their commitment to delivering objectives can be extended to a working agreement where people explicitly refer to their Working Style and preferences. They can choose to consult others with a different Style to achieve a more rounded approach, and learn to take account of what's important to others with a different Style.

7. *Remember the Allowers!*

The team working agreement can include noticing any pressure points or stressed behaviors and enquiring about these. As we move into Driver behavior unconsciously, it can be very helpful to have another person draw this to our attention and ask what we need in order to reduce tension and return to Working Style behavior. Asking an Allower question can be very effective in these circumstances (Fig. 1).

8. *Embed the New Way of Working*

Build in a process for team members to regularly review the working agreement, sharing their stories and successes, learning from each other's experience, and addressing any challenges too.

Summary

Working Styles are a useful resource for teams to maintain effective communication and connectivity, both within the team and with others.

Under pressure, we move from Working Style into Driver behavior. This can be counterproductive when we interact with others. Using Allowers we can invite ourselves and the people around us to return to Working Style and create more options to achieve results.

Leaders with awareness of Working Style preferences can encourage diversity of approaches to problem-solving, establish powerful teams, and generate greater mutual benefit.

References and Additional Reading

Hay, J. (1993). *Working it out at work*. Hertford: Sherwood Publishing.
Hay, J. (2009). *Transactional analysis for trainers*. Hertford: Sherwood Publishing.
Joines, V., & Stewart, I. (2002). *Personality adaptations*. Chapel Hill, NC: Lifespace Publishing.
Joines, V., & Stewart, I. (2012). *TA today*. Chapel Hill, NC: Lifespace Publishing.
Kahler, T., & Capers, H. (1974). The miniscript. *Transactional Analysis Journal, 4*(1), 26–42. https://doi.org/10.1177/036215377500500318.
Napper, R., & Newton, T. (2014). *Tactics: Transactional analysis concepts for all trainers, teachers and tutors* (2nd ed.). Ipswich: TA Resources.
Tudor, K., & Summers, G. (2014). *Co-creative transactional analysis*. London: Karnac.

Angel Investing and Connectivity

Alberto Casagrande

Abstract

This article focuses on the complex world of angel investing and on how our general framework applies in order to make angel investing a successful/profitable activity. It covers the whole framework of angel investing, the scope of the related activities, its economics, and the effort required to perform it. A special focus is on evaluation criteria throughout the lifetime of an investment and Alberto's personal experiences and insights. It is a glance at an amazing world in which solid evaluation skills are key. Alberto describes some tools that are already available to assist angels. It is interesting that all the pre-made tools he has encountered involve assessing whether or not the startup complies with the three pillar model success criteria.

The editors of the book introduce **Alberto Casagrande** who is actively involved in the angel investment ecosystem both in California and in Italy. For the last 15 years, he has managed The Core Inc., a boutique firm devoted to strategic, ICT, and economic consulting with advisory mandates at the World Bank and several central banks. Alberto was previously a project manager at McKinsey in Italy and economist at Italy's Central Bank.

A. Casagrande (✉)
The Core Inc., Rome, RM, Italy

© Springer Nature Switzerland AG 2020
P. Wollmann et al. (eds.), *Three Pillars of Organization and Leadership in Disruptive Times*, Future of Business and Finance,
https://doi.org/10.1007/978-3-030-23227-6_18

Introduction

The present chapter focuses on the complex world of angel investing and on how our general framework applies to it in order to make angel investing a successful/profitable activity.

In order to shed some light on the above, it is important first to understand the whole framework of angel investing: in section "Scope," we will describe the scope of such activity, in section "Economics" its economics, and in section "Effort required" the effort required to perform it.

In section "Angel investing and our three pillar model," we will focus on the general framework of angel investor's activity, focusing mainly on evaluation criteria throughout the lifetime of an investment. In section "Evaluation criteria for a candidate startup and three pillar model," we will look at all this business from my personal experience, drafting a quick history of my involvement. Section "Evaluation criteria for a follow-up investment in a startup and three pillar model" will wrap up the chapter.

Scope

Angel investing consists basically of providing financing to new or recently formed companies, together with some extra skill to develop the business and, in particular, in some technical capacity, be that horizontal (e.g., management, IT, legal) or vertical (startup sector), or access to a network of stakeholders that could potentially be beneficial to the company, be that for financial or technical reasons.

Such activity in reality has been there to some extent for quite some time. Even a few decades ago, at least in most Western economies, newly founded companies would offer equity to either advisors or well-connected friends in exchange for funds and some other supporting role such as facilitator, technical advisor, or something else.

What has changed over the last two decades has been the fact that, by now:

- There are many angel investors. Angel investors—both as individuals and in angel communities—nowadays constitute a well-established and important piece of the startup ecosystem, providing a crucial layer of financing (alongside financing institutions, venture capitalists, private equity, friends, and family) as well as any other type of business support (alongside technical advisors and employees among the others). Just focusing on the USA, angel investments have exceeded $20 billion since 2010, with average capital received per investment amounting to $328,000 (data from Center for Venture Research). In almost all early stage deals nowadays (but angels are present in expansion and late stage deals too), even the most well-known ones, it is very common to observe the involvement of some angels (be they individuals or communities, well-known personalities or even more local and less known angels).

- There are widely accepted tools to support deal-making for angels, for example, quick, cheap, and solid legal financing agreements such as SAFE or KISS (Simple Agreement for Future Equity resp. Keep It Simple Security), and to facilitate communication with various stakeholders even remotely (e.g., VOIP providers such as Skype or WhatsApp, e.g., make communication free to everybody almost all over the world), so barriers for outsiders to work with companies have disappeared.
- Angel investing has become a global activity. In fact, angel investors and angel communities are now spread throughout most countries in the world, with a great coverage in countries such as the USA and Singapore and increasing coverage in Europe (mainly London, Berlin, Paris, Barcelona), China, India, and Australia to name but a few of the most important ones.
- Angel communities have grown not only both in number and reach but also in the solidity of their regulation and operating mechanisms. In the USA, some communities have now notched up more than 20 years of existence, and working mechanisms are, in the meantime, smooth and function very well, including decision-making, budgeting, meeting schedules, due diligence techniques, deal making, and exit processes.

Economics

Angel investing is rarely a philanthropic activity. Most angel investors want a return from their investment, besides possibly getting involved in the business in one capacity or another. Since angel investments are often in startups, and realizing that—statistically—startups are more likely to fail than to survive for more than few years, it is quite obvious that this is a challenging world.

According to a recent survey from a network of angel associations in the USA, about 70% of angel investments have returns of less than the capital invested, most of them going close to 0 as, in such cases, the company usually shuts down operations; about 20% have returns of up to $5\times$ (5 times the capital invested); about 7–8% have returns of between $10\times$ and $30\times$; and about 2% have returns in excess of $30\times$.

Angel investments performed with an IRR ranging from 20% to 25% and an average investment duration ranging from 4.5 to 5 years depend on the investment pool.

By just interpreting the above statistics, it is quite likely that there will be failures for hopeful angel investors, as well as a good chance that the overall investment will not be repaid.

Given the high likelihood of startup failures, it is also clear that:

- It is not a business for inexperienced/unskilled investors (though you could be lucky, as I was with my first investment, but I was not aware of what I was doing). Many angels I have met told me that they made many mistakes with their first angel investments. Some angel communities I know even go as far as strongly discouraging new members from making investments in the first year of membership.

- There are high incentives for angels to form communities, as merging experiences and financial power help them navigate through the objective difficulties of such business. On this note, I have to add that I benefited tremendously from the opportunity of joining a well-established angel group on the West Coast of the USA a few years ago as I was really lacking some of the fundamentals I am now describing and making quite obvious mistakes (you can get lucky once or twice but not always).
- An angel investor needs to diversify its portfolio significantly in order to be able to compensate for losses with good exits. Experienced angels talk of the need to build a portfolio of at least 20 companies in order to be relatively safe. In fact, an angel investor needs very successful exits in order for the model to be sustainable. On the other hand, some angels argue against such a theory, stating that they cannot devote the attention to more than 7–10 companies.
- It is not advisable for an angel investor to invest everything at the same time, as good opportunities usually take time to appear. At the beginning, at least in my experience, most startups looked great, and then I started to appreciate some of the finer nuances; after all, most startups have some major pitfalls. Patience is key.
- Angels need to accept losses without missing a beat, i.e., they need strong nerves. Typically, a successful and meaningful exit takes 4 to 7 years. On the contrary, startups that fail to grow well/keep getting funded can fail quite quickly and the angel's investment can fall to zero! (As a matter of fact, an investor may even lose all their capital in less than a year. In my experience, I came close to losing all my money in one investment in less than 6 months). So, the beginner angel is likely to incur certain failures while hoping to get a good but uncertain exit. As you can see, it is quite a nerve-racking activity!

Effort Required

Angel investing can be either quite passive, simply getting involved financially in selected deals from time to time, or be more proactive, participating in some capacity in advising the companies in which one has invested. In most cases, angel investors mix between the two, especially if they are members of angel communities, because when it comes to passive deals they might be relying on another member's more active involvement.

Even if we consider the passive side only, the range of activities is quite extensive:

- Screening startups for first investment. Such activity needs to be run until portfolio does not get a sufficient number of deals that allow enough diversification. Once this number is reached, it still needs to be run as some exits happen and/or some companies fail (at least if the objective is to maintain a diversified portfolio and keep investing). Screening activities can be very intense if due diligence of the startup needs to be done and the angel gets involved actively in it (it can take only few calls, or it can go as far as talking to some clients of the startup/previous investors, analyzing reports, etc.).

- Screening startups for follow-up investments. I initially underestimated such activities. It turns out that there are several funding cycles for most startups, and good money can be made from investments in several phases of successful startups. Such screening is more based on the experience of the previous investment period but can be quite time-consuming as well (depending on how deeply one wishes to go), involving interviews with key personnel, reviewing, and commenting on projections and achieved results and so on.
- Being involved in the angel world, which implies: going to public events, participating in startup conferences, startup competitions, networking with other investors, be they funds or other angel investors, etc.
- (if part of an angel community) In order to be a "passive" member only, participating in at least some of the events organized every month, in order to build/maintain connections that can be useful for the future. "Active members" add to the above all the activity necessary to run such organizations, such as sitting on the Board of Directors, or undertaking other voluntary activities for the organization.

The more active side can also take some time as it requires:

- Following how the startup is going, including possibly mentoring key stakeholders (CEO, COO, etc.)
- (Possibly) If a member of the Board of Directors, participating actively in the Board's decisions
- Communicating with the angel community of reference on the deal

It is hard to quantify how much of each individual's time is spent on angel investing. There are not yet any public statistics available. Personally, many people I know spend well over 50% of their time on this, and some up to 100%.

In my personal experience thus far (both as an individual angel investor and "passive member" of an angel community), this takes about 30% to 40% of my time.

Angel Investing and Our Three Pillar Model

We will now deep dive into how angel investing activities ties in to the three pillar model described in the introductory chapters.

In general, it is safe to state that if any of the three pillars (sustainable purpose, traveling organization, and connectivity) do not apply to a candidate startup or to a follow-up round, no angel would invest in it for the first time or would follow up with it at a later stage. We are dealing a priori with extremely risky investments and

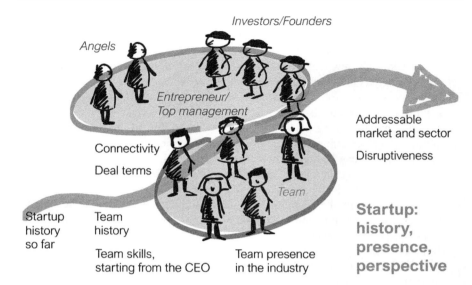

Fig. 1 The startup in terms of system and journey, perspectives, and criteria (Figure: Frank Kühn)

those success factors are supposed to be minimum requirements to arouse any investor's interest.

In this section we will map evaluation criteria for investing in a startup to the three pillar model (5.1); map evaluation criteria for following up in a startup to the three pillar model (5.2); and deep dive into connectivity focusing on how this generates new business opportunities for angels (5.3).

Evaluation Criteria for a Candidate Startup and Three Pillar Model

Each angel or angel organization has their own evaluation criteria to meet before they would invest in a startup.

Since I entered this arena, the most commonly acknowledged criteria are linked to a team and, in particular (Fig. 1):

1. Team skills, starting from the CEO
2. Team history
3. Team presence in the industry
4. Disruptiveness
5. Addressable market and sector
6. Deal terms
7. Startup history so far

The team focus—(1) through (3)—is particularly relevant because, in my opinion and experience, no matter how powerful the idea is if the team does not have it, you are not going to make it. More specifically, any startup (including some of the most successful Internet companies to date such as Facebook, Amazon, and Apple) goes through moments of crisis and/or moments where they might have to choose between going one way or another because of market changes, liquidity constraints, etc.

At that moment, no matter how good the advisors are, no matter what the liquidity status is/how much money the startup has in the bank, the team must decide and the team makes the difference. And they are more likely to be successful if there is a team who decides and acts fast, ideally with maximum cooperation, and if they move in the right direction and/or they correct their course quickly if they see it fit.

In most modern times, three profiles can be considered fundamental (sometimes condensed into one or two people because of budget needs):

- The CEO as the leading interface to investors and the wider business community
- The CTO/COO as the leading product/service changer
- The Head of Business Development as they lead the demand/business interfaces of the company

Without wanting to preempt too much from section "Evaluation criteria for a candidate startup and three pillar model," I would just like to mention that I always interview all of them in order to get a sense of how strong and resilient the team is.

With respect to our three pillar model, sustainable purpose and traveling organization best fit into the above criteria for angels.

Furthermore, criterion (3) above talks about relationships in the industry and with the angel communities ("connectivity skills"). This has to be considered as well, as the ability to close business partnerships and to secure funds for growth/survival are not only linked to the startup business but to the connections both in the business and in the funding industry.

Evaluation Criteria for a Follow-Up Investment in a Startup and Three Pillar Model

When dealing with follow-up investments, angels already have a working knowledge of the company, including performance, interaction with top profiles, track record of funding (this time internally), and a better perception of business and team potential.

All these factors come into play when deciding whether or not to invest.

One key factor to look at here is how the team has reacted to difficulties, how resilient the team has been (referring again mainly not only to our traveling organization success factor but also to that of sustainable purpose). This is difficult to ascertain only from formal communication with the startup. In order to overcome this, in my personal experience, I try to talk to CEOs as much as possible in order to understand it.

Another factor to look at is how stable the key team has been. Organizations with too high turnover of key employees at the beginning are not particularly appealing, at least to the angels I know. This has to do with our sustainable purpose criterion. For the record, it might sometimes be difficult to get this information from the startup as they know that it might not reflect well on them.

Finally, connectivity skills are to be assessed in greater depth in this phase, as, by now, the startup key personnel have demonstrated their ability to move both in the business and in the funding arena.

Connectivity and New Opportunity Creation/Business Development for Angels

Connectivity is essential for angels. Angels connect both in order to have successful returns as angels, and, more generally, because the expansion of their network can, in itself, create precious opportunities for them in the future (as either founders of new companies, or advisors, or executives of grown startups).

The main categories of necessary connections for angels are as follows:

- Connection with the entrepreneur/top management. This is the most obvious one, as it covers the whole experience of investing from selection to exit. Such connections should not be considered as happening only at the funding /deal making/beginning of the investment stage. In fact, angels are supposed to be more active during the investment life phase, which can take various forms: (1) informal chats; (2) formal advisory capacities remunerated by means of cash/stock options; and (3) seats on the Board of Directors.
- Connection with investors/founders who are familiar with the target startup's sector. This is extremely important and it is usually one of the key reasons why angels invest in some startups and not in others. Angels want to be confident that the startup is in an area in which they feel confident. Having already someone expert in the field or either a reputable founder or a reputable investor makes the investment less likely to crumble quickly. It is also worth noting that, at the same time, entrepreneurs compare some angels to others based on their connections. As an example (in a company I was screening), a startup selling infrastructure for hospitals is more likely to be successful if backed by an angel community consisting of reputable Medical Doctors.
- Connections among angels. Two angels who know each other can reach out in order to, for example:
  - Assess what each one thinks of one firm
  - Propose some opportunity unknown to the other
  - Suggest a community to reach out

  These relationships are very important and should not be underestimated. Obviously, exposure to other angels becomes much higher once an angel investor becomes part of an angel community.

My Experience as an Angel

Even before becoming an active angel, I worked as an advisor to startups (both for fees and for friends) since the late 1990s. Therefore, I know how difficult it is for a startup to be successful.

About 6 years ago, I started investing in a startup in Italy with some experienced friends of mine involving some other people to close an early-stage financing round. I liked the idea, though I perceived my role as being rather passive with respect to my desire of getting involved. Nonetheless, it turned out to be my first insight into this world, as I started discovering not only the beauty of it, its complexities (from closing to communication to follow-ups to exit), but also its potential rewards (I was able to get an exit in about 2 years, at slightly less than 5×).

I also started building relationships with other reputable business angels in Italy by participating in some startup competitions around Italy. This created an initial network for me from which I am still benefiting.

My main network of angels in Italy comes from the above-mentioned experiences and connections.

I then started to look for more opportunities in the USA, and I found—thanks to a tip from an Italian banker—an opportunity in the West Coast, with a micro fund investing in startups at seed phase. I first visited and then joined the fund. That was my second inflexion point in the startup world. I discovered a place where:

- Deals happen very quickly.
- Companies' ambitions are spectacular, usually with plans to conquer the USA within 5 years and the world within the next 5–10 years (of course all of this from the—slightly biased—point of view of the entrepreneurs, because most of them actually do not manage this!).
- Relationships too develop rather quickly, as it is relatively quick to get engaged on investing topics with local angels even without too many previous personal relationships, something that is not so common in Italy. Therefore, I was able to increase my angel network and secure introductions to some other startup opportunities.

I returned a few months later, and—while I was there—I discovered there was a startup week, i.e., a week of introductory meetings to the startup world for founders and investors, with testimonials from successful startups as well as from large corporations venturing into startups. I signed up and this was an ideal opportunity to improve my understanding of this world. On this occasion, too, I was able to expand my network and meet different types of profiles (entrepreneurs, fund managers, angels) with whom I am still in touch.

On my third visit, I was introduced to a startup that was very promising and about to be screened by an angel network. They looked spectacular to me, and I was ready to invest (I was about to ask them their banking coordinates to send my wire). After the angel community decided not to approve the deal, I asked the entrepreneur to introduce me to the community. I spoke to them and joined one of their screening events. I loved it, finding the startups' selection very accurate and the audience (angel investors) rather choosy and demanding. I asked to join the community and was accepted as a member.

At the moment, I am both active as a stand-alone investor and as a part of a structured community. Both settings have pros and cons. In my case the pros of being a stand-alone investor are:

- The ability to have a stronger impact on the entrepreneur and much more contact with the startup.
- The possibility of negotiating a tougher deal with the entrepreneur, usually because it is an earlier stage than that accepted by angel communities (everything else being equal, an angel community would have stronger negotiating power of course given the size of the deal).

The pros of joining a community for me have been tremendous:

- More deals: I now have access to more deals (from 3 to 5 per year before, to 12–15 per month now) and in a wider range of sectors than before.
- Learning and sharing: I can learn consolidated screening and follow-up techniques; previously I was forced to mimic such techniques using my own judgment and my own available time (less than the time an entire community would have available). I can share due diligence work with other reputable angels and benefit from their knowledge in areas I am not familiar with (e.g., the biotech sector, cloud computing). The angel community was able to spot problems/opportunities in certain startups that I would not have been able to spot otherwise (one very important example concerns the solidity of patents, another the structure of the deal, preferred equity vs. common stock, etc.).
- More networks: Both the ability to meet more angels (most of them more experienced than I am) and mingle with them and the opportunities that are available for the angel community from the local environment (e.g., external screenings, presentation of startup funds, and the like) allowed me to build an extensive extra network, something that I was already able to do on my own but at a much slower pace.

By looking at startups through both scenarios (inside or outside an angel network), I dramatically redefined my evaluation criteria for assessing a startup. As mentioned earlier, for me the team is the first fundamental asset, probably even more important than the idea. Even because, for all the startups in which I have invested so far, what you are left with, once the investment is finished (hopefully with success), is the people who worked on it, namely, the team.

This brings me to the role of personal relationships in angel investment. In my opinion, they are crucial. Without good personal relationships I can definitely affirm that I would not have invested in any of the startups I have invested in so far, because, at the end of the day, it comes down to reciprocal trust.

The first and most fundamental person to trust is the entrepreneur, closely followed by the team around him. Usually, founders have big egos, but either they somehow adjust to the egos of investors (which are also not that small in my experience), allowing the latter to both understand the business opportunity and be able to provide the right input to address the startup; or the startup is not going to receive funds, unless of course the business case is unbelievably successful (at an early stage, this is usually not the case).

Then in most cases there are some pivotal investors who are crucial. Recently, I was looking at a startup in the area of genomic computing, and while having some knowledge of big data, I did not know anything about genomes. It turned out that— among the angels—there was a gentleman who had a business in the exact same field. I decided to talk to him and—once I had understood his take on the business—I invested.

Finally, in an angel community, it is crucial to have a good relationship with the community managers, as they facilitate all the activities of the angel community, and can provide extremely valuable tips. They are a very useful asset and need to be considered as key to the business.

Conclusions

When dealing with startups, angels must choose a behavior/a strategy that deals continuously with the ability to best apply our general three pillar model on a daily basis.

Therefore, it is crucial for an angel to have solid evaluation skills. Some tools are already available to assist angels. Some angel groups with whom I have had dealings use a sort of "due diligence" questionnaire for all key questions. All the pre-made tools I have encountered involve assessing whether or not the startup complies with the three pillar model success keys.

Beyond any off-the-shelf tool, since decisions at the end are personal, in my personal experience, I do have a few questions I ask myself before I decide whether or not to proceed with the investment/follow-up:

1. Do the startup leaders (still) believe in the success of the target startup? What energy level do I perceive from the target startup?
2. Is the market (still) responsive/potentially ready for the target startup?
3. Would I regret it if I lose money in the target startup? Is this investment worthwhile compared with other available startup investment opportunities?

Finally, angel investing can be very rewarding, if the behavior/strategy identified allows to obtain returns measured by a combination of financial results, network expansion, and business opportunities generated.

Connectivity Challenges in the Pharmaceutical Industry: A Case Study

Marie Schmidt

Abstract

The article highlights the complexity of innovative processes and their demands on individual abilities using the example of market access for innovative pharmaceuticals, which she explains in detail. At a time when innovative companies must find flexible solutions to ever-changing market dynamics, the ability of connectivity constitutes a key success factor. Companies' strategic orientation and the operational goals of individual employees require continuous review and (re-)alignment. In the era of connectivity, strategies, organizational structures, and connected tasks of single employees must enable agility in order to create successful innovative processes.

The editors of the book introduce **Marie Schmidt** who is working as Associate Director Market Access EMEA in a global research-based pharmaceutical and device company where she is leading pricing and reimbursement processes of innovative medicines and medical devices. She studied Health Economics at the University of Rotterdam and SDA Bocconi School of Management.

Foreword

In the introduction chapter of the book, the three pillar model for organization and leadership was developed (shared sustainable purpose within the organization, ability to act as a "traveling organization" with high content-based and mental

M. Schmidt (✉)
Santen, Osaka, Japan

© Springer Nature Switzerland AG 2020
P. Wollmann et al. (eds.), *Three Pillars of Organization and Leadership in Disruptive Times*, Future of Business and Finance,
https://doi.org/10.1007/978-3-030-23227-6_19

flexibility in an appropriate moving environment and a huge connectivity mindset and skills). The interplay of these pillars can be well observed when studying the development process of medical products and the personal characteristics of project teams responsible for the respective processes for these are never linear but based on the aggregated knowledge of biochemical and other processes and often result from the failure of previous research hypotheses. Accordingly, the sustainable purpose as the general direction and the traveling organization as the necessary explorative and creative flexibility are a necessary precondition for successful innovations.

The case study below explores the need for collaboration across product development stages as well as organizational entities in order to ensure innovations have access to European healthcare markets. It therefore primarily focuses on the third factor "connectivity." It aims to illustrate the connectivity of markets (*environmental*) conditioning the connectivity demand on organizations (*organizational*) and the challenge for individuals (*individual*) working in this environment:

The mindset and skill set related to connectivity strongly conditions the commercial success of innovations and their availability to patients. The necessary "psychological preconditions for connectivity" are subsequently described in Hannspeter Schmidt's article "Psychological Capabilities Required for Connectivity" which was originally written as the second part of this article but removed because of its overarching importance for other articles too.

Introduction

Connectivity is a challenge for international, innovative organizations and their employees: International companies are challenged to develop consistent strategies for highly complex and interdependent markets; employees working in these complex structures require the personal abilities and psychological characteristics to successfully implement and achieve company goals. This article aims to illustrate the demands of successfully managing connectivity on companies as well as on an employee's psychological capabilities. It focuses on implications of connectivity for organizations with the example of a case study from the pharmaceutical industry.

The European pharmaceutical market is highly regulated by supranational and national authorities. In order to bring a new medicine onto the market, the *European Medicines Agency* (EMA) first needs to grant the market authorization (MA) approval based on available clinical data. The MA acknowledges that the product satisfies all scientific requirements and complies with the relevant European legal and legislative standards for it to be marketed in Europe. However, unlike other markets, MA approval of medicinal innovations does not automatically effect their usage and/or sales. As social security schemes across Europe require citizens to have health insurance, the cost of medicines is mostly covered by public health insurers. National reimbursement authorities in each European member state independently initiate clinical and economic value assessments referred to as *Health Technology Assessments* (HTAs), in order to determine the reimbursement status of the new medicine. Positive reimbursement status is the prerequisite for market uptake, based on patient usage through prescriptions. Subsequent to the HTA, authorities and manufacturers negotiate the price which is composed of, first, the HTA outcome and, second, the average price of a specific country cluster. The latter component, also referred to as *International Reference Pricing* (IRP), induces that pricing for pharmaceutical innovations is unique compared to other products as it reflects a high level of connectivity in terms of market alignment. IRP is performed by low-income as well as high-income countries applying different calculations using average prices, lowest prices among specific clusters or other paradigms. Strong connectivity of healthcare markets across Europe precedes the effective application of IPR which, in turn, demands intensive organizational alignment. International pharmaceutical companies are required to reflect the same level of connectivity as the market in order to anticipate decisions and ensure agility as the key to long-term profitability. Horizontal (affiliates) and vertical (departments) collaboration across organizational entities is one key factor to succeed in mirroring connectivity; the other key factor is collaboration across product development stages, which usually goes in hand with vertical collaboration. The following practical example aims to illustrate the connectivity of markets (*environmental*) conditioning the connectivity demand on organizations (*organizational*) and the challenge for individuals (*individual*) working in this environment:

Case Study

Environmental Connectivity (1): The European Pharmaceutical Market Reveals a Considerable Level of Connectivity

After having obtained MA approval from the EMA, a pharmaceutical company applies for reimbursement from the respective national authorities to ensure uptake at launch. Without reimbursement approval, the company's turnover with product A would rely on out-of-pocket payments or private insurance arrangements, meaning the market for the product would be considerably limited. As each country determines its own reimbursement process and coverage, the company has to apply for reimbursement in each country separately. The countries remain independent with regard to their reimbursement decisions, whereas subsequent IRP processes reveal a strong level of connectivity and, by definition, create dependencies across markets; by referencing prices of other country clusters, they base their pricing decisions on other countries' pricing decisions. Reference prices are calculated in various ways: either by building average cluster prices or using lowest prices of clusters as a reference price. Figure 1 shows the country clusters that each member state refers to in one or the other way when setting prices for new or existing pharmaceuticals.

More explicitly, when the company applies for reimbursement in Country X, as the first applicant country, the price setting is typically structured by using an existing competitor product (patent-protected or generic) as a price anchor. Sometimes, previous product clusters represent reference price groups to which product A can be allocated in terms of pricing as well. Apart from using competitor prices as a

	AT	BE	BU	CH	CY	CZ	DE	DK	EE	EL	ES	FI	FR	HR	HU	IE	IS	IT	LT	LU	LV	MT	NL	NO	PL	PT	RO	SE	SI	SK	UK	Add. countries	N. of countries
AT		■			■	■	■	■	■	■	■	■	■		■	■		■	■	■	■	■	■		■	■		■	■	■	■		24
BE	■		■		■	■	■	■	■	■	■	■	■		■	■		■	■	■	■	■	■		■	■	■	■	■	■	■	Or Country of origin	26
BU								■	■	■	■	■	■					■	■							■	■		■	■			12
CH	■						■	■					■										■								■		6
CY	■									■			■															■					4
CZ		■						■		■	■	■	■	■	■	■		■	■		■		■		■	■		■	■	■	■		19
DE	■	■				■		■		■	■	■	■			■		■					■			■		■		■	■		15
DK	■	■					■					■				■							■	■				■			■		9
EE															■				■		■											Country of origin	4
EL	■	■	■		■	■	■				■	■	■		■	■		■	■	■	■		■		■	■	■		■	■	■		22
ES	■	■			■		■		■	■		■	■			■		■		■		■	■			■			■	■		Eurozone but not regulated	16
FI	■	■	■		■	■	■	■	■	■	■		■		■	■	■	■	■	■	■	■	■	■	■	■	■	■	■	■	■	Liechtenstein	29
FR							■				■							■													■		4
HR													■					■											■				3
HU	■	■	■	■	■	■	■	■	■	■	■	■	■	■		■	■	■	■	■	■	■	■	■	■	■	■	■	■	■	■	Liechtenstein	31
IE	■	■					■	■			■	■	■										■								■		9
IS								■				■												■				■					4
IT	■	■	■		■	■	■	■	■	■	■	■	■	■	■	■			■	■	■	■	■		■	■	■	■	■	■	■		27
LT			■			■			■						■						■				■		■			■			8
LU																																Country of origin	1
LV						■		■	■						■				■								■			■			7
MT					■	■			■		■				■			■	■							■			■	■	■	Public sector*	11
NL		■					■						■																		■		4
NO	■	■					■	■				■				■							■					■			■		9
PL	■	■	■	■	■	■	■	■	■	■	■	■	■	■	■	■	■	■	■	■	■	■	■	■		■	■	■	■	■	■	Liechtenstein	31
PT											■		■																	■			3
RO	■	■	■			■	■			■	■				■			■	■						■					■			12
SE																																	n/a
SI	■						■						■																				3
SK	■	■	■		■	■	■	■	■	■	■	■	■	■	■	■		■	■	■	■	■	■		■	■	■	■	■		■		27
UK																																	n/a
Reference frequency	16	15	9	2	10	13	17	15	12	13	16	15	19	5	13	13	3	15	14	9	11	8	15	6	10	13	10	13	13	16	17		

*For private sector in Malta, data from 12 European reference countries, classified in a three-tier system, is used for ERP: Low- priced tier: ES; UK; PT; FR/Medium-priced tier: BE; IS; CY; IT/High-priced tier: DK; DE; IE; NO. AT, Austria; BE, Belgium; BG, Bulgaria; CH, Switzerland; CY, Cyprus; CZ, Czech Republic; DE, Germany; DK, Denmark; EE, Estonia; EL, Greece; ES, Spain; FI, Finland; FR, France; HR, Croatia; HU, Hungary; IE, Ireland; IS, Iceland; IT, Italy; LT, Lithuania; LU, Luxembourg; LV, Latvia; MT, Malta; NL, the Netherlands; NO, Norway; PL, Poland; PT, Portugal; RO, Romania; SE, Sweden; SI, Slovenia; SK, Slovakia; UK, United Kingdom

Fig. 1 Overview of country baskets as basis for IRP in Europe (Efpia 2017; European Commission 2013)

price anchor for product A, authorities in country X would further reference prices of product A in prior determined EU countries. Thereby, economically prosperous countries would reference high-price countries while countries with limited GDP would reference low price markets. In summary, the price is set in relation to the prices of the therapeutic product class including competitors as well as prices of the same product in other countries. This mechanism is referred to as *International Reference Pricing* (IRP) in the pharmaceutical industry.

Sequencing the launch and reimbursement applications of product A according to pricing potentials in the different countries allows the company to control prices at the time of the initial launch. Throughout the life cycle of product A, countries foresee regular price adjustments whereby the country basket prices are updated and prices in each country possibly adjusted in case of price decreases in other countries. This typically brings about a continuous long-term downward pricing spiral across countries. Recurring price revisions and adjustments are processes that illustrate the continual nature of connectivity.

Environmental Connectivity (2): Further Harmonization Efforts Are Required from Reimbursement Authorities to Ensure Equal Access to Innovations

The demand for increased connectivity of European reimbursement bodies is a consequence of price decisions not only being based on IRP but also on HTA outcomes. This leads to unequal reimbursement and pricing decisions and/or patient access across Europe. National diversity of methodological approaches toward study design and value assignment is criticized as jeopardizing investment in innovations. Currently, HTA decisions as well as prices for innovations are heavily diverging across member states, leading to unequal access to medicines for European citizens and uncertainty around return on investment for companies. Connectivity amongst HTA authorities as well as between HTA authorities and companies is necessary to reduce uncertainty around reimbursement and pricing processes. As a consequence, this would foster transparency in favor of innovation investment and patient care. The European Network for Health Technology Assessment (EUnetHTA) established its joint action 3, aiming to implement a sustainable model for scientific and technical collaboration on HTA between national and regional HTA bodies across European member states by 2020 (EUnetHTA 2017). Throughout the past, EUnetHTA's working groups have developed various tools to support the conduct of joint assessments with regard to evidence collection, validation, and benchmarking. However, in contrast to the common practice of centralized regulatory assessments performed by the European Medicines Agency (EMA), joint HTA assessments so far remain a theoretical concept. Member states are concerned that, by committing to a common methodological framework which defines thresholds and study requirements in relation to the additional benefit of innovations, they would forfeit their sovereignty with regard to price setting as well.

The flexibility of negotiating country-specific prices in relation to the assessed benefit and against the background of national ability-to-pay leads to strongly diverging prices across Europe, which would certainly be challenged when implementing a consistent HTA concept. Previous efforts to homogenize HTA approaches to increase connectivity showed that voluntary connectivity amongst European HTA bodies is perceived as being beneficial to gain transparency and improve information exchange but, when it leads to the establishment of binding concepts as a consequence of inconsistent access to innovations across Europe, authorities or member states prefer to preserve the sovereignty of evidence evaluation practices. This conflict of interests can also be transferred to the individual connectivity level, where individuals support connective action that does not conflict with their personal goals. The individual scope of connectivity will be addressed in a separate section below.

Organizational Connectivity: Companies' Response to Increasing Environmental Connectivity

In the interest of companies' revenues, Market Access departments require strong expertise with regard to formal and informal price setting, whereby long-lasting relationships with national and regional authorities and other key decision-makers support the anticipation of pricing and reimbursement developments due to political trends and referencing practices. In addition to relationship building with external parties, companies foster horizontal and vertical collaboration across their own organization. Companies intensifying the level of connectivity between the different affiliates are referred to as "horizontal connectivity" in this article, while the establishment of cross-functional decision-making structures bridging early to late product development stages is referred to as "vertical connectivity." While R&D is commonly allocated on a global level, Medical Affairs and Market Access often drive their activities from a regional or even local level. Traditionally, the different departments have been engaged in different product phases which did not demand such high levels of organizational connectivity. In the meantime, Market Access departments have become increasingly involved in new business opportunity assessments and early product development processes in order to ensure that clinical study design and product characteristics are appropriate when coming to the market, allowing for broad (non-restricted) reimbursement and optimum pricing. Recent developments have shown that the more companies experienced difficulties in safeguarding the return on investment for innovative products by achieving adequate pricing and reimbursement decisions at launch, the more the focus was drawn to including pricing and reimbursement insights in early product development stages. The early alignment regarding reimbursement benchmarks primarily aims to anticipate, and subsequently influence, future HTA outcomes as a major basis for price setting. The effects of study design on reimbursement and subsequent pricing decisions are increasingly the subject of political debates within companies and European politics.

Individual Connectivity: Its Challenges and Drivers

The awareness that over 10 years of R&D efforts may not translate into commercial success if the study setup does not fulfill HTA requirements has placed market access at the center of pharmaceutical activities. It requires various departments such as R&D, Medical Affairs, Marketing, and Market Access to collaborate much more closely and create connectivity across all organizational levels. Successfully establishing Market Access for innovative products relies heavily on the level of connectivity of the respective functions within the organization and to external decision-making bodies.

Looking at pharmaceutical companies, pricing functions typically allocated within the Market Access departments require strong connectivity with country affiliations or other organizational entities as well as external partners across markets to anticipate pricing decisions and envisage holistic pricing strategies. Increasing regulations for pricing and reimbursement processes across member states and their growing impact on core pharmaceutical business planning necessitate increasing connectivity of Market Access employees, who constitute central functions in *traveling organizations* (*Definition in introduction*), clearly advocating given reimbursement requirements across product stages while ensuring flexibility when facing political changes in healthcare systems has a strong impact on reimbursement opportunities. Compliance with reimbursement standards increases the likelihood of subsequent commercial success; however, flexibility with regard to reimbursement success is required when negotiating reimbursement. Achieving optimal reimbursement coverage for the majority of patients eligible for specific medical innovations represents *the sustainable purpose* of individuals and requires a well-balanced personal approach between adherence to standards and a considerable level of agility to be able to respond to political dynamics. Establishing a successful balance between regulation conformity and negotiation flexibility necessitates strong personal sensitivity with clear benefit awareness.

Discussion

The conflict between the loss of "information sovereignty" induced by strong connectivity and the divergence of political interests that need to be pursued constitutes a barrier to connectivity, between departments, organizational entities, and HTA authorities. Connectivity will ultimately be experienced by organizations and individuals when the consequences of connectivity are perceived to leverage value for them. Therefore, it is crucial to discuss the consequences of connectivity for people's behavior as much as the personal prerequisites. The psychological challenges for individuals working in high connectivity-demanding environments are described in Hannspeter Schmidt's article "Psychological Capabilities Required for Connectivity."

References

Efpia. (2017). Retrieved from https://www.efpia.eu/about-medicines/use-of-medicines/hta-relative-efficacy-assessment/

EUnetHTA. (2017). Retrieved from http://www.eunethta.eu/activities/joint-action-3/jointaction31/eunethta-joint-action-3-2016-2020

European Commission. (2013). Retrieved from http://ec.europa.eu/health//sites/health/files/systems_performance_assessment/docs/erp_reimbursement_medicinal_products_en.pdf

Purpose, Journey Thinking, and Connectivity in Large Global Consultancies

Nicole Hoenig de Locarnini

Abstract

Nicole Hoenig de Locarnini stresses—based on research conducted in 2016/2017 as part of an executive education program at Oxford Saïd Business School in collaboration with HEC Paris—how in a more complex, connected world, the context of management consulting is significantly changing. Globalization, digitalization, changing client demands, and the impact of new ways of working require the business model for management consulting to be redefined, especially within the context of a "Big Four" company. The differentiator for a successful organization in the future is a redefinition of the partnership in terms of its structure and of the role of the individual partners as connectors and shapers as well as the increased importance of individual development in this context. In her article, the author develops a modular framework for transformation across the three dimensions of the individual, the organizational, and the market context.

The editors of the book introduce **Nicole Hoenig de Locarnini** who is a senior advisory member within one of the "Big Four" companies moving toward strategy consulting. To date, she has devoted her professional life to developing deep technical insurance/reinsurance expertise at a major global insurance company followed by a successful career in management consulting. Her work spans companies and business units within the financial services, life sciences, and producing industries.

N. H. de Locarnini (✉)
London, UK

© Springer Nature Switzerland AG 2020   181
P. Wollmann et al. (eds.), *Three Pillars of Organization and Leadership in Disruptive Times*, Future of Business and Finance,
https://doi.org/10.1007/978-3-030-23227-6_20

Introduction and Link to Our Three-Pillar Model

Connectivity in large professional services firms: Unlocking the potential power of partnership—when individual leaders become an assembly of superpowers

As already mentioned in the general introduction to the book, the business world is changing both drastically and quickly. It is obvious that professional services organizations and here management consulting firms are both subjects and objects of this disruptive development. On the one hand, more than other industries, they must ensure that they are among the first to understand the direction, key content, and the opportunities and risks of the forthcoming changes so that they are able to support their clients as well as possible.

In terms of our three-pillar model, the *sustainable purpose* of management consulting firms is obvious: to serve their clients as well as possible in delivering expertise, knowledge, temporary project resources, and success in the clients' key initiatives and helping them to meet their overarching enterprise targets.

This also includes special support—expertise, knowledge, and resources but also coaching and mentoring—for the clients' journey, which means, in terms of our three-pillar model, professional support of the clients' *traveling organization*. On the other hand, we will see that the management consulting firm itself is on a journey as a result of external factors (e.g., the changing business world) and internal factors (e.g., changing workforce demands/the high staff turnover)—so the term "traveling organization" has two meanings for a management consulting firm: it is something to cope with as an organization in its own right, and it is also something to help other organizations to cope with. This means, among other things, that management consulting firms and clients have some overlaps in their development journeys.

Under these circumstances, connectivity capabilities—*connecting resources*—are key because cooperation and managing interfaces are dominant in a knowledge-driven business as we will see below.

Executive Summary

In a more complex, connected world, the context of management consulting is changing. Globalization, digitalization, changing client demands and the impact of new ways of working requires a redefinition of the business model for management consulting, especially within the context of a "Big Four" company.

The differentiator for a successful organization in the future is a redefinition of the partnership in terms of its structure and of the role of the individual partners as connectors and shapers as well as the increased importance of individual development in this context.

Research conducted in 2016/2017 as part of an executive education program at Oxford Saïd Business School in collaboration with HEC Paris provides a modular framework for transformation across the three dimensions of the individual, the organizational, and the market context. The aim is to develop a lasting partnership as "aligned autonomy" in a network structure that is characterized by collaboration, with an emphasis on individual development, a redefinition of performance management and organizational learning. For reasons of confidentiality, the original dissertation is not accessible to the public but is available in a redacted version. Any references to interviewees within or outside of my firm have been removed. This chapter is based on some parts of this research with a short introduction to professional services firms, the changing situation of a global professional services firm, sustainable purpose, providing examples of organizational changes (the journey) as well as showcasing the need for connectivity in this complex environment.

Introduction to Professional Services Organizations

About 7 years ago, I began to explore opportunities for my next career move after 5 years in a large multinational insurance company. My mentor advised me to learn something that I had not learned before, so I decided to acquire some experience in a professional services firm (PSF): I opted for management consulting in the financial services sector at a "Big Four" company.

The "Big Four" are the four largest accounting firms and they handle accounting, tax, and advisory services for many public and private companies. The "Big Four" consist of PricewaterhouseCoopers (PwC), Deloitte Touche Tohmatsu Limited (Deloitte), KPMG, and Ernst & Young (EY). The "Big Four" were formed in 2002 after a series of mergers reduced the original eight PSFs down to four. In 2015, the "Big Four" had a global revenue of USD125 billion across all service lines (audit, tax, advisory, legal) with about 838,000 employees. By comparison, the largest global company by revenue is Walmart with revenues of USD482 billion and 2.3 million employees in 2015. By way of comparison, Allianz Insurance had global revenues of USD123 billion in 2015 with "only" 142,000 employees.

When talking to some of my peers working in other "Big Four" firms or management consulting firms, I realized that many characteristics of the organizations and their partners are the same. It is not possible to make a generalization regarding what we do. The work experience depends to a great extent on the individual partners, who are responsible for the internal teams and the projects they can sell to clients.

From an academic and organizational point of view, Morris and Empson (1998) define a PSF as "an organization that trades mainly on the knowledge of its human capital, i.e., its employees and the producer-owners, to develop and deliver intangible solutions to client problems." In "Managing the professional service firm," Maister (1993) describes the two characteristics that make PSFs different from any other company. First, most of the work demands a high level of customization, and second, professionals engage in a great deal of personal client interaction. *The Oxford Handbook of Professional Service Firms* was published in 2015 by Empson et al. as a collection of articles about PSFs, including their context, their management, their organization, and their intercompany interactions. In publishing this handbook of up-to-date research, the editors want to legitimize PSFs as a relevant area for academic study. "Despite their empirical significance and theoretical distinctiveness, for many years, PSFs remained very much in the shadows of organizational research" (Empson et al. 2015). It is difficult, if not impossible, to gain holistic information about the size of the industry, as most organizations are privately owned and not legally required to disclose financial information. For example, financial information on non-"Big Four" consulting provided by strategy firms (McKinsey, BCG) or IT consulting (Accenture, IBM) was not included due to lack of information. Moreover, it is a challenge to decide which companies to include for the management consulting market, due to issues of confidentiality, size, and geographical coverage. Furthermore, the market itself cannot be clearly defined.

Due to the nature of the business, PSFs prefer to work closely with their clients but to operate "under the radar" of public information and interest. Another aspect that makes academic research about PSFs difficult is the lack of clarity of what exactly a PSF is and what distinguishes it from other organizations. Empson et al. provide an updated definition of a PSF considering multiple scholarly perspectives. This definition provides four characteristics of PSFs. Figure 1 shows a visual representation of Empson et al.'s definition.

First, a PSF's primary activity is the application of knowledge for the development of customized solutions to clients' problems. Second, this knowledge comprises both specialist technical knowledge and in-depth knowledge about their clients. Third, a PSF's governance is characterized by extensive individual autonomy and contingent managerial authority. Fourth, a PSF's identity is shaped by its clients and other peers. Professionals within PSFs establish their reputation as experts in certain fields and are therefore recognized for these skills by their clients, who are willing to pay for these skills, and secondly by their peers both within and outside their organization.

The editors state that while "many organizations will possess some of these characteristics [. . .] a PSF will possess all of them to varying degrees" (Empson et al. 2015, p. 9).

Empson et al. also provide an integrative framework for analyzing PSFs, highlighting the complex power dynamics and tensions within the PSF and outside it. This framework is illustrated in Fig. 2.

PSFs are interconnected with their professionals who are directly responsible for the success of the PSF. Client demands need to be mapped with the PSFs' abilities to conduct business. Competitors are directly competing for the most relevant resources. Following the idea of the traveling organization, PSFs will, with this "in mind," be able to navigate this complexity whatever the market or competitors come up with.

Maister states that "professional services firms compete in two marketplaces; they compete for clients and they compete for staff" (1993, p. 189), which are both equally important and intertwined. Professional regulators, especially in the context of a "Big Four" organization, provide potential challenges to the PSF due to its multidisciplinary structure. "Big Four" organizations are based on the traditional audit business and are therefore potentially always in a conflict of independence with their management consulting service line(s). The auditor's duty is to uphold the

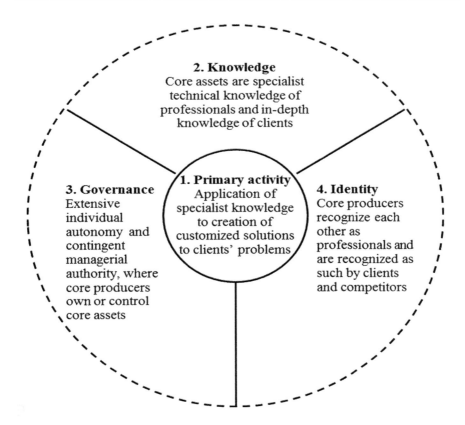

Fig. 1 Defining characteristics of a PSF as differentiator to other professions (Figure: from Author's thesis at HEC Paris—Oxford Saïd Business School "Unlocking the potential power of partnership—when individual leaders become an assembly of superpowers") [adapted by author from Empson et al. (2015)]

public interest, whereas the consultant's duty is client satisfaction. The different elements of a PSF shape its organizational practice, but their demands can conflict. Many professional services firms are managed as partnerships. With the creation of the public corporation in the nineteenth century, the partnership developed as the predominant form of organizational governance (Greenwood and Empson 2003). Gage (2004) states that "the most exciting advantage of partnership is the potential it creates for synergy" (p. 7) and that partners should handle their work according to their individual strengths and preferences (p. 9). In his view, the key factor for a successful partnership is simple: "ask people in a successful partnership what makes it work so well and they are very likely to respond with 'trust'" (p. 45). The concept of trust and psychological security was examined in great detail as part of this research but, owing to the narrower focus of this chapter, is not detailed here.

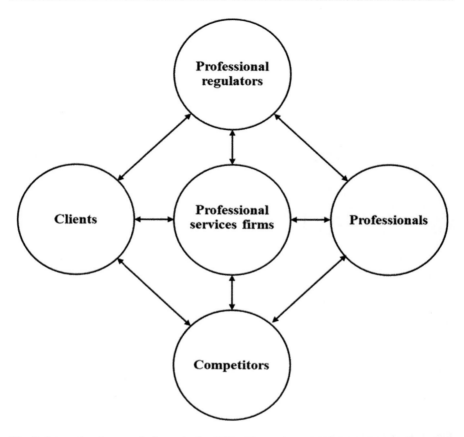

Fig. 2 Integrative framework for analyzing PSFs (Figure: from Author's thesis at HEC Paris—Oxford Saïd Business School "Unlocking the potential power of partnership—when individual leaders become an assembly of superpowers") [adapted by author from Empson et al. (2015)]

According to Maister (1993), every PSF has only three goals: "outstanding service to clients, satisfying careers for its people and financial success for its owners" (p. 223). When referring to owners in a PSF, in the "Big Four" and most management consulting firms, these are the partners. In Maister's view, PSFs mirror medieval guild structures, which used a hierarchy of apprentices, journeymen, and masters. The company's profitability drops significantly when senior people fail to delegate routine jobs to more junior people. He claims that "people do not join professional services firms for jobs but for careers" (p. 129). The turnover rates in organizations like my organization is about 15–20% on an annual basis. Some firms intentionally use a high turnover strategy to find and retain the best people. In this way, partners can make more money from junior people without the immediate prospect of promoting them. If a PSF has a good reputation, more people will want to join it and although they know that their chances of promotion might be small, they believe they can benefit from just being at the firm and having it on their resumé.

Today's Challenges for Professional Services Firms: Redefining Business Models and Transforming Themselves

Today's world is increasingly complex, due to a higher level of connectivity, a constant (over)flow of information, and the speed of transmission of all kinds of information. It is a VUCA world: a world of volatility, uncertainty, complexity, and ambiguity, which has a significant impact both on individuals and on society in general. PSFs in the management consulting sector have experienced growth over the last few years, despite significant changes in terms of technology and legislation. This has put the industry in a good position, but there are still challenges, and like every professional services industry, management consulting is defined by the needs of its client's—as they change, so too must the industry. For the upcoming journey, the focus of PSF must be on enhancing their operational processes and "doing more with less." For many, the key to success lies in implementing a comprehensive transformation and digitalization within a newly embedded ecosystem.

One of the primary challenges the PSF industry faces is the growing separation of the market into two distinct parts—a low-cost, commoditized business section which is more and more being covered by near- and offshore business units (often located in more emerging markets) and a high-value, holistic knowledge consulting section. Another challenge is that the speed of development in digital technologies is creating new business models at a faster rate than many current PSF company structures can cope with. Planning and completing a successful digital transformation means that larger consulting firms have to embrace an innovative mind-set to empower its organization to differentiate—and ultimately providing greater value to clients. Adopting a "fail fast" mind-set is not necessarily part of the skill set of today's management consultants. There are also other elements outside their own transformation that PSF firms must consider on their future journey as they work toward revenue and business growth:

- The first being the ongoing war for talent. Competition is fierce, and many firms have been forced to do one of two things—either explore service and product offerings that do not rely on their ability to sell people or look outside the traditional talent recruitment pool of universities and focus more on skills than qualifications.
- The second factor is the need for collaboration. As specialist and disruptor firms appear it becomes more apparent that, to succeed, PSF firms will need to partner with each other in order to meet the full breadth of client demands—within their own organization (as dispersed local firms and regions) and outside their own organization. This does not solely mean a large firm partnering with, or acquiring, various start-ups—more and more it is about a firm partnering with technology or academic partners to widen the scope of potential client experience.

- The third factor is the consideration on how to move away from traditional "body-selling"' business models to an output-focused model that shares risks and rewards with clients. Today's client requirements have changed in the sense that traditional consulting no longer works with "out-of-the-box solutions" that just have to be "plugged in" to the clients' organization. Increasingly, there is a demand for co-creation and co-design as neither the client nor the consulting firm has done exactly this project before; yet there is the trust that, somewhere in an organization of 250,000 consultants, someone might have conducted a similar project where the knowledge can be applied to this new client situation. This is the core strength of an international PSF when done well—connectivity.

For our clients, one of the biggest challenges is industry convergence. There is a need to be connected so as to cross-leverage and understand "connectors." Industry convergence is largely the outcome of evolutions in technology and consumer behavior. The disruption caused by digitalization and hyper-connectivity creates a business landscape where previously distinct or separate industries begin to converge—changing their traditional services and methods of operation because of competition from new, digitally enabled business models. We are seeing a new wave of industries being redefined as supplier and customer relationships continue to be challenged. Healthcare, energy, and financial services are prime examples of industries that were traditionally ruled by a few corporations but have seen new entrants from other sectors and start-ups. Industry disruption and convergence are happening at an unprecedented pace. Convergence is not only blurring the lines between industries, it is also creating new markets and new opportunities for companies or governments to grow and compete in a world where everything is connected. One of the most significant symptoms of convergence is ecosystems. Companies used to compete within one core industry; however, as issues become more complex and technology allows new entrants, ecosystem collaboration is becoming the new normal. Several large companies are investing in other entities to give them the opportunity to experiment with more agile processes, risky new propositions and cutting-edge technology. This is particularly prevalent in the healthcare industry where a lot of R&D is now being undertaken through alliances. The role of the management consultants, who have a holistic market overview, is to act as facilitators and connectors to create the "right" connections—thinking with, for, and one step ahead of our clients—through the different market perspectives and insights we get from our numerous projects. Various examples can be observed in merging, e.g., insurance and life sciences companies or bringing quantitative models used in the financial services industry to the producing industry with great success thanks to the increased use of data and predictive analytics.

Management Consulting as a Context for Constant Change: Being Continuously on a Journey

In his article, "Consulting on the cusp of disruption" in the *Harvard Business Review* (2013), Christensen highlights that a disruption of the management consulting industry is inevitable. Yet, many consultants interviewed stated the difficulty of "getting large partnerships to agree on revolutionary strategies" (p. 10). He stated that the primary assets of management consulting "are human capital and their fixed investments are minimal" (p. 5). The only asset or "product" the companies possess is their employees. These employees are directly linked to the company's performance measurement. The management consulting industry has a constantly high influx of new, highly motivated young talent. People are usually hired at the lower ranks of the organization. Internal growth opportunities are then provided by the organization and the "organizational pyramid" is maintained. A constant number of people also drop out of these organizations due to, for example, a change in lifestyle or because they receive other offers (Maister 1993). Consulting still has an "up or out" mentality, although this is currently changing with the ambition to attract diverse talent (from normal business management to strong IT skills) and to provide different career paths with more flexibility. Newer talent has different expectations and organizations increasingly struggle to attract exceptional talent as the organizational set-up is still very hierarchical and linear in terms of promotion. In his article "When McKinsey met Uber: the gig economy comes to consulting" (2016), Hill describes the rise of young freelancers that have been trained in large consulting companies and are changing the consulting market. According to his survey of 100 independent consultants, 59% stated a career change, higher flexibility and working with clients in a different way as main drivers for independence. In terms of future workforce planning, different engagement models need to be considered.

The average annual staff turnover rate in the management consulting industry is about 15–20% (Batchelor 2011). Every fifth or sixth person hired will leave the organization within a year. Management consulting organizations are trying to overcome this fact by establishing a unique "culture" for the members of the organization. My own organization recently rebranded its mission statement to "EY—Building a better working world." This statement is meant to express a common understanding that is built on shared assumptions and beliefs, and on the norms and interpretations of what EY is. Furthermore, it means that a person knows what they can expect when they work with another person from EY anywhere in the world. With increasingly complex activities and working across regional boundaries, the individual's contribution to the team success is hard to measure. "The more people collaborate, the harder it becomes to determine who contributed what to the ultimate solution" (Morieux and Tollman 2014, p. 14). Furthermore, new business models in consulting arise with the emergence of alternative PSFs working with (senior) freelancers on talent platforms that are often required to work with an existing project team (Christensen et al. 2013).

The Self in Management Consulting: Emotional Intelligence as Enabler for Connectivity

Runde (2016) claims in a *Harvard Business Review* article that the critical distinguishing factor for advancing in professional services is emotional intelligence. Emotional intelligence is the ability to monitor one's own and other people's emotions and to use this information to guide thinking and related behavior. Goleman wrote in 1998 that "without it, a person can have the best training in the world, an incisive, analytical mind and an endless supply of smart ideas but he still won't make a great leader." In today's more complex and global business environment, stronger communication across multiple boundaries is required. Emotional intelligence is described by Runde as a combination of adaptability (relationship with self—self-awareness), collegiality (relations with colleagues—collaboration), and empathy (relationship with clients). Self-awareness is the ability to understand strengths and weaknesses and to recognize emotions and how they affect thoughts and behaviors. In the management consulting environment, self-awareness helps one to adapt to several different supervisors, colleagues, clients, and working styles, which is inherently built into the management consulting working model consisting as it does of varying projects and project teams. Collaboration is essential in management consulting, as most of the work is done in teams, regardless of the rank of the individual. Teams are becoming global and diverse and the workplace itself is becoming more virtual. Teams are also becoming larger as they attempt to solve complex client problems that span functions and sometimes even industries. It is important for team members to respect each other's ability and perspectives. Goleman states that empathy is understanding what others are feeling. "Empathy allows you to build trust with your clients—and this is the most challenging and underappreciated part of any job in the professional services industry" (Runde, p. 3).

In management consulting, the challenge is to encourage the client to tell you their actual problem. From his perspective, similar to Maister, "the key to winning business is getting the client to trust or like you enough that they will tell you what issues are worrying them" (Maister 1993, p. 3). Runde (2016) considers the ability to listen the most important capability and he distinguishes two types—those who listen to respond ("encyclopedia") and those who listen to listen ("empathizer"). The encyclopedia listens to provide the client with his knowledge, whereas the empathizer listens to understand the issues and then asks the right questions. These are skills that can be learned, and they are an important success factor for partners in management consulting. In the past, "the lone wolf" was a common pattern for highly successful partners, yet today "hunting in a wolf pack" is required as large scale, and complex problem-solving skills are not the remit of just one partner but rather of teams of subject matter experts covering all angles of client issues. In the research, the partnership in a PSF was compared to a football (soccer) team. In the past, the German football team, for example, would have had two or three stars, and the rest of the team would have comprised good yet run-of-the-mill players. In today's national team, every single player in each position is a highly trained, excellent star in his own right. Yet, the common team purpose is aligned around winning the match.

Partners are co-owners of the organization, and following various statements by key managing partners from my own, but also other management consulting organizations, the partnership is still viewed as the best possible company model since it provides a key sense of ownership and responsibility among the individual partners. This influence is much higher than in a normal corporation and provides a high degree of flexibility and agility.

From my perspective, there is often not yet enough leadership and understanding of the new era of complexity. This is especially evidenced by the fact that partners are often not yet able to think in network and collaboration structures and have old belief systems rooted in "hard" facts, such as their own incentivization. Empson et al. (2015) highlight that PSFs present distinctive leadership challenges given the professionals' traditional expectation of liberation from organizational constraints. It is argued that leadership in PSFs manifests itself "explicitly through professional expertise, discretely through political interaction, and implicitly through personal embodiment" (p. 19). However, they state that these traits are "rarely combined in single individuals, which gives rise to the prevalence of collective forms of leadership supported by embedded mechanism[s] of social control" (p. 19).

Instead of maintaining the "old" ways of partnership, where co-ownership is seen as having control over a portion of the (local) business, I am redefining the main role of the partners as connectors for the business (Fig. 3). It is their main role to connect the old and the new, technology and people, different business fields, and people with different knowledge and expertise. In this way, partners encourage others in the organization to collaborate. Diverse partners connect different areas, and, in this connection, they increase productivity. Accordingly, the focus lies on connections and not on single boxes drawn on organizational charts. In this model, accountability is achieved through a limited number of roles and responsibilities with clear decision-making power and simple KPIs.

I do not intend to go into too much detail here (as this would be an entire new chapter) yet the mainly dominant individual performance management system for partners in the management consulting industry was highlighted in the interviews as being one of the main inhibitors for collaboration as well as a lack of lack of long-term business focus as the incentive scheme is based on an annual result basis. Different metrics and objectives must be developed between different roles (sales roles, delivery roles, development roles) as one cannot exist without the other (and not all skills are usually found in one individual partner) and the interplay is crucial, creating reciprocity.

To create an approach for developing an innovative and collaborative culture to lay the foundation of a future-proof traveling organization, I am leveraging the concept of alignment and autonomy. Individual partners put their autonomy at the (best) service of the group. The "best service" is defined by a sustainable purpose and translates to a compelling vision and strategy. Alignment is used in the sense of alignment toward a common purpose, goal, or vision. Today's most successful

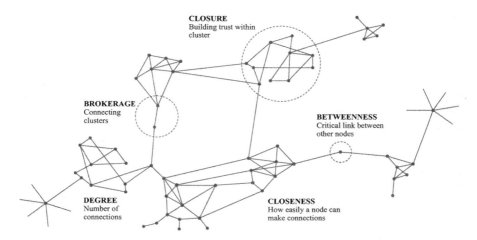

Fig. 3 The connected company—[Figure: adapted by author from Gray and Vander Wal (2012)]—It shows a general architecture of a connected enterprise. This architecture must be concretized and tailored for each industry, and even each enterprise, to make it operational

technology companies operate under this paradigm. Spotify's agile coach Kniberg (2016) developed a model (Fig. 4) to explain Spotify's successful business model.

An organization with low autonomy and low alignment is a micromanaged organization with an indifferent culture. High autonomy and low alignment lead to an entrepreneurial organization with a chaotic culture due to the lack of clear direction. Low autonomy and high alignment form an authoritative organization and lead to a conformist culture. High autonomy and high alignment—in short, aligned autonomy—lead to an innovative organization with a collaborative culture aiming for a common goal.

Full autonomy in any organization can lead to a duplication of tasks. Therefore, appropriate communication and knowledge-sharing mechanisms need to be in place to ensure organizational learning without sacrificing too much autonomy in the organization.

The disruption of management consulting is not hypothetical despite having already undergone periods of change on all sides by competitors and new technologies. Management consultants have maintained status and growth through prestige, branding, and long-time client relationships but, ultimately, they are no more immune to the forces of disruption than any other industry especially because of the forces relating to the future of work and various emerging facilitated networks of well-trained and specialized freelance consultants. Every day, there are more ex-consultants pursuing a more balanced lifestyle who are ready to share their expertise. Every day, the tools that companies can use to form their strategy improve and become more advanced. And every day, consulting firms need to prove that they can be relevant in this new world—and not simply because of their prestigious name. With a sustainable purpose, with the understanding that the organization is on a continuous journey in pursuit of the optimum outcome and finally with better ways

Fig. 4 Organizational implications of autonomy and alignment [Figure: adapted by author from Kniberg (2016)]

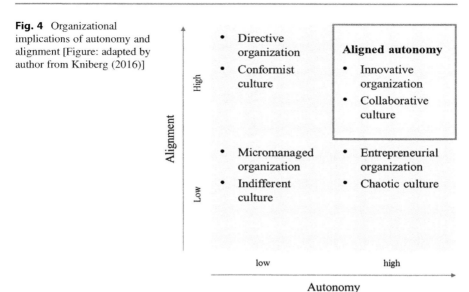

of connecting available resources within and outside the organization, I believe that PSFs are nowadays well equipped to play a redefined role in today's exponentially changing world.

References

Batchelor, Ch. (2011). *'Up or out' is part of industry culture*. Retrieved from www.ft.com, http://www.ft.com/cms/s/0/d42434b2-6b69-11e0-a53e-00144feab49a.html#axzz4GZZRwI00

Christensen, C., Wang, D., & van Bever, D. (2013). Consulting on the cusp of disruption. *Harvard Business Review, 91*(10), 106–114.

Empson, L., Muzio, D., Broschak, J., & Hinings, B. (2015). Researching professional service firms: An introduction and overview. In *The Oxford handbook of professional service firms*. Oxford: Oxford University Press, pp. 1–24.

Gage, D. (2004). *The partnership charter*. New York: Basic Books/Perseus Books.

Gray, D., & Vander Wal, T. (2012). *The connected company*. Sebastopol, CA: O'Reilly & Associates.

Greenwood, R., & Empson, L. (2003). The professional partnership: Relic or exemplary form of governance? *Organization Studies, 24*(6), 909–933.

Hill, M. (2016). *When McKinsey met Uber: The gig economy comes to consulting*. Retrieved from ft.com: https://www.ft.com/content/a5419fca-7f24-11e6-bc52-0c7211ef3198

Kniberg, H. (2016). *How Spotify built one of the best engineering cultures*. Retrieved from highfive.com: https://highfive.com/blog/how-spotify-built-one-of-the-best-engineering-cultures/

Maister, D. (1993). *Managing the professional service firm*. New York: Simon & Schuster.

Morieux, Y., & Tollman, P. (2014). *Six simple rules*. Boston, MA: Harvard Business Review Press.

Morris, T., & Empson, L. (1998). Organisation and expertise: An exploration of knowledge bases and the management of accounting and consulting firms. *Accounting, Organizations and Society, 23*(5–6), 609–624.

Runde, J. (2016). Emotional intelligence. Why young bankers, lawyers, and consultants need emotional intelligence. *Harvard Business Review*, 10/2016 (HBR account download).

Revisiting Shared Governance at a Community College in the USA

Sharon Lalla

Abstract

Sharon Lalla describes a striking case of a College in the USA, the environment of which presented significant weaknesses that resulted in isolation, loss of trust, lack of transparency, and lack of empowerment among its constituents. As this situation started to become a risk for the College's accreditation, urgent measures had to be taken with a focus on shared governance. Sharon Lalla shows that when shared governance is missing or ineffective, a radical transformation of the College's culture is crucial. Effective shared governance has been proven to create a sustaining traveling organization in higher education systems. This is why accreditors require it. When there is no or weak shared governance practices, there are few or even no checks and balances in place. Members at all levels, including the highest decision-making levels, need to be transparent about issues and policies that can potentially have an impact on the organization.

The editors of the book introduce **Sharon Lalla** who has worked in industry and higher education for over 30 years. After being awarded a doctorate in education technologies at Pepperdine University, Sharon became a college professor and took a leadership role in the administration of education technologies at New Mexico State University. Currently, Sharon is a New Leadership Academy Fellow and was Vice President of Instruction at Luna Community College at Las Vegas, New Mexico, from July 2016 to June 2019.

S. Lalla (✉)
Luna Community College, Las Vegas, NM, USA

© Springer Nature Switzerland AG 2020
P. Wollmann et al. (eds.), *Three Pillars of Organization and Leadership in Disruptive Times*, Future of Business and Finance,
https://doi.org/10.1007/978-3-030-23227-6_21

Executive Summary

Upon my arrival at the College 3 years ago, it was obvious that the college environment exhibited significant weaknesses which resulted in isolation, loss of trust, lack of transparency, and lack of empowerment among its constituents. To ensure that every higher educational system is prepared to deliver quality education, accreditors are periodically assigned by region to evaluate the fiscal and educational quality of an institution. In October of 2017, our accreditor found significant reason to place our College on a Show-Cause notice—a sanction that is closest to shutting down the institution. Among severe findings was a lack of shared governance. It is well known and commonly practiced in higher educational systems in the USA that shared governance is not only a best practice but also a requirement. According to Bahls (2018), alignment created by shared governance is ineffective if important constituencies are left out of the process (p. 14). As a result, accreditation reviewers explicitly look for shared governance in a number of key criteria which are used to evaluate the quality of a higher educational institution. Without a formal shared governance model in place that is fully transparent and explicit, it is commonly believed that the institution will have a severe breakdown in (1) trust among its leaders and with one another, (2) essential communication, and (3) buy-in to new ideas and changes.

When shared governance is not present or ineffective, the practice of shared governance can require a radical transformation of the College's culture. This article supports the importance of a formal shared governance model, describes the model, and presents experiences toward this transformation. The revised shared governance model is embryonic in its implementation; however, the campus groups are working together to re-create the axle necessary to sustain a traveling organization.

Introduction

The ultimate mission of higher education systems is to disseminate knowledge and prepare students to become productive citizens (Gerber 2001); however, a shared governance structure plays a significant role in determining the effectiveness of a College in supporting its ultimate mission. The concept of shared governance is not new. Its intent is to give voice to the major groups in a higher education system. These major groups not only include the governing Board of Trustees and the President, but also the Students, Faculty, and Staff. If these internal members of the higher educational system participate in the decision-making process, it is believed that trust and a greater degree of buy-in will occur (MacTaggart 2018, p. 9) despite the continual changes and major disruptions afforded by societal challenges.

The Problem

In 2015, the College accreditation report acknowledged a gap in the College's shared governance structure. It was listed as a concern and would require attention prior to the next accreditation review which was to occur in 2019. While it was identified as a concern, it was not escalated at the time. In 2016, several essential committees were established that included involvement from the student body, faculty, staff, and administration. The committees were approved by the President and then formed. In those committees, issues were discussed and decisions or recommendations were made in areas concerning classroom technology, tutoring services, distance education, and institutional analysis. Minutes were recorded and placed on the College website. In 2017, when our Accrediting agency received a number of complaints regarding the Board of Trustees' actions, they made a second visit followed by a serious sanction against the College. It had been common knowledge that actions by Board of Trustees and leadership had been questionable for several years, yet, the campus and its community remained silent. It was not until the accreditation team placed a Show-Cause order on the college that a sense of urgency was imminent. The College had 90 days to respond to the findings and present evidence of substantial change or close campus.

A Sense of Urgency

There is nothing like an ultimatum that could potentially result in devastating results to create a sense of urgency and lead a diverse group toward action. This is what the sanction did. At the time of the show-cause, an Interim President was in place. To make a transformation quickly, it was imperative that a large number of people work together and quickly. As a result, an initial committee consisting of 13 faculty, staff, and administrators was created to begin the work of finding evidence for 5 criteria consisting of 21 core components.

We began by appealing to the committee members recollection of "better days" to produce a collective vision for the hard work that was yet to come and that was essential to a sustainable practice. Although accreditation was the impetus for a much needed and speedy transformation of the College, it was essential to hone in on the vision that first bound the initial accreditation committee of 13 to a shared vision.

Scenario: Describe a Shared Vision

As part of an initial exercise, the 13-member accreditation team, which consisted of faculty, staff, and administration, were asked to shift their perspective from anger to possibility. We only had 90 days, and it was essential that all 13 members were committed to the work on which we were about to embark. Through a process of self-discovery, each member used narrative to describe what they considered to be exceptionally positive moments as a College employee. Some committee members discussed the "good old days" when the College had high enrollment, felt very inclusive, and maintained an overall feeling of being connected with the students; some members spoke about the loss of educational opportunities for students who would normally not be afforded an education; some members described their profound gratitude each day in service to students. The discussion was thoughtful and heartfelt and it continued for a couple of hours. What stood out was that the committee members basically reaffirmed the mission statement "opportunities for you." Opportunities was a key word, which described what was often the first and perhaps the only chance for rural students with little access to financial, social, and cultural resources, to succeed in the workforce and in society. This shared vision is what propelled each member into action. Once the committee of 13 was separated into five teams, each team proceeded to collect the evidence to support their criteria.

Next Steps

Team 5 addressed Criteria 5 (below) which included shared governance. Team 5 was initially comprised of four committee members: one administrator, one faculty member, one academic director, and one staff member. This subcommittee was responsible for addressing the topic of college resources, planning, and institutional effectiveness. Criteria 5 consisted of four core components, and one component, 5B, was targeted at leadership and collaboration:

> 5B: The institution's governance and administrative structures promote effective leadership and support collaborative processes that enable the institution to fulfill its mission. (Higher Learning Commission Policy) https://www.hlcommission.org/Policies/policy-index.html

This core component looked for the institution's governance and administrative structures that promoted effective leadership and supported collaborative processes that enabled the institution to fulfill its mission (HLC Assurance Argument). This team was responsible for providing evidence that there were campus-wide collaborative processes in place that were aligned with the College mission. The team expanded its size by adding approximately 15 more members consisting of additional faculty, staff, and students. This larger team reviewed other college shared governance models with a goal to create a model that would support the unique characteristics of our rural college.

Within 2 weeks, the team put a model together which included a number of formal groups and committees that it felt best met the needs of the College. This model reflected a horizontal approach to ensure participation and transparency. A significant inclusion in the model was a Shared Governance Council. The purpose of the council was to act as a check and balance between the Board of Trustees and the College constituency. If the Board of Trustees agreed, the Board would have to present their new or revised policies to the Council prior to taking any action.

The model was presented to the campus community and discussed, and modifications were made based on the collective feedback. Within 35 days, the shared governance model was created, vetted by the College, and officially approved by the Board of Trustees. Existing committees were rolled into these larger committees, and the work began to implement shared governance in the decision-making process.

Our Shared Governance Model

The College's shared governance model comprises five constituent groups—Board of Trustees and President, Academic Leadership, Faculty, Students, and Staff. Additionally, three committees were formalized—Shared Governance Council, Strategic Planning and Institutional Analysis, and Retention and Completion. A brief review of each of the constituent groups and committees follows.

The purpose of the Faculty Senate is to facilitate effective communication among the faculty and between the faculty as a whole and the administration of the College. The Senate, which consists of elected faculty, presents the views and recommendations of the college faculty to the administration and to the College Board of Trustees as they relate to academic policies.

The Student Government represents the students at the College. To enhance the quality of student life and encourage student retention at the College, its purpose includes encouraging cooperation and communication between the students, faculty, administration, Board of Trustees, and all campus organizations.

The Staff Advisory Senate consists of elected employees at the College. The group serves as a source of input regarding issues and decisions of the college as they relate to all regular full-time/part-time, and nonfaculty people.

The Academic Leadership consists of the Vice President of Instruction and all Academic Directors. This group provides leadership and vision in the planning, development, and implementation of all academic areas led by the College's strategic plan—including faculty and support human resource development, curriculum, instruction, budget, completion and retention, and institutional analysis.

Shared Governance Council

The purpose of the Shared Governance Council is to serve as a collective unit with equal representation from all college governance groups including the Faculty Senate, Staff Advisory Senate, Student Government, and Academic Leadership. The Council reviews policy proposals, issues, concerns, and other institutional matters that are presented by these governance groups.

Each governance group is represented in the Shared Governance Council: The Student Government and Faculty Senate already existed, while the Academic Leadership and Staff Advisor Senate were newly formalized groups. To create the Shared Governance Council, two elected members of each of these constituent groups were its first members. The general idea is that each of the constituent groups would contribute to issues and discussions in their own groups; they could then bring ideas to the Council, other constituent groups, the President, or the Board where institutional discussions could continue. Decisions can be shared at the group level, or the council can be used to further discussion with administration such as the President or Board of Trustees when a new or revised policy might be required. It should be noted that any group can bring forth concerns or discussions to anyone at any time.

Strategic Planning and Institutional Analysis Committee

This committee measures the appropriateness, strength, and relevance of the College's strategic plan, ensuring it proactively seizes opportunities and addresses challenges of uncertainty due to changes in the organizational environment. This committee also develops and implements metrics and strategies for measuring the institution's progress toward its strategic goals and provides recommendations on how the College broadly embraces the strategic plan as the basis for driving operations. Members were selected from all constituent groups of the College.

Retention and Completion Committee

This committee examines existing methods for recruiting, advising, counseling, retaining, and evaluating student experiences. It determines needs and identifies problem areas pertaining to retention and completion as well as researching and making recommendations for solutions. Members were selected from all constituent groups of the College. The following graphic illustrates the model in place (Fig. 1).

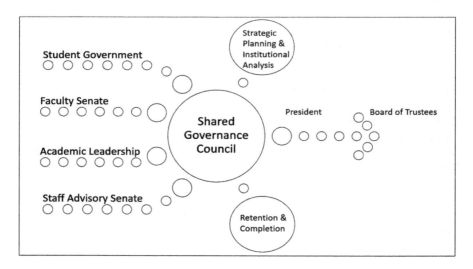

Fig. 1 Shared governance model (authors' own figure)

The Importance of Interconnectivity

Effective shared governance is hard work; however, when active, it energizes a number of individuals within the system to participate, facilitate, become informed, and have the necessary conversations. Also, the construction of a shared governance structure has allowed the senate groups and committees to begin the long process of trusting leadership again. Although there were elements of shared governance within the College before the construction of a model, formal approval by the Board of Trustees meant that the Trustees were willing to be more inclusive with all stakeholders in College decisions. In addition, the new shared governance structure has also increased motivation and buy-in across campus.

Connectivity between individuals and resources can be very complex and time-consuming. There are numerous social structures that either allow or prevent those interconnections to be made. Once a model like shared governance is created or revived, new work begins.

As a newly formed Shared Governance Council, the Council was excited to participate in the decision-making process; however, the model is not as easy to implement. Effective communication is crucial to its success. The first test of shared governance occurred when a Board of Trustee member resigned; consequently, one of the first requests by the Council to the Board of Trustees was to participate in the temporary selection of a new Board of Trustee. This temporary Trustee would serve for a year until the next community election. Since responsibility of the temporary selection of the Board of Trustee ultimately rests with the Board of Trustees, the Board accepted the Council's offer to participate. As a result, the Council members interviewed the lone candidate. As a group, however, they recommended to the Board of Trustees that the candidate not be selected as a Trustee. The Board of Trustees reviewed the recommendation from the Council but nevertheless chose to vote the candidate in as the temporary Trustee.

The result of this opposing decision led the Council to question the validity of their contribution to shared governance. The Board, on the other hand, believed they had given the council voice but believed their decision was theirs and was made appropriately. Defeatist conversation about the decision began to travel across the campus. Smaller and larger meetings were held to share concerns and feelings. As a result of these conversations, the College members had a clearer understanding of the purpose of shared governance and group roles and responsibilities. While some members of the council and constituent groups believed that the shared governance meant that the College would utilize a democratic approach to decision-making, they began to understand the participative nature of shared governance. This is an example when expectations and communication can anchor harmony or distrust. Continued conversation between members of the council and the board resulted in a better understanding of each perspective. As a result, the Trustees, the Shared Governance Council, and other campus members will need to continue to learn the balances of power and the potential value of the collaborative nature of shared governance.

Summary

Effective shared governance has been proven to create a sustaining traveling organization in higher educational systems. This is why accreditors require its presence. When shared governance is nonexistent, there are little to no checks and balances in place. Members at all levels, including the highest decision-making levels, need to be transparent about issues and policies that can potentially impact the organization.

Changes to enrollment numbers, funding formulas, and state and national initiatives in higher education continually challenge the College. For shared governance to work successfully, its constituents must be invested, self-evaluative, and prepared to improve its ability to participate in the decision-making processes of the College. As a result, more work needs to be done both at the group level and across campus groups with the intention to improve communications within and across the groups. By reviving a shared vision, building the connections among the various groups, and validating shared responsibility horizontally, vertically, and ubiquitously, the College is better prepared to address the challenges.

The shift in performance and participation was initially required because of the sense of urgency placed on the campus by the accreditation team. Most likely, the natural response once a sense of urgency abates is to revert back to the "way it used to be." Nevertheless, competition in higher education cannot be ignored, and the College will need to collectively forge ahead, challenging the status quo and actively contributing to institutional needs. A re-focus on shared governance at our College has potentially opened ubiquitous avenues for participation, communication, and transparency. Leadership decisions at all levels need to reflect the interests of the organizational mission. This is why effective shared governance is essential; it makes everyone accountable for its success. When actions at any level conflict with our mission, it is up to each member from the maintenance team to the Board of Trustees to recalculate.

The importance of leadership cannot be overemphasized. The College is in a position to thrive because governance groups are beginning to trust the opportunities they have to participate and contribute more effectively to the decision-making processes of the college. The College will be hiring a new President to lead the College into future opportunities. Currently, the Shared Governance Council is leading the selection process that will invite five qualified presidential candidates to the campus. This is a crucial time for the College and the shared governance process. Excellent communication skills, self-assessment, and ability to embrace conflicting views and to make readjustments are essential in the presidential leadership as well as other areas of leadership. Governance groups must continue to trust and actively engage in and contribute to the needs of the College.

The College survived the 90-day charge; however, the College is not over the hill. The College is expected to forge ahead and continue to do the hard work. Leadership at all levels with effective shared governance as its axle will become the driving factors that can ensure sustainable results. The College will continue to be monitored until it becomes a traveling organization.

Recommendations

The following minimum recommendations are suggested to support a shared governance framework:

1. Leaders should practice leading from the sidelines. This can be very difficult when one finds comfort in a top-down power structure or is focused on the end result. Leaders must be more cognitively present to identify when to jump in to facilitate and support and when to be patient with the process (when possible).
2. Trust your employees, but provide professional development opportunities to develop their leadership skills. It is not enough to expect employees to raise their contribution level to that of participation. Skills need to be developed so all members can effectively facilitate meetings, create measurable goals, take minutes, analyze data, and write reports.
3. Make sure all governance groups own the responsibility of being transparent. One purpose for shared governance is to extend the conversation and knowledge across the organization. Leaders should provide clear requirements to groups about their responsibility to be transparent with their discussions and recommendations, remaining open to differing opinions.
4. Leaders should encourage ubiquitous ways to support institutional conversations, including offering different ways that groups can facilitate conversations.
5. Leaders should communicate simply and often such as by sending emails regularly, conducting meetings, and/or holding all-hands meetings to discuss new policies and current issues.
6. Make sure everyone knows where to get records of meetings. Minutes should be posted on the website within 48 hours of a meeting.
7. Revisit the shared governance process to ensure they are effective and continue to evolve. Provide an annual feedback mechanism regarding the effectiveness of shared governance structures and practices. Digital surveys can be made available to get a broader response from the campus community. Make adjustments to the shared governance process or structure when results identify common concerns.

References

Bahls, S. (2018). Evolving workforce expectations. *Trusteeship: Shared Governance, 26*(3), 14–19.
Gerber, L. (2001). "Inextricably linked": Shared governance and academic freedom. *Academe, 87* (3), 22–24.
Higher Learning Commission Assurance Argument. Retrieved November 4, 2018., from https://www.hlcommission.org/Policies/criteria-and-core-components.html
MacTaggart, T. (2018). Nontraditional presidents. *Trusteeship: Shared Governance, 26*(3), 9–13.

Part V

Practice Cluster: Talents and Capabilities

The three pillars for organization and leadership applied to organizations in disruption need talents and capabilities for success. Bob Dignen and Tim Burmeister show the importance of learning and development (L&D) and the needed disruptive change in its direction. From a different perspective, Volker Hische links the pillars to the question of how to develop and connect people with their company. Finally, Christal Lalla exemplifies how alienated interventions can help to improve purpose, journey, and connectivity thinking for individuals and teams.

Learning and Development in the Organizations of the Future

Bob Dignen and Tim Burmeister

Abstract

Digitalization seems to threaten numerous business models and raises deep questions about the meaning and practice of Learning and Development (L&D) functions that many see as disconnected from core business activity, pushing somewhat linear solutions into organizations traveling in multiple directions. The article explores the current and future realities of learning in organizations. Three conversations with L&D experts investigate the need for new forms of collective and connected leadership required to steer the "traveling organizations" of today and tomorrow and the potential for more values-based organizational cultures driven by sustainable purpose. On-demand performance support is expected to replace classic static L&D curricula. Leadership is on the verge of transcending leader, and newly relevant learning communities are about to emerge.

The Editors of the Book Introduce:

Bob Dignen who works as a director of York Associates, an organization that supports clients with leadership training, C-suite and executive coaching, international team-building, and consultancy on learning design. He recognizes that digital transformation threatens to bring yet more disruption to his clients' ability to perform. Bob is the author of several books.

(continued)

B. Dignen (✉)
York Associates, York, UK
e-mail: Bob.Dignen@york-associates.co.uk

T. Burmeister (✉)
GP Strategies, London, UK

© Springer Nature Switzerland AG 2020   207
P. Wollmann et al. (eds.), *Three Pillars of Organization and Leadership in Disruptive Times*, Future of Business and Finance,
https://doi.org/10.1007/978-3-030-23227-6_22

> **Tim Burmeister** who has been working in Learning and Development (L&D) for 18 years, thereof the last 2 years as a learning transformation manager for GP Strategies with a focus on Europe, the Middle East, and Africa (EMEA). Tim sees the learning profession and learning industry on the verge of a profound change driven in part by emerging digital technologies.

Introduction

Conversations About the Future of Work in the Era of Digital Transformation and the Role of Learning and Development
    "What Got You Here Won't Get You There."—Marshall Goldsmith

The authors of this article, Bob Dignen and Tim Burmeister, first struck up a conversation in an office in Germany approximately 10 years ago. Tim was head of eLearning for a major retailer in Europe. Bob had been hired to deliver intercultural training. Tim now no longer believes in the efficacy of the eLearning he developed at that time. Bob no longer believes in or delivers the form of intercultural training that he was hired for at that point in time. Using the slogan of Bob's current main client, "Change happens."

Bob and Tim's experiences with change, along with their history of abandoned beliefs and discarded practices, teach a fundamental message: Change is always happening, and L&D professionals must always prepare for the total abandonment of what they might hold most valid and dear at any present moment. In this article, Tim and Bob again converse among themselves and significant others in Tim's organization (Adam Stedham, president of GP Strategies, and Christopher Smith, director of Consultancy, Strategy, Organization, and Leadership Development at GP Strategies) to explore the current and future realities of learning in organizations today and the role of L&D as a function.

This time the focus is on the disruptive forces of digital transformation, which appear to many as a serious challenge, potentially with some form of silver lining, on the horizon of corporate life. Digitalization seems to threaten the business models of the most established and successful global organizations and raises deep questions about the meaning and practice of cross-functions in L&D, functions that many see living an inverted version of the three-factor model: disconnected from core business activity, pushing somewhat linear solutions into organizations traveling in multiple directions.

The following three conversations with global thought leaders deeply involved in the world of L&D at different levels offer a moment to explore the future of the L&D function in corporate life and the opportunity for its better connection to "the business." The conversations investigate leadership, one of the classical domains of L&D, and the need for new forms of collective and connected leadership required to steer the "traveling organizations" of today and tomorrow and the potential for more values-based organizational cultures driven by sustainable purpose. Bob plays his favorite role—asking questions. Adam, Chris, and Tim play their role admirably—sharing excellent insights.

And remember, these conversations are stories. They are narrative discourses, forms of language that convey and conceal. Let not the tangibility of print and the seeming permanence of an object, which we might call "book," disguise the reality that authors as narrators ultimately create fictions that are ephemeral spirits on the one hand, yet worthy guides on the other, as we transverse a complex territory. So, no pretence of the finished article here (pun intended). You are invited to a number of conversations and are also invited to join the authors in Montalcino, Italy, to continue the said conversations if you so wish. Let the conversations begin.

Conversation 1: Talking to Adam

At my core I believe that helping people fully develop their knowledge, skills, and capabilities is the key to helping them live fuller and richer lives, because I've seen it in my own life. I'm a living example of this. —Adam Stedham

Key Ideas in the Interview
The following is a summary of the key ideas discussed during the interview:

- Increasingly, management sees L&D as a function which can enable organizations to perform better.
- L&D has lived apart on its own island separated from the mainland of the business for many years, with the separated communities evolving different languages.
- Vertical disconnect in organizations—senior leaders losing touch—is happening alongside new forms of horizontal connectivity: new grassroots-collaborative patterns.
- The leadership challenge of today and tomorrow is to create the conditions for performance to happen.
- Learning and marketing share many similarities in that both act to influence the behaviors of key stakeholders to improve the profitability of companies—watch out for the rise of the learning agency.

Interview

Bob: *What's your assessment of where L&D is at the moment in large organizations?*

Adam: It's an amazing time of amazing opportunity, but it's also a time of unparalleled expectation. So, L&D has emerged as all the more important and as a differentiator for the success of companies. Now, that's a double-edge sword. On the one hand, it means the learning function and the ability to deploy learning and human resource development inside of an enterprise is more core and more critical than it has ever been. On the other hand, there is much higher scrutiny than there has ever been. You know, for many years, the CEO never really paid much attention to what was happening from a learning and people development perspective. Now the CEOs are increasingly aware, and they are knowledgeable; they're focused on it. So, it all brings opportunity and expectation.

Bob: *Does it also bring a threat? The current reputation of L&D in many larger organizations is problematic, to be honest, in many of my client companies. Can L&D deliver on these expectations?*

Adam: I think the biggest threat that L&D has is partly from its own history. The fact that it was never viewed widely as a strategic component of the enterprise has meant that L&D's language was free to develop in and of itself. So, L&D developed a language that was different to the language to the rest of the business. It's almost like having a different island offshore from the main coastline, and you don't have interaction. Over time, the language and behaviors are going to be different. But now that the island and the mainland are connected by a firm bridge, we have a communication problem. So, I think many of the concerns can be remedied by L&D understanding how to speak the language of business. I don't believe L&D is broken. I think L&D has a hard time speaking a language that Business understands.

Bob: *Is that a similar challenge faced by ourselves in the learning industry? Do we need to learn a new language to connect again with our clients?*

Adam: I think we do need to learn a new language to connect with our clients. With that said, some core parts of our own success in the past few years have been based on the business fundamentals of our clients—it's training outsourcing, it's our lean Six Sigma practice, it's some of our strategy work. So when discussing outsourcing, clients want to know whether we can deliver services at a higher quality for a lower cost than if the client did it themselves inside. They also ask, within lean Six Sigma practice, are you able to help us run the plant or the operation with lower overhead costs? That's also a business conversation. So, I do think parts of the business of our industry do this already and will drive more conversations in the future.

Bob: *Where do you see digitalization playing into this complex situation? It produces increased expectation, on the one hand, but also increased ambiguity.*

Adam: There are a couple of ways to look at digitalization within learning, and I think a lot of people talk about digitalization and learning at a very superficial level—almost like digitalization is a conversation about modality. For me, digitalization is really part of a broader conversation about the entire changing of power, and how power is disseminated and controlled inside organizations, even inside society. What digital change is doing is really shaking up some of the hierarchical structures inside of companies. And this is very challenging from a learning perspective. You know if you are used to going to a person who runs this, and they understand the strategy, and they understand what they are trying to accomplish, then you put together curricula and programs to help the organization execute on their vision. That's a model we are used to. But this much flatter emerging world where reality is a series of connections, a series of matrices, there are multiple stakeholders, and you have five or six people collaborating to create something . . . so which of these five or six people created that? Who gets credit for it? Who needs to be the one trained? So, it's now simply more complex for learning providers to deliver value in this environment.

Bob: *Yes, and I guess you would also see, as I do, many clients were quite fragmented in multiple ways in any case, and now digitalization and more fuzzy structures bring more fragmentation. So, learning providers will find it difficult to land and sell coherently and holistically in such an environment. Do you see this as a challenge for your own organization?*

Adam: I think it is, but I think you said a very important word. And this is the paradigm shift that is difficult for all of us, including me in my role. So, while organizations are becoming more connected in new ways in a digital world—people working horizontally, people collaborating in matrix work teams, people just working together. . . grassroots movements—as all those connections are happening, it feels at the top like disconnection. No longer do you have vertical connections driving results; you have horizontal connections in organizations that are driving those results. So, in some ways the feeling of the organization being disconnected is actually a result of the organization becoming all the more connected. It's just getting connected in a new way—a horizontal way.

Bob: *That's interesting. Most of my clients are experiencing things as fragmentation, I would say. This is perhaps because many of the new connections* *are not emerging within classical job structures, management structures, or incentive structures. It's almost counterculture in some ways and is yet to work its way to a happy balance.*

Adam: Oh, absolutely. You know, in my own world, I was walking along a corridor recently and I happened to look in the room and I see—wow—all these people, this group of leaders from across the company. So, I thought I'd better walk in and find out what this meeting is about. So, I go in and they explain to me what they're working on, and what the meeting is about. Then I walk out and call our CEO and ask who called that meeting. He says, "I don't know." So, I call the Chief Sales Officer and ask the same question and he says, "I don't know." Historically, if you called together senior leaders for a strategic meeting, it was facilitated from the top. This happened as a grassroots movement to solve a business challenge. They all came together, met, and came up with solutions. So, on the one hand, it's an example of the amazing connectivity—the horizontal connectivity of the organization. On the other hand, it's a very awkward feeling to the vertical connection of the company. It's a new paradigm. That's the future of where we are going. That's how organizations are going to be agile and get things done. But how you provide training and leadership development as well as competence development inside this organizational dynamic is very difficult to answer.

Bob: *Well, Adam, that's exactly my next question. What can leaders and those providing learning do to create an environment where this new paradigm can flourish?*

Adam: At the end of the day, we have to be able to learn how to prepare the land. There's nothing I can do that's going to turn a seed into a stalk of corn, nothing. Only nature can do that. What I can do is to prep the soil, make sure we have the right kind of chemistry, and ensure we have the right kinds of nutrients. I can say which land looks fertile and which not. If I see a storm coming, I can try to protect my crops. I can do a lot to give my crops a best chance of success. But at the end of the day, the crops are going to have to grow. So that's where we are as leaders going forward.

Bob: *Is what you just described part of the leadership culture in your company?*

Adam: This is not fully fleshed out. It's emerging. We're working with partners who are thought leaders in this area. What we are working on with some of our entry-level leaders is really about connection and enabling. So, you connect with the people who work for you and you enable them to be successful, whether that's through coaching or through processes or clarity of purpose or alignment of skills to job role. But it's not command and control. You can't command and control on a sustainable basis. With that said, there are times when you have things that need to get done, so you need to adopt more of a command-and-control culture—like, we have to get this done in this way by this time. But that's not sustainable over the longer term.

Bob: *Coming back to digital and your natural metaphor, it seems that digital promises only perpetuate storm and destabilization, and in that environment, it's difficult for people to feel that their way of doing things has validity. Do you sense that digitalization will bring a sense of uncertainty that might push people back to a safe zone rather than embrace a more emergent approach, paradoxically?*

Adam: But I don't think that uncertainty is a problem. Discomfort and lack of performance due to uncertainty is a problem. Look, we can't impact the rate of change in the world. What we can do is to equip people with the skills and capabilities to function in this kind of dynamic environment. But this is just my opinion.

Bob: *So, the issue of performance becomes ever more critical. And this brings us back to a new emerging mandate for L&D to focus less on learning and more on performance.*

Adam: Yes, I think you're exactly right. And I think you actually said the critical word that represents the change of our world from an L&D perspective. The job of L&D is to no longer develop, deliver, and control learning. It can't be done any more. The job of L&D is to enable, track, and report out learning. We're enabling learning. Now, we might do that by developing curricula or by curating curricula. We might enable learning by doing job rotation assignments. We might create collaboration groups by having people with different skills coming together to solve problems—an actionable learning environment. There are many ways in which we can enable learning.

Bob: *So, a kind of learning culture?*

Adam: Yes, you know there is research coming out that says that the desire to control learning in an organization can be the single biggest impediment to having a learning culture, because a learning culture in this digital world has almost a grassroots element to it. Whenever you try to control a grassroots movement, it doesn't work.

Bob: *This is interesting because it raises a number of paradoxical elements. There's a desire from the business to have higher levels of performance, but what you're describing is a shift to a more decentralized kind of role for L&D, not guaranteeing learning but simply creating an environment where people will learn if you can trust them to do it.*

Adam: Yes, but I'm an enormous fan of metrics for learning. The key question is, what are the metrics for learning? For years, and this is where we started our conversation, on our island, we came up with our own language, whereas on the mainland, they talked a different language. Nobody on the mainland ever talked about level one or level two or learner satisfaction. On the mainland, people talked about business results. At the end of the day, if I am doing more training at a car dealership, the metric that I should be measuring is, Did we sell more cars? That's the only metric that matters. So, I always say to customers, if you want to develop learning metrics, let me see what you measure right now, because that's what's important to you. Then let's see how this learning intervention correlates to what you are already measuring, and then let's evaluate the impact of this learning intervention on the things that you are measuring. There's no need for me to come up with a learning metric that you don't already track as important to the business. This metric is not important to you.

Bob: *Yes, in many ways learning metric is a kind of oxymoron. What is needed is to understand business metrics and track learning impact to those.*

Adam: Absolutely. On the island we talked about learning metrics, and on the mainland, they talked about business metrics. And over the course of time, we have the situation where these two definitions are different. That's a real translation issue. If learning wants to show value to C-suite, it's not a question of whether people liked the training or not. It's more about answering, Were more cars sold? Did safety improve?

Bob: *Yes, I guess you can have learning that people really don't like having a positive impact on business results. That's a possibility.*

Adam: Yes, there's a lot of research that says there is no correlation at all between learner satisfaction and overall business results. Look, I've been a stand-up trainer, and your feedback can go down because you stop serving cookies at lunch. And on top of that, forcing people to be in a room away from the day job, forcing people to do pre-work, demanding that people concentrate and participate can have a very negative effective on your scores as a trainer. Yet it can have a huge impact on the knowledge transfer that occurs during learning.

Bob: *Yes, and therein lies another problem. Is the learning industry itself ready to stand up with a greater integrity, or is it part of maintaining a false language and believing that learner satisfaction matters?*

Adam: I think the learning industry is stepping up. I have a friend at the moment who is doing his dissertation (we compare learning notes) on how to prepare a head of learning for someone who comes from the business versus someone who comes from learning, and who would be the best choice, etc. What I think is happening, not only are learning heads starting to understand the business better, but business people are starting to understand learning better. So, I think the gap between learning and business is shrinking.

Bob: *What I'm also seeing is convergence of learning between industries in value chains where, for example, in insurance, it makes sense for the insurer, the broker, and the customer to sit in the same room and do learning together because they do business together. This is a new collaborative learning process.*

Adam: Absolutely. Take the insurance industry as an example; one of the best ways an insurance company can influence its profits is by training its customers around healthier lifestyle. So, if I am providing car insurance and I train my customers to drive more safely so that they have fewer accidents, it improves the profitability of the firm. And I could show many examples in many industries. But it kind of shows that the way L&D has been designed does not support the kind of more horizontally connected world where all stakeholders are together. And when I say horizontally connected, I am bringing the customer into that. So, we've done a lot of work with insurance companies on how to train their customers.

Bob: *This feels very optimistic. What we're discussing here shows the immense opportunity of L&D to expand its scope and impact in very innovative and meaningful ways.*

Adam: Absolutely. This is a huge area of fertile ground. What is the goal of L&D? We want to influence the behavior of employees in a way that is beneficial to the productivity of the firm. At our core, that is our charter. And if you look inside of the business, there is a function that exists to influence the behavior of our customers to improve the productivity of the firm, and that organization is called marketing. But if we look at what marketing does, and you look at what training does, it's very similar. They just have a different target audience. And at the end of the day, marketing's target audience is multiples bigger than learning's target audience. So, I think there is a tremendous opportunity for the learning industry to step into what was classically the marketing domain.

Bob: *Is that a service line you see clients open to and willing to explore?*

Adam: Absolutely. In fact, I'd never heard of a learning agency before until about a year ago. We just purchased one. And some of our competitors are calling themselves learning agencies because what they are doing is trying to affiliate with the marketing-agency type of relationship between client and provider. And I think this concept of learning agency has a ton of opportunity for learning professionals and our industry.

Further Questions for Reflection
The following issues were either touched upon directly or raised implicitly during the interview and may be interesting to think about further alone or discuss with your colleagues and contacts.

- How can L&D learn to speak the language of its business stakeholders?
- Who is best placed to lead the learning function in companies: learning experts or business experts?
- How far will horizontal leadership emerge as a future paradigm, replacing outmoded vertical models?
- How can marketing and learning experts inside organizations cooperate to influence their respective stakeholders?

Conversation 2: Talking to Chris

Key Ideas in the Interview
The following is a summary of the key ideas discussed during the interview:

- We need to rethink our core assumptions around how learning happens in large companies, as the nature of organizations is changing. In complex organizations it is difficult to drive learning outcomes in mechanical ways with classical curricula pushed at people. Moreover, we may need to focus less on the individual and much more on social learning.
- It is likely that new learning communities with high revenue impact, e.g., customer and strategic business partners, will be targeted by L&D in the coming years as well as those inside businesses.
- Leadership will grow in importance over "leader" as a focus for learning and development, reflecting the dispersed yet interconnected nature of organizations.
- Organizations are being constantly reinvented in response to a dynamic environment. In a fundamental sense, organizations never fully align to their environment and always remain partly realigning or in flux, a phenomenon which may generate internal conflict.
- Business leaders are increasingly likely to reflect more on the 'why' of business—ethics and sustainable purpose—as the impossibility of exponential growth in a finite world becomes apparent.
- Passion remains key to leadership, and a galvanizing force which drives transformation.

Interview

Bob: *What's your thinking of where L&D is at the moment and where it might be going?*

Chris: Okay, so where are we? I think we're at a place where there is a real challenge for the learning industry, which is partly around trying to understand what the L&D role is going forward. Today's modern learning organization is looking to create an environment in which people can pull through what they need, when they need it. This is rather than trying to define through lots and lots of analyses what people need and then trying to push people through that. So, I think there's a fundamental shift from a push to a pull model.

Bob: *So, L&D got it wrong in the past?*

Chris: Arguably, L&D has always been kidding itself that it can do the analysis and understand what people need, and then tell them to go do it. In other words, there's an argument that L&D has always worked under some false premises about what it does and can do. And this is linked to an under-standing (or not) of the nature of organizations, and what happens in organizations, and the model that has prevailed in people's minds to a large extent is an industrial and, I guess, a mechanical kind of model, that if we can figure out what the problems are and then tweak the people in a slight way, then this will make the difference, which I think is a false premise.

Bob: *So, a better metaphor for organizations is biological, more like an organism?*

Chris: Yes, organizations are a social system, and so you can't control things in the way suggested by more mechanical models. And linked to this, I think another very important thing is the fact that we tend to locate learning in the individual. And a lot of that comes from our schooling. Yes, of course, there is learning at an individual level, but you also need to look at socialized learning, at how we learn together. And learning isn't knowing in your head. I know a lot and I've forgotten most of what I've heard. Life's like that. Learning is only real when you've used it or applied it in some way. Knowing is relatively easy. Finding the right times and opportunities to use it and connecting it to what you need to do with others is much harder. And I've seen this so many times in learning over the years; people see things that are useful, but then struggle to use it in meaningful ways and at relevant times. Learning is ultimately all about doing stuff with others.

Bob: *So, to put it more brutally, are you saying that a lot of L&D may not be fit for purpose, particularly with the new challenges and opportunities arising around digitalization of organizations and their learning?*

Chris: I wouldn't narrow it to the L&D function in that way. Is it fit for purpose? Well, it needs to evolve and adapt. But then it's doing this in a context when pretty much all functions need to evolve and adapt as well. So, it's not alone in that. And I have to say, I'm unsure here if the change is really very different, or is this something that has always been there and we're just seeing it through our own particular lens? And each generation always thinks its world is completely different from the one before.

Bob: *But organizations are changing?*

Chris: Yes, the nature of organizations is shifting, particularly large organizations, but in different ways. I saw some statistics recently around increases in employment around the world—large organizations are not growing. The number of people they employ has been pretty much static or falling. That's not to say they aren't growing in profit; they just don't need so many people to do that growth. But the boundaries of an organization are also changing and are now much more porous with people moving in and out, and that brings a challenge to L&D. Should they just be developing people inside the legally defined boundary of the organization, or should they be thinking much more broadly and look across boundaries to develop communities that will be part of our success but that don't technically work for us. So, not fit for purpose—that's a bit harsh. The whole world is changing.

Bob: *You mention this idea of learning communities, which I see some of my clients addressing internally within their own organization but also in relation to partners, suppliers, and customers. Do you see addressing new and related communities, even connecting these communities, as something significant about the way L&D will develop?*

Chris: Yes, but this is not entirely new. Car companies have been doing this with their showrooms and dealerships, which may be independent businesses, for many years. The car company does the training because they want to be sure the that training gets done is right. And then you can look at the franchise world. So, there are models out there that people have already seen in this way. But connectivity in a new world of social media adds challenges. For example, I think one of the big challenges for businesses, and this is really heightened by all the social media stuff, is that their reputations may be damaged by bits they don't immediately control. So, you can have airline companies suffer brand damage when the outsourced company providing meals goes on strike, and a video of a lack of a meal on a plane goes viral. This means L&D potentially has to take a broader view of what its organization is, its learning community, and which levels of expertise are necessary at different points for the customer and brand.

Bob: *That sounds challenging. Challenges to get cross-functional training going inside companies is rigorous enough with the fragmentation that exists in terms of aligning needs and management expectations. Talking about connecting across companies sounds very challenging.*

Chris: Yes, although the new technologies potentially allow us to connect people in innovative and more seamless ways than was true in the past.

Bob: *This leads to one obviously important topic: leadership. Where are we with this, and where do you see it evolving in the environment we've just discussed?*

Chris: I think there are some of the same trends. For example, although we talk a lot about leadership development, we are generally talking about "leader" development. So, we focus on the individual, and we believe that if we could just fix the individual with more knowledge and more skills, then that could make a difference to the business. And, of course, it will help, but much more important is leadership development, which is the capacity for leadership across an organization and across its boundaries. And that is much more collective than individual and involves a complex mix of ways of thinking and doing.

Bob: *Is leading and leadership getting better?*

Chris: You know, on average, I think the quality of leadership in most organizations now is much better than when I started in my career 20 years ago. I still hear about and see things that are horrific and not where they need to be, so still lots of scope for us to help. And I do think the world in which people are trying to lead is more complex. I was talking to someone the other day about the VUCA world (Volatile, Uncertain, Complex, and Ambiguous), and we were discussing if it was all real or whether we were just kidding ourselves. And yes, it's always been there, but I think the pace of change has accelerated. You can't take so long now to think about and do things. And the scale and multidimensionality of global businesses and coordinating the different levels of leadership through a business are more complex now. We've gone through a kind of centralizing model in which organizations tried to control things from the center. And now I think there's a recognition to breathe out and let go of that and create an environment; so, I think this is where senior leadership is at—creating an environment where others can succeed. And that means enabling, not controlling and directing, creating the culture, responding to resource requests, and enabling people locally to get on and do the job.

Bob: *I sense that is true. Companies are increasingly pushing back to regional and local structures. Yet they retain very centralized IT, finance audit, and compliance functions.*

Chris: Yes, because you need to do that. It shouldn't ever be an "either . . . or." It's definitely "both . . . and." I've seen a lot of companies using centralization, focused control, clear lines of responsibility, and so on to drive efficiencies, consistencies, and effectiveness, and end up with one core program or key process. The advantage of that is cost efficiency and consistency of thinking and mind-set inside a business. And I think that's helpful in creating common attitudes and behaviors toward the market, but then retaining enough freedom and flexibility when it comes to decision-making. But it's always a struggle. Smart companies have to look at where they need consistency and where they need to allow flexibility and autonomy. And there are some areas, finance and governance, you absolutely need to be in full control. Interestingly, some of the tech companies operating out of California have the reverse problem. They're used to free-wheeling, growing, no rules around here, etc. Their risk is that they don't have enough visibility on what's going on, and things happen that are not good for us.

Bob: *Yes, there's almost an intellectual paradox here between the values of control against flexibility. It's the balance that is key, which is more art than science. And one of the key messages in my own training and coaching is that organizations are never going to get it fully right. This means you're never going to work in an organization but probably in what you feel is a disconnected disorganization. The notion that you are ever going to hit that sweet spot, particularly with environmental volatility and the human weakness inherent in leadership, is an illusion. The need is to connect to colleagues and work with them through the system, your organization, sometimes against the system, all positively, to produce results for you, your team, and maybe for other functions that, although with KPIs not aligned at all to yours, it makes sense for them to "win" in some way over you. And for me, this is a kind of discourse, a kind of language, that I don't hear in leadership thinking today—the dysfunctionality of things. Organization, we need to realize, is an abstraction.*

Chris: Well, it is an abstraction. What is an organization exactly? Is it the legal entity? Not really? Is it the physical assets? Not quite. It's a kind of legal fiction. So, yes, there's a fundamental philosophical question here when we talk about the notion of organization and what we really want from that as individuals. What are we looking for from this, from our connection to this thing, and the people in this thing? There is that level. And some leaders, but not many, think in this way; they see everything in the flow and their job to intervene and steer the flow but that they don't control it. And they can let go of the anxiety that they've got to be in control. Most leaders struggle with that in my experience, partly because they have the paradoxical situation in that they are seen to be in control; they have the most senior position; other people are looking to them to provide control; and the reality is that they are not. And the other thing you triggered in me is around the notion that organizations are always being invented; they are never "there" as a finished thing.

Bob: *So then can leadership be seen somehow as a constant and continuous process of co-creation? And that is then very tangible around, how do we collaborate? or what do we need to do together to be successful?*

Chris: Yes, but all of this takes quite a thoughtful person, and someone who is quite robust in terms of their own ego and sense of self-worth who can begin to say, "I know that doing this doesn't help me in terms of my objectives, and anyway, those objectives are mostly a fiction. And I'm okay for another part of the business to get more of what they want from this because that's in the wider interest of what we are trying to achieve around here." That's a rare mind-set.

Bob: *And we cannot forget the pressures from paymasters: shareholders and financial markets.*

Chris: Yes, the financial markets drive a lot of this. They drive a whole sense that you've got to hit certain revenue targets or return-on-investment numbers. And that's not such a bad thing, but it's also part of the game.

Bob: *Yes, it's their KPIs that seem to pull leaders sometimes away from a more sophisticated view and back sometimes to what are almost organizing fictions.*

Chris: Yes, and this is very much driven by the financial markets and the interpretation of numbers. And it's part of the process, and you need to put this in its context; it's one need inside of the whole system. And leaders in businesses must manage a very wide range of stakeholder needs with a very wide range of timeframes—next week, next month, next year, and next decade. You know, one of the things that I have become increasingly focused on is that we live in a world with a post-industrial capitalist model with a logic of continuous growth. And I think we're going to have to adapt to how we live and what we do in the world before we kill ourselves off. And I do think that business leaders compose the one community of people who can do most to make a difference. I don't think politicians can, although they can help. I think some business leaders are becoming increasingly enlightened, as are investors in the financial markets who might have to take a 50-year view of the world, and so want to be sure there will be a world in 50 years' time. So, there are people who are increasingly aware that this is a core part of what they are accountable for.

Bob: *Yes, this is one of the components of the three-pillar model in this book— the need to create and work with sustainable values. And perhaps we are seeing a growing interest in ethics in business and leadership. There's a tone, a color that is emerging, which is beyond corporate social responsibility (CSR).*

Chris: I think that's right, which came to a head in 2008. Before that it was almost, If it's legal, it's okay. My job is simply to maximize value; that's why I was appointed. And many leaders are still in business for the notion of self-fulfillment, What can I get out of this? It's still very strong in certain cultures. But I do sense an underlying change after 2008.

Bob: *You mentioned the word "culture." It's a word that I often have a problem with, as people often use national cultures to make sense of their international world—Germans do this; my American boss did that. And I always try to disrupt that narrative, as I think it too simple and frequently a false way of seeing the world. Many corporates use a narrative of corporate culture to create a sense of bind and sense of clarity and momentum to move forward together. What's your sense of this word "culture," where it's at, and where it's going? Is it always used constructively, or is there a dark side?*

Chris: I think for a long time, organizational development, which is around culture and culture change and was big in the 1970s and 1980s, got a bit of a bad name. It was a lot around conformity. Now culture is talked about again, often when explaining bad behaviors in companies—it was a culture of corruption, a culture of overworking, which caused certain problems. For me, culture is a way of talking about what is happening around here, what are the rules, ethics, ways of doing and behaving. For me, ultimately, it is about the patterning of relationships inside and externally to an organization, and what helps to make a difference. Yes, culture is part of that; but so is structure and so are processes. They inform the culture but they are also shaped by it. And I do see cultures in certain sectors of industry with common patterns, e.g., in banking, in retail, in pharmaceuticals, etc. Culture does make a difference.

Bob: *So, if culture matters, are you involved in helping companies build a better culture for themselves?*

Chris: Yes, and the question brings to mind a recent merger and integration. Both sides felt that the best thing was to have the best of both cultures. And we said, "No, that's the last thing you want, or you'll spend all your time arguing over whether mine is better than yours." Our advice was to focus on purpose: What are you going to do now with two merged businesses and strong brands. What can you do differently now as a bigger player in the marketplace? What culture is needed to support that purpose and strategy? We always link strategy, culture, and leadership. Strategy implies change. The world around you is changing, so you need a new strategy. In order to deliver that strategy, you need a new patterning of the relationships in the business—that's culture. And to achieve that, you need to look at how you view leadership. So, it's a triangle, and each part of it is important.

Bob: *So, purpose is important in all of this.*

Chris: Very much so. The need finds the leader; the purpose finds the leader. It's not the other way around, that leaders go out and find a purpose. There is often a purpose there, and someone feels passionate enough to get involved and make a difference around it. And that 's really stepping into leadership. It's not about qualifications, experience, or training; it's much more about interest, curiosity, the willingness to try to engage others around the purpose, and the desire to work with others' energy and feed off it. That's what leadership is about as opposed to management. Actually, if you have the passion and interest, you'll find a way to communicate in a way that you engage others. And you'll gain the skills; you'll go through the feedback loop and see that some things are not working. And that's leadership—passion, actively caring and trying to make the difference.

Bob: *And I guess the same with you and those inspirational leaders you meet— they just have that innate passion for the cause.*

Chris: That's part of it. And that passion itself becomes energizing and engaging for others. Sometimes leaders articulate a need that is already felt. People often feel they can't go on as before. Leaders will articulate that, and create a language, so people will say, "Yeah, that 's it. That's what's not right. And I want to change it."

Further Questions for Reflection

The following issues were either touched upon directly or raised implicitly during the interview and may be interesting to think about further alone or discuss with your colleagues and contacts:

- Which forms of social learning can best be connected and orchestrated by L&D?
- How can cross-organizational learning processes be developed and deployed to enable L&D practitioners to act beyond a single-company focus?

(continued)

- What will be the cultural impact in organizations of focusing more on leadership than leader? How can leaders be prepared to give up their historically privileged position?
- How will farsighted and progressive business leaders position themselves in contexts driven by short-term profit and financial gain?
- How can we distinguish between passion (as a progressive force) and personal obsession (as a risk) when analyzing the motives of senior leadership?

Conversation 3: Talking to Tim (Again)

Key Ideas in the Interview
The following is a summary of the key ideas discussed during the interview:

- L&D needs to refocus away from slow development of learning solutions to the rapid deployment of relevant forms of performance support.
- The "why" of companies needs to become more ethically driven in order to attract next-generation talent.
- Performance-based experience replaces learning and focus in three main buckets: formal training, social collaboration, and on-demand on-the-job performance support in the flow of work.
- Artificial intelligence (AI) and machine learning technologies produce a rise in collaborative decision-making processes between human and computer.
- Learning and performance analytics are rising in importance, feeding useful data to those developing strategic targets for businesses based on current learning trends as indicators of future business opportunities.
- A major role for L&D going forward is to enable the new modes of collaboration that are emerging in organizations.

Interview

Bob: *Before we start properly, Tim, tell me one thing. L&D still has an important role. Is it worth discussing this?*
Tim: Yes, of course. L&D has a very valuable role in supporting the business to achieve results. This means that L&D has to engage—to understand the mission of the company, its strategy, the game the company is playing today, and what it needs to play tomorrow. And the core question is how

L&D can support that. But, and this is the key paradox, L&D is not there to do L&D, to do learning; it's there really to enable performance. To support the company effectively, L&D needs to transform itself. And it has to do this in an age when transformation, perhaps fortunately, is not an option.

Bob: *So what transformation do you see happening in the world of work today, and how is that affecting L&D today in large organizations?*

Tim: So, what I see as a kind of red thread globally, already 5 years ongoing, is this digital transformation disrupting all industries and all functions, in some cases radically. This is having an impact on the way work is done, which then has an impact on HR and L&D. And the approach that L&D took the last 5, 10, or 15 years doesn't work anymore, so L&D needs to change to a different approach to be able to support the digital transformation.

Bob: *Can you tell me more about the transformation that L&D needs to make?*

Tim: Speaking to many clients and corporations, there is a common theme. What L&D has done in the last 10 years is mainly event-based. They send people to events, once, twice, or three times per year, and the focus is on learning, on training. Put simply, a new approach is needed for the future. Now it has to be about continuous engagement; it has to be always on. You don't switch learning on and off any more; it has to be there always. The focus has to shift to performance support because, no one has time today to do learning. So, the question that L&D needs to answer is how to move learning back into the workplace and turn it into real performance support.

Bob: *This shifts the focus quite fundamentally.*

Tim: Yes, in the past it was all about L&D pushing out training to the business. But now it's employees and workers in organizations demanding what they want to know and what they want to do, and then they pull this know-how from inside and outside of the company (Fig. 1). So, in the past L&D was composed of content creators who designed courses. But now it's all about being curators of resources; curators in the sense that there are so many resources available that designers don't always have to reinvent the wheel. There is a lot of leverage in existing sources. It's not now about courses but more about resources at the moment of need so that people can get material to help them do their job better, which is performance support.

Bob: *Is what you are describing independent of the digital transformation? Is what you're describing needed, and did it need to happen anyway?*

Tim: Yes, it needed to happen anyway. But, looking at it at rather negatively, some will say that L&D got along doing their work for the last 10 or 15 years without really supporting actual performance, and they are still around. And

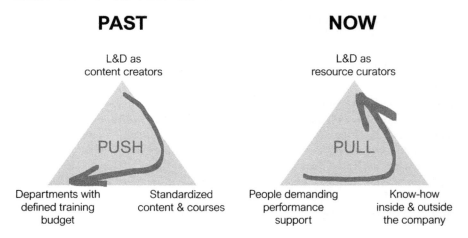

Fig. 1 Shifting the focus from push to pull (Figure: Frank Kühn)

it needed this radical and drastic shake caused by digital disruption to change the way things are being done.

Bob: *So, it needed a digital trigger to be pulled to change things?*

Tim: Yes, because the digital trigger being pulled is causing disruption across all industries and organizations now have to reinvent themselves, the solutions fall on L&D.

Bob: *So, you're talking a lot about disruption and change. The three-factor model identifies many responses to that change: the need to focus on sustainable purpose; the need to become a "traveling organization," adaptive and flexible; and the need to connect people and resources through the organization to enable performance. Does this model capture something important for you, and do you see a role for L&D in this?*

Tim: Yes, absolutely. On sustainable purpose, I think things are going beyond profit and the next quarter that organizations have to consider. Today, workers are selecting the company that they want to work for based on what the company believes in, what it stands for, that is, what is the "why" of the company? This is important for the younger generation today. So, this "why" is going to be one of the main factors to attract talent.

Bob: *And on "traveling organization"; the notion that companies have to be dynamic and stay agile. Does that make sense?*

Tim: I believe that this is just a starting point. I think things are going to get more dramatic in the years to come. The movement that we are seeing today means that no fixed point is really fixed. Business models are continuously evolving, so organizations need to make built-in flexibility more a part of the culture. Today you do something; tomorrow you will have to do something else. If you don't do that, you're out.

Bob: *On connectivity, so many business leaders experience their own organization as disconnected, fragmented, and so deeply problematic. Can L&D play a role in helping the silos and departments connect, share, and perform?*

Tim: Yes, so I believe this part of the analogy is also important. The future will be very much about collaboration, connecting workers across all kinds of borders and boundaries and connecting different seniority levels. It is about breaking down the silos of different business units and having people truly work together, even across organizations; integrating customers into the creation of products; and meeting their real demands, which are becoming even more customer-centric. And L&D needs to put the learner as customer more into the center, too. And this takes us back to the "traveling organization," because demands are always changing, so you need to be "traveling." And in this world of change, the only constant is what you stand for, the sustainable purpose, which will attract the talent and let you keep on doing what you are doing.

Bob: *Okay, taking again a more negative perspective, if L&D has been slow to embrace change in the past, what's to say it won't be slow again and be left behind by digital transformation? Is there a risk of failure?*

Tim: Yes, there is a high risk of L&D failing here. I see many learning functions that have lost the connection to the business and that are siloed in what they do. We also see this as a vendor. To enter new companies, to get new clients, we can't enter via L&D because L&D has lost a lot of credibility. So, we need to sit at the table with the business directly.

Bob: *How is your role in the business transformation different to classic L&D? What do you bring to the table as one of the largest pure learning companies in the world?*

Tim: Our advantage is professional experience, connected with our focus on performance and passionate people in the field of learning innovation and transformation. Importantly also, we are tool agnostic. We don't own any technology. We are connected with partners that are tool developers and vendors, which is an incredibly competitive landscape. It's so difficult to keep pace. These days, every couple of days, a new vendor emerges. You know, two students finishing university have a great idea, they find some venture capital, and in a couple of months, they have an app that is disrupting the whole industry. Therefore, it is crucial to know the market, understand what is going on, come up with a suitable learning strategy and approach, and be able to connect clients with the right technology to enable performance—focusing on making employees better and faster. Thus, it is a connectivity story of its own.

Bob: *So, this is not technology for the sake of technology? It's technology that really makes a difference for the customer?*

Tim: Yes, there are so many emerging technologies, you really need to understand their value, the outcomes that they bring, and the benefits of using them. If not, you run the risk of shiny gizmo syndrome and L&D heads hiding behind AI or virtual reality (VR), and not really delivering any outcomes. So, as a learning company, we are very focused on the "why": Why should we use this technology?

Bob: *Can I ask a question at this stage about this infamous 70:20:10 idea popular in L&D today around learning, as it seems your company is aligned to this?*

Tim: Yes, as this is so controversial for many, I use the model but don't mention the numbers 70:20:10. I mainly talk about a performance-based experience, which consists, I would say, of three buckets. One of them, as you say, is formal training, which is webinars, web-based-trainings and ideally a flipped classroom approach instead of just classroom/lecture style. This contrasts with the traditional classroom where the time is used to deliver content; in the flipped classroom approach, there is a pre-phase to deliver the content and the time in the classroom is then used to focus on skills application, learning by connecting to others and being highly interactive.

The second bucket is social collaboration, and this is like learning from others, chats, coaching, FAQs, buddying, and so on. It's interesting, our company just introduced a new software system that we all (4,000 people) need to use. And people are just asking each other, how does this work? It's what I did today at my desk; I just asked my neighbor, which became a 15-min conversation. So, social collaboration is happening anyway and it's important, so L&D needs to embrace it.

And the third bucket, and most important, is on-the-job performance support, which means, in the flow of work, at the moment of need, people get something to help them do their job better—could be an app, a fact sheet, or a place that is easy to access. I call this a performance-based experience. L&D needs to embrace all three buckets.

Bob: *So, you mentioned digital in all three buckets. Do you have any doubts about digital? Are there risks embedded in digital that we need to be cautious of?*

Tim: I would say, yes and no. Overall, I'm not so worried about digitization, as this is the new normal that is also called consumerization, which means, all employees in organizations have a certain way of consuming products and services. And almost all of that is digital. We still go to stores to test or maybe feel a product. But things are primarily digital. So, this is happening anyway everywhere. We go to work, and we use our smartphones to consume products and services. We use our computer to access stuff. And you know, the training rhythm of learning, waiting and then going to a classroom, doesn't align with how we consume other products and services. That's on the one hand. Even the iPhone can give us analytics about how we consume—our email use, our browsing history, which apps we are using, and how much time we spend on all of that. We kind of have our 10,000 digital steps available to see and to control. So, we still have the freedom. And even some companies in Germany with this data are shutting down email servers after 6:00 p.m., a digital cut to protect people. Look, the pace of change is amazing. What we're doing now will look like a dinosaur in 10 years' time. But still, as we get this technology, comes awareness and controls.

Bob: *You mention new technologies a lot. Are there one or two that are going to really make a difference? What is exciting? Which is out there?*

Tim: I think there are several. For instance, there are chatbots. This is, like, kind of a buddy who reminds you about things. For example, thinking about learning, the learner goes to a classroom session, and learn lots of great things, but when they go back to work the next day, they just continue as they did before. But with a chatbot, which they can configure, they go back to their desk with a buddy who can constantly remind them of what they should be doing and how they should be changing. So, I see the bot buddy coming more and more a part of a blended learning experience. There are also augmented reality (AR) and VR, which help you really immerse yourself in a reality that you can't easily access at a given moment. So, you can put on a headset, turn on the smartphone, and engage. AI is the third one, and making the impossible possible. These three tools together will enable us to blend humans and machines, taking decisions in new ways supported by the data processing of AI, which gives better recommendations than you can ever learn in a training. Many learning leaders think this is the future. But I can tell you it's not the future—it's already today. The most important thing still, though, is that all this must deliver an outcome. There must be some benefits to using the technology or it's just a shiny gizmo.

Bob: *So, final question, if I am sitting in L&D and I am convinced to transform, what is the roadmap? Is there a template to do all of this?*

Tim: There are a few things to mention here. High-performing learning organizations or learning functions that are very successful share common threads in terms of what they have been doing. First, L&D needs to align to the business and ensure that they are delivering on business outcomes. L&D needs to come up with KPIs at the very beginning of new projects, and understand what good looks like. If that is done in a professional way, L&D can become a business facilitator. Another idea is to use design thinking, which really helps to connect to actual customer needs. In the old world, the business would ask for something, and L&D would go away and come back after 6 to 9 months with a solution, and the business would say, "Hey, after such a long time, the situation has changed totally; we don't need that anymore." L&D needs to perform to the speed of the business and develop a fast minimum viable product (an MVP) with the users involved in the design. You build it for the user, who is with you, deliver it to the user quickly, get feedback, and then do the next iteration. You can be very agile. And with the business user with you while building the thing, you create something that customers can use.

Things are also getting shorter. Digital learning used to be 45-minute eLearning sessions or webinars that were boring and, today, are simply too long. It's now about telling a story in around 4 min. This is the amount of time people still accept. Then it's about user experience and interface design, crafting something easy to understand; you don't need a handbook. It's good to look at.

Another is the data analytics. There is so much data available—things like liking and rating—you can almost call it a "digital body language" in the sense that users, learners, give feedback. The learner can quickly identify what the top content is and what they should read. They can also use learning analytics to develop forecasts for the business, and report, based on the data, what users are learning and where we are heading or should be heading. So really in this way L&D can be seen not just as an investment, but also as a future-oriented business enabler.

Many new roles are emerging as a consequence of all this: the data analyst, the user experience designer, the content curator, and so on. It's a dramatically changing landscape.

Bob: *What does this mean for learning management systems (LMSs)?*
Tim: LMSs will remain for some time, mainly in the mandatory and compliance training field, but the future will be in learning experience systems, in which the experience of the learner journey is the focus. LMSs were built mainly for learning administrators, not for the users, the learners. The next genera-tion of performance platforms will have features that are a little like LinkedIn, with sharing and liking features, ratings, user-generated content, and so on.

Bob: *Where does culture come into all of this? We're talking about a learning culture revolution, aren't we?*
Tim: Yes, this needs a culture that almost abandons the term "learning" in favor of "performance." In a way, if L&D is doing its job well, people won't

experience learning as learning. They will just see whatever they see as "stuff" that helps them to do their job better. But they wouldn't necessarily see this as useful learning. Already, everyone goes on Google, browses for new information, and asks colleagues how to do things: People don't normally describe this as learning. And this new philosophy focuses on performance; this is what L&D needs to embrace.

Bob: *On the metrics side, do you think L&D will ever be able to prove it has an impact on the bottom line? This is the Holy Grail of learning.*

Tim: Yes, I strongly believe this, yes. But it's not about proving learning; it's about proving performance improvement. So, I think we will see in the next few years what happened a few years back when marketing managers went digital. Before, marketing was billboards and magazines, and you never knew really who read what—you had to guess. But with going digital and using the available data, marketing teams were able to predict impact from different channels, for example, if you put this message out via this channel at this time, then this socioeconomic group will make this decision. This was good analytics enabling marketing to make predictions. And I think this will happen in L&D: As the function becomes more digital and gets more data, L&D will be using the data to drive performance in predictable ways. And that's a revolution.

Bob: *I hope all this data transfer doesn't lead to more emails.*

Tim: Not at all, and this is another important point. More and more people realize that email doesn't work anymore. The reason—too many emails and too little time. So, the way we communicate must change, which will have an impact on learning. We will use new platforms. There are quite a few already collaborative platforms, for teams, that can become learning platforms, too, because isn't that the job of L&D—to bring people and communities together and have them aligned and connected in teams? So that's another area that will change and evolve. Even more revolutionary is the impact on leadership. The future is about putting the best people together digitally so that they can perform, to do a job. It won't matter who they report to, who leads them, but simply how well they do. Maybe we are seeing the end of leadership as we know it, not only L&D.

Further Questions for Reflection
The following issues were either touched upon directly or raised implicitly during the interview and may be interesting to think about further alone or discuss with your colleagues and contacts.

(continued)

- How can vendors of new learning and performance solutions engage with L&D functions strongly rooted in the past?
- How will companies ensure employees have time to acquire relevant knowledge and skills to perform in new ways while imposing ever higher workloads?
- Which new learning and performance metrics will establish themselves in the future with increasing data available to track performance impact?
- How can companies decide which new technologies will bring real added value and avoid the shiny gizmo error?

Conclusion

As the stories come to an end, we take this moment to express heartfelt thanks to those who shared their experiences and their reflections and stimulating insights into the world of work and L&D today and the future. Looking forward, it seems that sustainable and ethical purpose is likely to play an increasing role. The timeless organizational constellation of control and flexibility will continue to morph, now having to engage with digitally accelerated forms of change in the business environment. We will experience a world in which humans strive to structure—digitally and face to face—new forms of connectivity and connectedness. This world will enable people to thrive in ways good for themselves, their immediate teams and networks, and still broader stakeholder groups, who have perhaps never met but who have positively imagined.

Firm predictions have been made. Interestingly, the growth of powerful new L&D entities and processes is imagined—the rise of the learning agency (partly present among us already). The triumph of on-demand performance support resources is foreseen to replace classic static L&D curricula. Leadership is on the verge of transcending leader. Newly relevant learning communities are about to emerge, that, once addressed, can add value to revenue and brand beyond a classic FTE (Full-Time Equivalent) perspective. Of course, a messy coexistence of the above is probably a safe evolutionary forecast, which will bring further fog to the fogginess of today's organizational experience for many. But, we can hope the fog will lift slightly as evolution occurs.

So, there are no clear answers, no safe predictions ... perhaps an unsatisfactory ending to a tale involving three conversations and four protagonists. However, answers were never the goal. Our purpose is to step off the merry-go-round, connect for a moment, and ask meaningful questions before hopping back aboard refreshed and rejuvenated. That's how we feel. We hope you feel the same.

The important thing is not to stop questioning.—Albert Einstein

Training of Journey Capabilities

Volker Hische

Abstract

The purpose of this article is to better understand the psychological and sociological ingredients of feeling connected, and how to make connectivity happen in times of volatile businesses, moving targets, and transforming organizational shapes. It interlinks the three pillars with well-regarded concepts such as self-efficacy-expectation and Flow experience, a milieu approach, and the resonance concept. Finally, it offers an agile leadership check and gives hints for effective management techniques.

The editors of the book introduce **Volker Hische** who has been working as a consultant, trainer, and manager/managing director for more than 25 years in a global American technology company. Nowadays, he works as a leadership coach. He has already published and written books on leadership and project management.

Background, Purpose, and Structure of This Chapter

From resonance deserts and resonance oasis—a psychologically and sociologically inspired cocktail to make people feel connected with their company in times when business challenges are more volatile, corporate targets are more movable, and organizational shapes are transforming quicker than ever before.

V. Hische (✉)
Volker Hische Business Coaching, Binningen, Switzerland

© Springer Nature Switzerland AG 2020
P. Wollmann et al. (eds.), *Three Pillars of Organization and Leadership in Disruptive Times*, Future of Business and Finance,
https://doi.org/10.1007/978-3-030-23227-6_23

Let's start with a thesis. The most relevant impact on our working morale is the answer to a simple question: to what extent do we *feel* connected with and in our company. Sounds too simple? Just imagine the effect on our working morale if we do not feel connected with our company—feeling disconnected means leaning back, stopping engagement, and making management responsible for whatever happens in the organization. If we agree that a company is only as good as its people, the consequences are devastating: lack of energy, mental stagnation, and resignation. A cocktail of poisoned chalice for each company.

Companies invest vast sums of money in providing technical platforms or open space architecture to ensure that people *are* connected within the organization. This is fine. However, economic realities—e.g., global labor markets, increased internal competition, global value chains, teams working 24/7, and digitalization agendas—put a lot of pressure on the organization (see *travelling organization*). Good morale requires more than a technical or organizational environment that helps people to be connected.

Companies need to do more to have people *feel* connected with them. Leaders know: high team spirit, a common vision, and an open culture are the psychological ingredients of the antitoxin to prevent people from stagnation and resignation. These ingredients stimulate growth and success in our companies. Consequently, in the 1970s, psychologists like Albert Bandura and Mihaly Csikszentmihalyi developed well-regarded concepts to highlight the psychological aspect on connectivity. Today's social scientists like sociologist Rosa Hart have developed a theory of *resonance* as a holistic concept of connectivity, and the concept of *Becoming an Agile Leader*, developed by Evelyn Orr, shows the silver lining of how to create a company as a resonance oasis. This is the purpose of this article: to better understand the psychological and sociological ingredients of feeling connected and learn how to mix and dispense an appropriate cocktail to the organization.

The Ingredients: What Do We Need to Mix Our Cocktail?

Imagine you are appointed as new CEO. Your new company—let's call it Company A—has had a solid financial track record in the past and is well known in the industry thanks to a strong brand. You are highly motivated and looking forward to your new mission. However, within the first weeks in your job, you become a little nervous. No breakthrough innovation in the last years, no internationalization at all, no clear vision, no entrepreneurial spirit, and no growth perspective. In your first meetings with your management, you realize that people are behaving rather cautiously and reluctantly. In the past, mountains of PowerPoint slides have been generated. However, no visionary decisions have been taken. The former CEO launched lukewarm initiatives which came to nothing. External consultants have generated costly analysis to identify the underlying issues which everybody already knew, coming up with cost-saving initiatives evaluating the company from an investors' point of view. Results have not been discussed in depth with the management team, the truth being limited to a set of KPIs. In a next step, you start interviews with long-term employees to discover that there are a lot of structural problems which have not been tackled for years. Managers who did engage in true turnaround initiatives were dismissed. The workforce has completely lost faith in its leadership team and conducts *business as usual*. In the context of our topic: neither management nor employees still feel connected with this company. You conclude that it is only because of the conservative and stable industry that your company is still alive.

Let us look at a second example in the same industry. Imagine you are about to enter a company—let's call it Company B—as newly appointed member of the Board overseeing Production and Technology. For the first 2 days of your new job, you are invited to attend the annual management meeting. You find out that this company has enjoyed strong growth for decades. Acquisitions abroad have led to an external revenue of more than 50%. Profit is above the industry average. You realize that the operational issues to be solved in the meeting are simply down to the tremendous growth the company has experienced in recent years. The company is on a joint journey towards sustainable success, closely synchronizing with the opportunities provided by the market and its customer needs. During the meeting, you sense the high entrepreneurial spirit within the management team, empowered and fueled by strong leadership from the Board. You conclude that is obviously because of the strong leadership and laudable team spirit within the management that people feel connected with this company and its purpose and contribution to future-oriented solutions.

When you look at both examples, the difference is obvious. It is all about team spirit and leadership! Both companies operate in the same industry. Size and financial resources have been comparable in the past. Both companies are still owned and managed by families. So, the key differentiator is not financial power or size. It is all about team spirit and leadership. Nothing new, right? Agreed. And still it is worth having a deeper look at the leadership approach and its link to connectivity. There is strong mutual loyalty between CEO, management, and workforce based on three key values: entrepreneurship, personal development, and open communication. The Board has a clear vision and takes calculable risks to realize growth opportunities in international markets. Each manager is empowered to shape the future by him or herself in the framework of authority matrices. Everyone believes in the purpose of what they are doing; they know about the dynamics of markets and businesses along their corporate journey. There is a cross-functional operations management to overcome silo thinking and allow joint real-time adaptations to changing conditions in the markets. Finally, there is a deep understanding of the need to connect all resources with the company's development. This creates trust and responsibilities at all levels in the daily work instead of following the sweet illusion of certainty due to long-term planning in uncertain times.

The Psychological Ingredients of Connectivity

There are three ingredients developed and described by famous scholars of psychology that help people to feel connected with their company. These examples are to show how our approach of sustainable purpose, travelling organization, and connected resources is linked with other sound concepts of organization and people development.

Self-Efficacy-Expectation

Albert Bandura developed a concept which is, in his view, the main driver for succeeding in a task: the level of *self-efficacy-expectation*. According to Bandura, it is decisive to what degree people believe in their capability to have an impact when they carry out a task. Sounds abstract? Think about sport. When you start playing golf—for example—you will figure out quickly what it means. You start enthusiastically at the driving range, take a couple of hours with the pro, manage several nice swings, and dare for the first time to play on the golf course. You will probably realize very quickly that—as you used to believe—swinging a club automatically means hitting the ball no longer applies, not to mention hitting the ball in the right direction. Now it depends on your expectation of whether or not you will be able to hit the ball in the right direction sometime in the future. If your expectation is low or

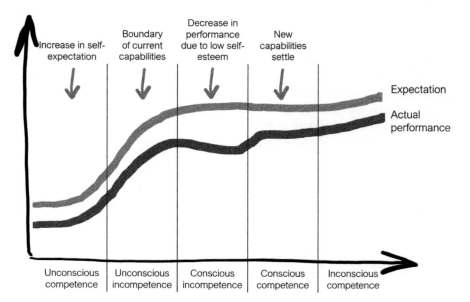

Fig. 1 The effect of expectations on performance regarding one's own capabilities [author's own figure, adapted from Dilts (1994)]

zero, it will not happen and you'll give up. The graph in Fig. 1 explains Bandura's concept in detail.

The graph demonstrates that there is a clear link between expected performance and real performance. At the beginning, people do move in the right direction. They are motivated and believe in their capabilities to adopt a new task because they have not yet realized that they might not be competent enough. Bandura claims that it becomes particularly critical in the phase of *conscious incompetence*. If the initial motivation is replaced by frustration due to continuous failure, people lose confidence and stop performing. They start to believe that they are not as competent as assumed (conscious incompetence) and give up. So, for leaders, it is crucial to understand what we need to do to avoid ongoing failure in the phase of conscious incompetence. The theoretical solution is obvious: help people to develop a new strategy and/or new skills and capabilities, particularly during the phase of conscious incompetence. This will increase the belief that their engagement will deliver the expected results.

To underline and strengthen this concept, we would say the challenge is not only about expected and real performance in terms of output and results. The frustration of people willing to engage themselves is even more critical, if they want to contribute to a higher purpose and then fail, because market and business needs, personal motivations and individual competencies are not connected with each other. Leadership means enabling and encouraging people to continuously create connectivity of relevant resources—needs, motivations, and competencies—even in volatile environments and in uncertain conditions.

Flow

Mihaly Csikszentmihalyi elaborated Bandura's concept and came up with the idea of *Flow*. He described *Flow* as situations where our attention (mental energy) is focused on realistic objectives and where our competencies fit our options to act (Csikszentmihalyi 2008). He found out that the following criteria support the Flow experience:

1. Objectives are clearly defined.
2. Work does not swamp nor underchallenge me—thus.
3. I believe that I will be able to control what I am doing.
4. Focus lies on the action (the doing) itself.
5. Experience of own competence.
6. Self-effectiveness—belief that I am the one who makes the difference.
7. Direct feedback as to whether or not what I am doing is successful.

Although Mihaly's *Flow* concept is self-explanatory, this does not mean that it is easy to put into practice. In their studies of managing virtual teams, for example, Hertel and Konradt identified typical problems that sabotage any Flow experience (Hertel and Konradt 2007):

1. Team members feel isolated.
2. Unclear team targets.
3. Difficult to motivate team members to review the achievement of their own goals.
4. Lack of feedback within the group—insufficient information about the performance of other team members.
5. Insufficient informal contacts.
6. Lack of clear rules.
7. Trust is a prerequisite for the participatory management style and is more difficult to achieve and cultivate in a virtual environment.

Obviously, it seems to be far easier to become familiar with the Flow concept than to apply it effectively in daily business.

Again, we have to connect the Flow concept with VUCA conditions and re-understand Csikszentmihalyi's criteria. For example: what about clearly defined objectives in uncertain circumstances? That is why we emphasize the purpose that enables employees to explore and agree to the most effective objectives with their managers. This is more iterative than ever before, focused on "minimum viable solutions" and underlining the relevance of direct feedback for quick re-adjustment. Thus, the flow experience addresses two levels of self-experience, i.e., it connects two competencies: effective execution of a task and continuous synchronization with the transforming business and organizational circumstances.

Big Five

The *five-factor model* of human psychology differentiates between five personality traits:

1. *Introversion* versus *extraversion* differentiates between whether we are more oriented to the "inner" or the "outer."
2. *Openness* refers to what degree we embrace new experiences.
3. *Agreeableness* refers to our willingness to cooperate and our capability for showing empathy to others.
4. *Conscientiousness* describes the degree of self-discipline, goal-orientation, planning, and control.
5. *Neuroticism* is the tendency to emotional instability.

As those five personal traits do have an impact on our day-to-day behavior, they merit being taken into consideration when we mix our connectivity cocktail.

What seems interesting here is the dual approach: on the one hand, the openness to change and, on the other hand, the degree of goal-orientation, planning, and control. These two aspects have to be connected and re-thought in a way that we have to understand objectives, organize tasks, and connect the resources in a more iterative way, regularly questioning and re-adjusting what we do. At the end, we will even have to deliver solutions that we weren't able to define when we started our work. The emotional stability will be provided by the purpose and meaning of our journey, our readiness to accept uncertainty and to enter unknown territory, and connecting with others and involving them in our joint endeavor.

The Sociological Ingredients of Connectivity

Based on the ingredients condensed from insights in psychology, it is worth looking at two sociologists who developed those ideas by conceding that we are not only individuals but part of teams and milieus. This is important to understand when we want to ensure purpose, change, and connectivity within our companies. In addition, both examples show how these three pillars are linked with other relevant theories.

Milieus

The sociologist Gerhard Schulze (2005) asked the following question: Are we only a product of our characteristics, or are we a product of our environment? As a result of his empirical research, Gerhard came to the conclusion that it depends to a great deal on our belonging to a particular population group ("milieu"). The *milieu* prescribes how people deal with chances, changes, and difficulties in their daily lives. Gerhard claims that the milieu we are socialized in determines how we handle problems. Let's take an example: Imagine you are an average mountain biker. You are used to going for a ride in your environment in the forest. Now one of your friends, who lives near the Alps, asks you to cross the Alps with him this year. Gerhard offers you five different ways of how to deal with this challenge (describing them as "normal existential problem definitions"):

1. A first reaction could be that you take this as a *threat*. Dangerous trails, uphill all the way, probably the most unfit member of the team. No way! You stick to your home trail. Schulze describes this as *harmony milieu*.
2. A second reaction could be that you take this as a *challenge*. To cross the Alps by bike is tough and needs you to be very fit. Let us see how the other bikers will cope. You will do your utmost during the preparation phase to end up as one of the best in the team. Losers are everywhere! Schulze describes this as *niveau milieu*.
3. A third reaction might be that you take this as a *stimulation*. This is cool, isn't it? Hopefully, this will be great fun. Schulze describes this as *entertainment milieu*.
4. A fourth reaction might be that you take this as a *self-actualization*. Wow, this is a great opportunity to figure out how I'll manage to climb 1300 m a day on a bike and how it will feel to navigate those difficult downhill sections. Schulze describes this as *self-actualization milieu*.
5. A fifth reaction might be that you take this as a necessary *adaptation*. It is a mega trend to be fit and active, and the TransAlp is a must for any mountain biker.

And—you do not want to let your friend down as it is normal for friends to do as the other one asks. Schulze describes this as *integration milieu.*

As this is only hypothetical please relax, nobody wants you to cross the Alps. However, according to Gerhard Schulze, it is our "normal existential problem definition" (NEP) which determines how we react to a changing world. Do we seek the chances and opportunities in our daily lives, or do we avoid every new situation? And it is easy to apply our personal NEP to new situations in business, isn't it?

The milieu approach is highly relevant when we discuss the aspect of travelling organizations. How are individuals prepared to face uncertain business development and organizational needs such as flexible structures, iterative decision-making processes, and practices for solving workplace conflicts? Such findings will influence the company's transformation strategies and even support approaches of transformational leadership.

Resonance

One of the latest concepts in the context of *connectivity* has been developed by Hartmut Rosa (2018), which he calls *resonance.* He claims that people can only feel connected with other people, with their jobs, with their company, with their families, and with their environment when there is some *resonance.* In general, Rosa claims that resonance will only occur when positive affection and emotion are triggered by our work, when there is an intrinsic interest and an expectation of self-effectiveness in a working situation. According to him, *resonance* is not an echo, but a response relationship. In their specific working environment, employees should play an active part in day-to-day decision-making processes, in the improvement of working conditions, and in the creation of ideas and new concepts. Finally, he says that *resonance* is possible when strong values are affected. So, a good match between company's and employees' values allows more resonance and more connectivity.

Could we generate resonance or even install *resonance oases* in our modern working environment?

Let us go back to our successful Company B. I ran the management workshop which was attended by the newly appointed Head of Production and Technology. Topics included strategic aspects like the future setting of the company, underlying critical success factors, and corresponding values. The second day was dedicated to key issues like supply chain management as Company B was facing operational issues due to its rapid growth. Hartmut Rosa would probably be pleased to testify that there was a lot of *resonance* in the room. All participants were highly engaged and contributed to the results. There was an atmosphere that was conducive to very open and constructive discussion. Everybody was touched by the positive energy, and at the end, we even witnessed a transformation from enthusiastic and engaged individuals to an enthusiastic and engaged team. Why did this happen? Let's check the resonance criteria:

1. *Affection*: There is a high degree of affection towards the company itself. All members of the management team have a positive personal relationship with the owner (who is CEO) and the family and identify 100% with the company.
2. *Emotion*: Each member of the management team is highly emotionalized. People are proud of the company's success story, its brands, and its future perspective. They fight hard for their needs and objectives. Once a decision has been made, though, people stick to it.
3. *Intrinsic Interest*: Everybody's intrinsic motivation is high as people are convinced by the products, the vision, and their own personal contribution. The challenge is rather to overcome individual interests and transform them into common, shared goals.
4. *Self-Efficacy-Expectation*: There is high a degree of ownership and self-responsibility. An authorization matrix clearly defines the framework within which each manager decides and acts on his or her own.
5. *Response Relationship*: it is part of the company's DNA that people are entrepreneurs. Decision-making and communication are a two-way street, and that was demonstrated in the workshop by ensuring that all participants raise their voice.
6. *Strong Values*: The company DNA is written in the form of three key values (entrepreneurship, continuous development, open and respectful behavior). As CEO and the Members of the Board have continuously emphasized these values for years, they have become implicit behavioral guidelines. Thus, people identify strongly with the culture of Company B.
7. *Momentum of Unavailability*: Everybody knows that this culture is not a no-brainer, nor is it self-evident. Thus, they appreciate that the Board and/or the owner pushes and ensures that the ingredients for resonance and connectivity are in place.

In other words: Rosa's resonance concept describes the pure connectivity that is for employees needed to go the company way together, to set up the team who are willing to go on a journey. Even if they don't know what is round the next bend. They are in resonance with the entrepreneurial purpose and with each other, trusting they will make it.

The Recipe: *How* Do We Mix Our Cocktail?

We have described the need to share the purpose of the organization's journey, connecting the resources such as business insights, individual motivation, corporate strategies, and processes. How do we develop the competencies that a travelling organization needs to be successful?

We came across several psychological and sociological ingredients from great scholars to mix a connectivity cocktail for our company which helps people feel more connected. Now we need the right recipe. If you expect a cookbook with a set of fantastic recipes, you will be disappointed. Leadership in a travelling organization is continuously on a journey as well and, thus, too dynamic to use recipes. However, there is some silver lining: *learning agility*. J. Evelyn Orr has published a great book about *Becoming an Agile Leader* (Orr 2012). Orr understands learning agility as

> the willingness and ability to learn from experience, and subsequently apply that learning to perform successfully under new or first-time conditions ... learning agile people do know what to do when they don't know what to do.

Which competencies help us to become an *agile leader*? Evelyn Orr lists four competency dimensions of being agile:

1. *Mental Agility*: describes people who think through problems from a fresh point of view and are comfortable with complexity and ambiguity and explain their thinking to others
2. *People Agility*: describes people who know themselves well, learn from experience, treat others constructively, and are cool and resilient under the pressure of change
3. *Change Agility*: describes people who are curious, have a passion for ideas, like to experiment with test cases, and engage in skill-building activities
4. *Results Agility*: describes people who get results under tough conditions, inspire others to perform beyond normal, and exhibit the sort of presence that builds confidence in others

You might add *self-awareness* which Orr defines as: *we know what we are good at and not so good at and actively address the not so good*. If we agree that those learning agility dimensions are vital, it is worth running a self-check. Be aware, though. It is certainly worth answering this questionnaire by yourself. However, it is also useful to ask others to give you open and constructive feedback on these indicators. This assessment is a great starting point to work on your own *learning agility* (Fig. 2, Table 1).

And? Are you the *agile* hero or are you rather disappointed? Relax. Usually, nobody is the "special one" (except—perhaps—a select few in sports or arts); we are rather the "normal ones." Nobody is *agile* in all four dimensions, and it is probably impossible to be agile in all dimensions. As a leader, though, it is worth connecting the individual strengths-weaknesses profile of your employees with the appropriate job profiles of a travelling organization. It is useful to connect the company's purpose and its needs for agile resources with the individual development plans for the people. Why not ask your team members to run their own personal strengths-weaknesses profile and start to work on the strengths and connect them with the company's journey? Why not give people who are strong in dealing with tough problems challenging operational tasks? Why not give people who are creative and innovative appropriate start-up projects? Why not give people who are strong in supporting others people development tasks? Why not give people who are strong in performing under first-time conditions pioneer jobs? Again, there is no simple

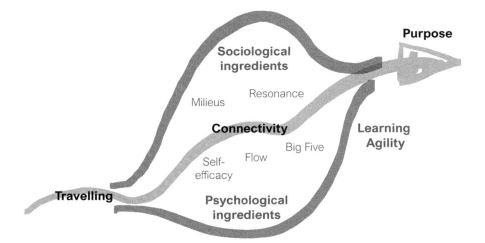

Fig. 2 Blending your learning and development cocktail from psychological and sociological ingredients, aligning it to the purpose, using it as a connectivity exercise, and pacing it with the travelling organization in terms of learning agility (Figure: Frank Kühn)

recipe. However, if we agree that we are all on a joint journey, the best survival kit in our travel baggage contains a good deal of *learning agility*.

A Cocktail Called *Resonance Oasis* to Feel More Connected with Our Travelling Company

We all know: we work for money. Companies reimburse our work by paying us a salary. That's it. Anything else? Nice to have. If we need *resonance* experiences (or—to put it more profanely—some fun), we have our families, our friends, our partner, our environment, our sports, our retail therapy attacks, movies, cinemas, museums, books, and arts. We do have our work-life balance, right? So—why bother with a romantic-sentimental metaphor such as *resonance oasis* for companies to enhance our working lives?

Let's assume a young talented and ambitious professional gets three competing offers to start their career. Company A is a start-up. The young professional got the advice from a friend to apply for a job there. Instead of running through a structured recruiting process with telephone interview, assessment center, further interviews, etc., he only had lunch with the guy who he would be working for in the cafeteria of the company's headquarters. A rather informal but inspiring conversation about life, work, aspirations, visions, and values. The next day he receives the call from this guy, telling him that he has got the job. Company B is a global corporate player to which our young professional also applied. After the telephone interview, our young professional is invited to take part in an assessment center which he successfully passes. The HR consultant responsible for the department in question—not the

Table 1 Questions on the basis of learning agility, acc. to Orr (2012)

Indicator	Description	Low or does not demonstrate 1	Sometimes demonstrates 2	Often demonstrates 3	Consistently demonstrates 4
Mental agility	Is more fascinated, amused, or intrigued by tough problems and challenges than stressed, troubled, or strained				
	Quickly understands the essence and the underlying structure of a situation				
	Can combine the best parts of more than one idea or solution from multiple people and sources and transform it into an overall improved solution				
	Functions as effectively under conditions of ambiguity as well as certainty				
	Is a curious person; is intellectually adventuresome				
Change agility	Is creative and innovative				
	Does not let others' reactions to his/her mistakes and failures be a deterrent to proceeding if he/she thinks something will eventually work				
	Knows how to get things done				

(continued)

Table 1 (continued)

Indicator	Description	Low or does not demonstrate 1	Sometimes demonstrates 2	Often demonstrates 3	Consistently demonstrates 4
	outside of formal channels as well as within them; is savvy about who to go to and when				
	Lives with the negative consequences of being ahead of others on change				
	Quickly picks up the need to change personal, interpersonal, and managerial behavior as required				
People agility	Can articulate complex ideas and concepts to others				
	Makes quick and mostly accurate judgments about people				
	Watches others for their reactions to his/her attempts to influence and perform and adjust				
	Has seen this person substantially change after receiving critical feedback, making a mistake, or learning something new				
	Seeks and looks forward to opportunities for new learning experiences in				

(continued)

Table 1 (continued)

Indicator	Description	Low or does not demonstrate 1	Sometimes demonstrates 2	Often demonstrates 3	Consistently demonstrates 4
	business or personal areas				
Results agility	Performs well under first-time conditions; isn't thrown by changing circumstances				
	Exudes self-confidence, has a significant, noticeable presence				
	Can state his/her case or viewpoint with energizing passion				
	Is willing to work hard and make personal sacrifices to get ahead				
	Has high internal standards of excellence in addition to being tuned to outside standards				

manager—informs him afterwards that the organization needs to decide which job offer might be best for him and that he will be informed within a couple of weeks. After 4 weeks he still has not heard anything. Company C took another approach. Instead of recruiting and selecting applicants, Company C *applies* itself for candidates like our young professional. He found out about Company C at a fair where Company C presented and introduced itself. Company C's idea is that the candidate is in the driver's seat, and it is him or her who selects the company and not the other way around. After the fair, our young professional is invited to attend an annual networking meeting, an invitation that the company extends to all its employees who were hired in the preceding 12 months. After this meeting, our young professional is expected to decide either to join the company or not. Reverse concept—well, guess how our young professional would decide or even better, make your own choice, how would you decide?

Take a second example. You work as General Manager for the country organization of a corporate global player in the IT service industry. You are accountable for profit and loss in this country. Although you have financial objectives concerning revenue and profit, you do not have the authority to take a decision that impacts on the company's costs. When you want to procure external services, hire new recruits, invest in product development, send offers to clients, etc., you need to run through a formal purchasing and/or approval process with numerous approval levels. All internal processes are centralized and managed via corporate headquarters. The company's matrix organization does not have an official authority matrix in place regulating accountabilities of senior executive roles across the various functions such as sales and delivery—so you have to have everything approved. Or you work as General Manager for a country organization of a hidden champignon in the food industry. You have agreed with the CEO, who is the owner of the company, the country's strategy and the annual financial objectives in the context of the company's overall vision. You are authorized to make any investment decision on your own concerning issues such as product innovation, new hires, procurement, product pricing, or new machines, aside from IT and controlling. Again—which company would you like to work for as General Manager? And why?

You would probably choose the company where you feel more affection and to which you have a closer emotional bond. Hartmut Rosa would argue that the degree of affection and emotion depends on the degree to which a company allows us to "transmute with" it. By transmutation, he means that we actively adopt and shape our environment and/or company instead of just passively experiencing it. Take an analogy from gardening. Let's take a typical couple. The husband does not understand why his wife likes *her* garden that much. It is fun for him to spend the evening together with her on the patio. However, he doesn't enjoy mowing the lawn, while she does enjoy digging, planting, weeding, and watering. Year after year. While she knows all the flowers, the sequence when each type will blossom, her husband can—at best—tell the difference between roses and tulips. While she is actively transmuting with the garden and is, thus, affected and emotionalized, he is merely "consuming" it. While he is just an observer and visitor, his wife feels deeply connected with their garden. She takes responsibility for the further development of the garden, while her husband remains "unattached."

The same effect is valid for our work life. Companies that enable their employees to transmute with them increase the likelihood that their people will get more connected. Those companies create a vibrant culture where people are invited to actively adapt to it by offering communication platforms, involvement concepts, and shared accountabilities. We feel more connected with the purpose and vision of our company when we are empowered to take own decisions in the framework of clear and transparent accountabilities and where we do have our own voice to participate in the development of the (travelling) company's future along its journey.

So, what is the secret of a cocktail called *resonance oasis*? Honestly, there is no secret. It is all about management attitude and effective management techniques.

1. *The CEO* should be deeply connected with the company. He (or she) represents the face of the company. People can directly talk to the CEO. He defines a clear vision together with his Board and sells this vision to the employees.
2. *The DNA* of a vibrant culture. The Board should develop and prescribe the travelling company's values (i.e., entrepreneurship—open communication—personal development) itself. Afterwards, the values can be discussed and modified by management and employees.
3. *The learning agility* as a key competence becomes the core of leadership development programs and measures.
4. *The accountabilities* are to be clearly defined by job descriptions and authority matrices at all levels.
5. *Empowerment* of all management levels. Management should be invited and empowered to actively contribute to the future development of the company.
6. *Pride* cannot be prescribed but is the best indicator of a vibrant company culture and whether the five management techniques above work or not.
7. Last but not least you will need to take *a deep breath!* This is (unfortunately) a must if one is to establish a vibrant culture. To change and transform a culture is not a matter of months but of years. After all, Rome wasn't built in a day!

There are probably more "building blocks" which help to create a culture where people feel more connected with their companies. You may be able to you create your own cocktail to stimulate connectivity in your company. Remember, only transmutation generates resonance—not just consumption. So, start mixing and you will feel the resonance.

References

Csikszentmihalyi, M. (2008). *Flow—The psychology of optimal experience*. New York: Harper.
Dilts, R. B. (1994). *Die Veränderung von Glaubenssystemen*. Paderborn: Junfermann.
Hertel, G., & Konradt, U. (2007). *Telekooperation und virtuelle Zusammenarbeit*. München: Oldenbourg.
Orr, J. E. (2012). *Becoming an agile leader. A guide to Learning from our experience*. Lominger/Korn Ferry.
Rosa, H. (2018). *Resonanz. Eine Soziologie der Weltbeziehung* (3. Auflage). Berlin: Suhrkamp.
Schulze, G. (2005). *Die Erlebnisgesellschaft. Kultursoziologie der Gegenwart*. Frankfurt: Campus.

A Striking Analogy: Journey Thinking, Connectivity and Wine, Spirits and Special Pairings

Christal Lalla

Abstract

In her article, Christal Lalla shows that it is possible and beneficial to create an approach to the (global) management of dynamic organizations in a VUCA world with the three fundamental pillars described by a new framing and interpretation in the context of wine and food pairing or gin mixing, allowing a new, out-of-the-box, deep understanding in a business context. One key outcome is about the importance of an experimental mindset to find special, unexpected new fits and potential connections in complex and partly controversial or contradictory environments. Especially the journey to achieve results is as exciting as are the linked exercises to develop teams and leadership skills in this context.

The editors of the book introduce **Christal Lalla** who is a certified sommelier, working in Italy, Germany, France and the USA since 2012. She has established a fast-developing, innovative business around wine, wine services and wine education as well as providing out-of-the-box leadership training. Before 2012, Christal worked in the entertainment industry in Las Vegas and Nashville.

About Christal Lalla: An Additional Foreword by Peter

Christal is, from my perspective, one of the rare persons with 'absolute tasting skills', not only when it comes to wine, but she is also amazingly creative in her ability to combine it with all kinds of food. She follows a holistic approach which

C. Lalla (✉)
VinAuthority Sommelier Services, Bonn, Germany

© Springer Nature Switzerland AG 2020
P. Wollmann et al. (eds.), *Three Pillars of Organization and Leadership in Disruptive Times*, Future of Business and Finance,
https://doi.org/10.1007/978-3-030-23227-6_24

understands wine as something that appeals to all the senses including music, the winemaker's philosophy and approach, the visual and haptic sensations of the vineyards and the cellars with their barrels and the taste of the wine combined with different varieties of food. Moreover, she has explored and experienced in various ways the benefit that a workshop or business meeting can gain from being combined with a wine and food pairing or, for example, a gin mixing session. The combination of alienation and analogies in this context leads to amazing results.

Thanks to her travels around the world, Christal has developed a broad understanding of the cultures of the world, and the diverse understandings and interpretations of wine making and wines, but also of food in different countries and region. Christal's case study explores the striking analogies between the pairing of wines and food on the one hand and achieving connectivity of content, resources, people in developing organizations on the other. Recently, Christal has additionally focused on gin mixing, choosing the right ingredients from a nigh-on infinite portfolio of options and balancing them to prepare the right gin for a specific situation. Gin making is always a journey—you have to go drop by drop with the different liquids to find the best result.

You will see that core theoretical items for (global) management of dynamic organizations in a VUCA world like the three fundamental building blocks or better pillars find a new framing and interpretation in the context of wine and food pairing or gin mixing and allow new access to a deep understanding back in a business context. A key outcome is about the importance of an experimental mindset to find special, unexpected new fits and potential connections in complex and partly controversial or contradictory environments. Maybe it opens your mind when you try to transfer surprising experiences such as the fit of Brunello wine and dark chocolate or the fit of highly acidic and fruity Riesling to spicy Asian food to potential constellations in business you never imagined would be possible. Especially the journey to achieve results is exciting.

As always, this 'out-of-the-box-thinking' and its outcome have to be carefully interpreted, adopted and tailored to the specific contexts. The important advantage is—to act according to de Bono and put your 'provocation hat' on—to try something new with no limits of thinking in the beginning, but when the idea is reflected on and detailed to do everything to integrate it into the concrete context in a way which will let it fly in the relevant 'terroir'.

Introduction

How to give Purpose, to Create Movement and to Connect People by Pairing Food and Wine or by Mixing Gin

In the first chapter of this book, three fundamental keys or main success factors for business in these days are described to support managers and leaders in their challenging work, we call them the 'Three Pillars Of Organization And Leadership In Disruptive Times'.

The underlying ideas seem to be simple and easily adaptable and applicable but this thinking could be an illusion. In business, things that seem obvious and easy are very often the most difficult ones. This is a striking psychological phenomenon which has often been discussed and explained but it remains challenging as it is, at the end of the day, a matter of alignment 'between brain and soul'. To understand something intellectually does not necessarily mean it can be applied by you.

So, a metaphorical and/or an 'out-of-the-box' approach might help to bridge intellectual and emotional intelligence. Let's talk about something even closer to life than business: pairing wine and food.

Why does this article belong in this book? This is easy: you need a fundamental mindset and conviction to do so, you should be open to experiments and you should have a serious understanding of connection. What does this mean? For instance, even those people who never seemed to fit in their businesses might be brought together under another headline which is very similar to food and wine pairing or gin mixing: one additional ingredients could form a very balanced and harmonious result.

Link to the Three-Pillar Model in Detail

It makes sense to go into a little more detail to interpret the aforementioned three fundamental pillars in the context of wine and food pairing.

Sustainable Purpose

An important sustainable purpose of humankind is to enjoy life with all, or many, senses in parallel. It is something which connects us very closely with life. We all love those films when a large family gathers in the garden under old trees at a table to enjoy a great meal with great wines. It gives us the feeling of the life we would love to experience as often as possible, and it is not surprising that—beyond love—this is something that we flag as a really fundamental experience which stimulates our eyes, noses, palates and our haptic senses—even our ears especially if we add the right music.

Very often, following a sustainable purpose in an enterprise, a programme or project, we can be connected with wine and food pairing as well as gin mixing or similar activities to celebrate a start of a journey, reaching significant interim targets at the end of development phases, etc.—the more abstract business success or motivation is connected to fundamental life experiences. In this context, it might make sense to mention that the variety of tastes and the variety of flavours have significantly increased over the last couple of years and that people are focusing on experiencing all nuances (Fig. 1).

Fig. 1 Pairing food and wine (Source: pixabay.com, JPG 3219845)

Travelling Organization

Food and wine pairing or gin mixing is always an adventure, especially if new constellations have to be explored. There are some basic and well-known settings in place which you will find in famous cookbooks and descriptions of special award-winning restaurants. But if you want to invent something new, it is like going to a 'scientific laboratory'. You never know in advance exactly what will happen and what will be the outcome, only an assumed direction.

If we stay on the 'liquid' side, we might reflect on the example of how to blend an exceptional gin out of 3–65 ingredients. There are some basic ingredients which one might combine as a starting point but, afterwards, you must add, drop by drop, the more 'exotic' ingredients—and you realize that one drop more might create an outstanding gin or ruin everything. It takes days to check all realistic combinations and you need outstanding tasting capabilities, something like 'the absolute palate'. Experienced sommeliers have to have the right mindset: they are open for experiments, they know that this will be something akin to a 'trial and error' experiment and they are patient and confident. Whatever happens, they will achieve something amazing and will ultimately understand during this journey what fits best for a special situation, such as for instance an Asian/German bar or an Argentinian/Italian restaurant.

Connecting Resources

In this context, we have two layers to reflect on: on the one hand, connecting different wines and different food—or different gin ingredients—and on the other hand, connecting people in tasting events.

The adventure of connecting different wines and food components or gin components has already roughly been described above. Nevertheless, some additional thoughts on connecting people are needed.

Wine and food pairing events have a strong overarching relevance:

- People might 'portray' themselves with their individual preferred tastes (e.g. a participant in a game might say: 'I am more the vanilla type than the cherry type').
- People learn about others besides the abstract business interaction.
- People might playfully learn who would fit to them from aspects other than business ones.
- In general, people learn to think and feel in analogies to open up new perspectives.
- And finally, it is great to have a conversation about things that stimulate the senses and enforce communication.

Pairing food and wine or spirits—and people—on a stage other than the business one has a lot of advantages. The context is very human, exciting and different compared to the business world and is thus an interesting base for new connections.

Gin mixing events have the same strong overarching relevance in another context:

- People learn about their own perception (their judgement of taste) in relation to the perception of others.
- People learn about balance: how one drop more of an ingredient might change the whole impression, which is a good analogy for the working of teams.
- People might 'portray' themselves with their individual preferred tastes (e.g. a participant in this game might say: 'I am more the pepper dominated gin than the lavender blend'.
- People learn to talk about themselves and their perceptions in general.
- People learn about others besides their abstract business interaction.
- People might playfully learn who would fit to them in situations outside business.
- In general, people learn to think and feel in analogies to open up new perspectives.
- It is thought to be great to have a conversation about things that stimulate the senses.

Three Exciting Cases

An Unforgettable Workshop: Testing a New Format

An international programme team whose members do not know each other very well meets for a workshop on interface analysis, stakeholder identification and team development. The team members only know each other on an abstract and formal level so far.

The purpose of the workshop is to develop a deep understanding of the team and its members in their cultural contexts and to effectively and efficiently draft an interface landscape and a stakeholder map with concrete follow-up measures.

The feeling of a journey into an uncertain environment is built up by a creative idea on the first afternoon and evening:

The team is given the task to prepare a sophisticated dinner. For this the team members are divided into three (very diverse) sub-teams who will not be allowed to contact each other for the next couple of hours before the final dinner:

(a) Team A writes the ingredient list for dinner and passes it to Team B.
(b) Team B goes shopping and creates the detailed menu and passes the menu to Team C.
(c) Team C decides the wines for the menu and does the wine shopping the wines.
(d) Team D will do the cooking on the basis of the ingredients.
(e) Team A does the service for the dinner at the table.

There is no personal communication between the teams, only formal exchanges (the written ingredient list, recipes, the written shopping lists, etc.).

During dinner, the participants reflect on several topics around diversity, identity and results of formal communication (handover of documents without personal interaction):

(a) How do we evaluate the consistency of the overall result, which was achieved only on the basis of formal communication?
(b) To what extent did the work of the groups meet the expectations of the other groups?
(c) Which dish do i like best, which dish best represents my cultural background and why? Which dish is the most surprising and why?
(d) Which wine fits best to which dish and why as a personal 'preference' (without right or wrong)?
(e) If you were a dish and a wine—which one would you like to be? And why?
(f) What are the take-aways/outcomes in the overall experience?

The results of the reflection are collected and evaluated by the facilitator and the sommelier. A 'food and wine' preference and combination landscape positioning the team members is developed. People with similar positions are 'encouraged' to have closer conversations and make stronger and sustainable connections—and a better understanding of your working environment.

The outcome in general shows: a journey into a quite unknown and uncertain environment might lead to interesting results, new insights and, especially, new connections.

On the basis of these experiences, the development of interface landscapes and stakeholder maps are more open and creative as usual general patterns were broken the evening before. And these experiences might create a relaxing atmosphere which would allow people to be more open for changing the usual business patterns which might be indifferent in the past.

Pairing Food with Brunello

The famous Brunello di Montalcino is produced from a Sangiovese clone (Sangiovese Grosso). Its flavour comes, on the one hand, from the grape (notes such as cherry, violet, etc.) and, on the other hand, from the aging in the oak barrels (hazelnut, tobacco, vanilla).

In a professional Brunello tasting in one of the more than 200 cellars in Montalcino, it can be usual to taste a Brunello wine before and after eating some pecorino cheese, salami or even dark chocolate. It is amazing how your tasting sensation can be changed. The whole wine tastes different—which means that the perception of a first-class product depends on the framing. This is a strong analogy to the perception of people—so sometimes reframing is helpful—and to the perception of performances of teams, etc. And it shows that the whole context is quite relevant, not only the impression of the wine but also the food, the environment, the ambiance, etc.

Another pairing experience of Brunello is at meals with courses consisting of (strong and old) cheeses like pecorino, with game like wild boar, deer, rabbit (with its characteristic intensive taste) or fatty meat. Interestingly enough, fat and salt change the taste of the wine. Fat, for example, can significantly smooth the tannic tasting notes of Brunello and produce a harmonic balance.

Also, Brunello has just begun to be tasted with chocolate because some winemakers believed in a special pairing aspect to be explored with different sorts of chocolate. This is still under review.

A key outcome is that the perception of the same thing (Brunello) changes tremendously depending on the environment, on the personal mood and on the interfaces (here, with food). This is a great analogy to perceptions in working environments; maybe you sometimes need 'wine and food analogy' to cope better with your work (e.g. a positive person with good, but different views and energy).

A Gin Masterclass

The participants, potentially arranged in small groups, have 4–6 ingredients (liquids) for gin, of course the main ingredient, juniper, and 3–5 others such as coriander, orange, pepper, lavender, etc. They add the ingredients drop by drop to the basic juniper to find their favourite results. If they are in a small group, they have to discuss the interim outcome each time and decide together how to proceed.

After all participants/groups are finished the results are mutually tested and the differences evaluated and documented.

At the end, the process and the overall outcome are evaluated to find lessons learnt—always with the idea of identifying relevant insights for daily work in a business context.

Summary of the Key Insights: Learnings and Takeaways

In general, it is obvious that the exercises described above bring people together. The interaction and conversation in the group and between the people is very often convivial and relaxed—and quite personal. Especially in project teams with people from those different cultures which are based on mutual relationships and trust, these events are very beneficial.

If you regard organizations like a living organism (and not like a machine), it makes a lot of sense to learn from nature and its—refined—products, especially if they represent global and local diversity and personality. This diversity can be also found with wine and artisan food.

It is obvious in large transformation processes that individual personalities have to be seriously respected and the right matches for them in terms of roles, tasks, objectives, teams etc. should be found.

Sensitivity for 'good matches' can be trained in general by wine and food pairing or by gin mixing, as well as curiosity, openness for unexpected outcomes, readiness for trying unusual things—or for journey thinking and a connectivity mindset for people and organic products. Each new combination is exciting and could have the potential to be explored.

The problem is the transfer—even very adventurous people in private contexts often avoid risk in business, but in an era where a startup mindset is called for in enterprises, this has to change. The affinity of a wine and food pairing to business situations can help if the transfer from one area to another should be proactively discussed and analogies be found to create transparency.

Regarding food and wine, there is, on the one hand, a scientific level description, for instance, what happens when fat meets tannins on a molecular level (see above). This might have a quite common effect for all people. On the other hand, individual tasting habits can be further developed and extended which means what people like and understand.

Just as it is hard to develop one's personality in general it is also hard to develop tasting capabilities and an individual sophisticated taste.

Part VI

Conclusion

How the Three-Pillar Model Can Be Applied in Practice

Peter Wollmann, Frank Kühn, and Michael Kempf

Abstract

As a kind of summary, this article describes the link from the beginning of our journey to the set of key questions that we could conclude from the discussions in our author community and from the articles written for this book. The respective answers to these questions are crucial for each organization and have to be updated on a regular basis on the organization's journey. The readers are offered a careful selection of two dozen of those key questions that underline the relevance of the three pillars and, additionally, provide them with helpful success factors and takeaways for building their own steps which support their organization's journey.

The Editors of the Book Introduce Themselves

Peter Wollmann is now acting as a senior mentor, sparring partner, trusted advisor and catalyst for leaders in new roles and responsibilities and for organizations. Before, he had been over nearly 40-year diverse senior positions in the Finance Industry, the last years as program director for global

(continued)

P. Wollmann (✉)
Consulting Partner, Bonn, Germany
e-mail: pw@peterwollmann.com

F. Kühn (✉)
Consulting Partner, Dortmund, Germany
e-mail: fk@kuehn-cp.com

M. Kempf (✉)
Consulting Partner, Bad Honnef, Germany
e-mail: michael@kempf-cp.com

© Springer Nature Switzerland AG 2020
P. Wollmann et al. (eds.), *Three Pillars of Organization and Leadership in Disruptive Times*, Future of Business and Finance,
https://doi.org/10.1007/978-3-030-23227-6_25

transformations within Zurich Insurance Company (ZIC). He is the author and publisher of a range of books and articles on strategy, leadership and project and project portfolio management.

Frank Kühn has been facilitating projects on transformation, organization and leadership for over 25 years. Frank graduated in engineering and received his doctorate in work science. After gaining leadership experience in research and industry, he became a partner at HLP in Frankfurt and ICG Integrated Consulting Group in Berlin and Graz. Today, he is a self-employed consultant and business partner of ICG and is associated with further development and project partners. He has published a wide range of publications and teaches courses at universities.

Michael Kempf has been an experienced Management Consultant for over 20 years. His career has spanned various jobs in social work, 10 years as a manager (HR and logistics) in industrial and retail companies and, since 1998, in advising people, leadership teams as well as working teams and organizations. Michael has co-authored numerous publications in the field of leadership and organizational development.

How It Developed

How has this book and its focus on pillars for organization and leadership emerged? Coming from our latest professional experiences and urgent business questions, the author community explored the transformation of organizations in the VUCA world, how to manage the transition from illusions of structural stability to agile set-ups, how to overcome the working and leadership styles we have been taught over the last decades and centuries.

In our community, we discussed various perspectives and experiences from different industries, enterprises and institutions, professions and personalities. How to tackle the challenge? Thus, we came to the hypothesis of the three pillars for organization and leadership in disruptive times and wrote this book for a deeper dive and practical evaluation.

The first pillar—Sustainable Purpose—is the core, the 'raison d'être' of organizations. It creates the identity, the enthusiasm and the pride in being part of something valuable—a company or institution—that solves a relevant problem in the world. The purpose must reach the hearts, heads and hands of the people and provide them with a strong direction and positive energy. The more the flexibility of structures and the change readiness of humans are called for, the more a true purpose is needed that makes it worthwhile for the people to be part of a journey into unknown territory.

The second pillar—Travelling Organization—is the key to keeping pace with the VUCA world. The organization has continuously to move and synchronize with the development of markets, technologies and society. If we cannot foresee the future, we have to take smaller steps and explore the land, accepting back-loops, instead of clinging to the illusion of well-known business dynamics, stable development, smart strategies or highly effective structures.

The third principle—Connecting Resources—makes the substantial difference to Caesar's and Taylor's paradigms of 'divide et impera'. The synapses make the difference rather than the cells: the connections between strategy and market opportunities, processes and skills, financial targets and customer satisfaction. In our discussions with professionals, we have been affirmed that this is common sense but—even worse—that it contradicts both our socialization and organizational patterns.

Thus, the articles—with their various views and approaches—underline the relevance of the three pillars and, additionally, provide us with helpful success factors and takeaways. As a conclusion, we made key recommendations in the following. Apply them from your personal view or go through them together with colleagues and discuss the outcome. Perhaps—inspired by the proposed items—you will find additional aspects that you consider crucial for your organization. Build your own action plan or transformation process that supports your organization's journey.

Playbook: Two Dozen Key Questions on How to Drive the Three-Pillar Model

Awakening for the Journey

How do you. . .

1. Explore and discuss the VUCA world, new market opportunities, business disruptions and changing customer needs—with which friends, colleagues and experts, in which circles, communities etc.?
2. Create a shared understanding of your entrepreneurial journey in your enterprise and what it needs in terms of readiness to keep pace and adapt, connect and transform?
3. Define, share and check a sustainable purpose that creates passion and inspires your leadership teams, employees and your customers for your joint journey, enabling them to align their ambitions and competencies?
4. Create a transformation process that involves all stakeholders and leads your company from a business perception that is limited to mid-term targets towards a travelling organization with passionate teams that are synchronized with real business development?

Interlinking for the Journey

How do you...

5. Involve and align all your teams and individuals, and make them define their purposes and contributions to the corporate purpose and goals, connecting their journeys with the travelling organization?
6. Develop an agile mindset empowering and encouraging your teams to experiment with quick failing and learning loops, involving your top management as a role model and taking an active part?
7. Use differences as learning opportunities and connect them in valuable discussions: e.g. global vs. local organization, regional and structural orientation and benefiting from experience vs. fresh thinking and from diversity in maturity, culture and competencies?
8. Exchange on the success and impact of this joint endeavour and further develop it?

Exercising the Future

How do you...

9. Connect all your resources with each other: purpose, strategy, ambitions, competencies, products, processes, technologies, architecture, rooms, structures and roles?
10. Overcome managerial silo thinking by solution-, process- and project-oriented working in alternating contexts supporting your employees to travel and collaborate across organizational borders and deploy their expertise and creativity?
11. Respect and connect different working styles, encourage diversity of people and their approaches to problem-solving, establish powerful teams from this and generate greater mutual benefit?
12. Develop trust arising from personal exchange of opinions and mindsets, experiences and expectations, even touching on sore points and controversial fundamental beliefs—and how do you reinsure the growth of trust in your organization?

Leadership on the Journey

How do you...

13. Clarify that leadership is to serve connectivity and collaboration as the absolute precondition of the company's, teams' and people's success—and not to delimit from others?
14. Connect your own leadership practice to the corporate purpose, every day and with radical consistency?

15. Communicate clearly and often use chats, social media and meetings to discuss how the three pillars are realized in new policies and daily work?
16. Care for clarity and involvement, respectful behaviour and psychological safety which come from true collaboration instead of the illusion of structural stability?

Building New Practices

How do you...

17. Align your strategic innovation and project portfolio and roadmap to the purpose, keep them flexible and connect them to other management processes (such as knowledge management, strategic HR development, business and organization development, etc.)?
18. Introduce agile platforms and practices to support cross-organizational communication and collaboration, such as slack times and workhacks, scrum, prototyping, micro projects?
19. Apply creative, powerful interventions with quick insights and long-term effects that support the commitment to the new quality of organization, collaboration and leadership?
20. Evaluate success and calibrate such new practices on a regular basis?

Enabling

How do you...

21. Recruit people who have the will to go on a joint journey, bring in their curiosity, openness and agility, contributing to the corporate purpose and success?
22. Provide learning and development opportunities so that people can take flexible leadership roles in the organization, manage processes and projects, facilitate meetings and cope with conflicts?
23. Install goal setting and reflection, feedback and learning procedures that help to align the travelling organization, teams and people and keep them connected?
24. Evaluate success and calibrate development on a regular basis?

Closing Words

Finally, coming back to one of our initial statements, radically speaking: Invest your valuable energy, deep motivation and scarce capacities in (co-)working on an inspiring purpose, contributing to the corporate journey, building connections. Be aware that the impact and value of a resource are zero if it is not connected and does not interact with others. And that even structural hurdles are cultural ones—otherwise, somebody would have already removed them.

We travelled through numerous considerations and a joint process; connected our experiences, ideas and feedback; and followed our purpose: to contribute questions and recommendations to organization design and leadership development. We concentrated on three pillars and found that they have been substantial in our businesses.

They are not surprising because they are so natural, obvious and simple. But they aren't consistently and systematically applied in many companies. Therefore, we want to make a difference: release the organizational overkill that has been constructed over years to face increasing complexity, but has failed its purpose. Today, many people have the feeling that they are serving the organization (instead of the other way around), that they are serving their superiors (instead of their customers), that the organization is fragmented and not kept together in order to co-create a contribution for a better world.

Thus, let us radically change this and go on this joint endeavour.

To all 'travellers in mind'—
Thanks for joining our journey.

Printed by Printforce, the Netherlands